Avarice

A HISTORY

Avarice

A HISTORY

By Stanton A. Coblentz

Public Affairs Press, Washington, D. C.

INTRODUCTION

If our whole modern western civilization were spread out on a laboratory table for analysis, what would we find to be its chief aim
and interest for the great majority of us?

When we watch the typical modern in the street or marketplace,
the store, the office, the factory, the bank, the stock exchange, the
answer is not hard to find. We see it flaring before our eyes in newspaper and magazine advertisements advising us where and how to
spend our money, and where and how to increase it; we face it in the
salesman ringing the doorbell, breaking in upon our peace via the
telephone, the television, or the radio, or clogging our daily mail with
unwanted appeals. We observe it in the rush and scurrying of business, the crowded thoroughfares, the dashing feet, the clicking of
typewriters and adding machines, the fevered conferences, the suppressed air of excitement that invades our commercial centers. And we
notice it most vividly of all in the quarrelings over money, the con-
tested wills, the claims for damages, the suits for non-support and for
alimony, the charges of fraud, embezzlement, tax evasion, and corruption, the labor disputes and all the perennial bitterness between employer and employee, landlord and tenant, and seller and buyer.

In other words, our age is peculiarly concerned with *getting*. It is
concerned not so much with the getting of culture or ideas as of bank
notes and bank credits; it is much less interested in a gratifying inner
life than in the accumulation of wealth. To a large extent, the same
has been true also in other periods; but we cannot point to many previous eras in which the child, almost from the cradle, has been so
thoroughly taught that life's flower and summit is acquisition.

One or two personal examples may indicate the attitude of mind
which, though known to us all, never so truly reveals itself as when
we observe its results.

Take the case of the elderly woman who sometime ago asked my
opinion of an offer made her for the sale of her house.

"But are you not contented where you are?" I asked.

"Perfectly."

"And do you need the money?"

"No, thank God."

"Then why are you thinking of selling?"

A faintly avaricious glitter came into the faded old eyes, a gleam
as of sly and appetizing expectation.

"Oh, but they offered me a wonderful price!"

A few days later, I met the same woman again. She greeted me with tears. "Oh, Mr. C.," she mourned, "I don't know what I'm going to do. I've sold my house, and have to move by the first of the month. It's terrible, Mr. C., an old person like me not having a house any more, nor a place in the world to put my head!"

The reader may suggest that what this old woman needed was not so much a place to put her head as someone to examine her head. Nevertheless, was she not being true to the popular faith—the creed that, making money a destination rather than a mere aid toward a destination, sacrifices the primary life values to the secondary? In other words, was she not a typical exemplar of the age, and of its philosophy and attitude of mind?

But even if she was in her dotage, what of the middle-aged couple I knew who had a home in a beautiful suburban residential district? By virtue of years of loving toil, they had developed a garden that was a joy to behold; while the house itself, couched beneath the gentle rolling foothills, was ideally arranged and situated. One day, to my surprise, I learned that the place had been sold. "Ah, but they made a splendid deal!" reported a mutual friend. "Originally, way back before the war, the house cost only $6,000, so of course they couldn't resist selling when someone offered $26,000."

Sometime later I saw the ex-suburbanites. Pinched and worn, they had aged years in a few months—they were living in a basement in the city, having been unable to obtain more suitable accommodations at a "reasonable price." But they would return to the suburbs—sometime, when they were able.

It would be preposterous to suggest that such cases have been confined to our times or even to our civilization; the legend of King Midas is proof that we deal here with an ancient aberration. But a former period could at least mock at Midas.

Just how far, then, do we differ from other centuries and lands in our veneration for possessions—our quest of acquisitions for acquisitions' sake? In just what shrines and temples have the great gods To-Have and To-Hold been honored throughout the ages? What fruits have they bequeathed to the world?

It seems to me that it will be interesting to answer these questions beginning with savage life, and proceeding through the marauders, merchants and millionaires, the seekers and squanderers of fortune that have filled so many pages of history. Thus, with the perspective of other times, other customs and other points of view before us, we may be able to see ourselves in a clearer light.

CONTENTS

I

THE EARLY HISTORY OF "I HAVE"

Here in the modern West, whose laws and institutions and ways of thought are built about the words *me* and *mine*, it is hard for us to picture a state of society in which these very pronouns have not been invented, or, if invented, are little used. Imagine the situation, for example, if a man spoke only of *our* land, *our* house, *our* food; and if he meant, literally, that he regarded the land, the house, the food as possessions-in-common of a group. But this, you will exclaim, is Communism! No, it is not Communism in the sense in which the term applies to Russia and other Marxist countries; but it is communism with a small letter, the communism of primitive peoples.

Even in our own civilization, we have traces of the old primitive sharing. Even today many a married couple pour their receipts into a common fund, without a thought that "so much is John's, and so much is Mary's"; even today there are parents who share unstintedly with their children, and relatives who give with a free hand to relatives, and religious groups that provide for those of their persuasion. In so far as such persons ignore the strict barriers of *This Is Mine* and *This Is Not Yours*, they hark back to our ancestors of thousands of years ago, and to primitive peoples throughout the world.

Of course, we moderns have much to covet that was undreamt-of by the simple savage with his fish-hooks and arrows, his tent of bark, and his clothes made of the skins of animals. Our own period, representing the multiplication of the average man's possessions beyond anything within the grasp of kings a few centuries ago, has given you and me so many opportunities to use the words *my* and *mine* that the attitude of early man has become harder to understand than it would have been in almost any previous age.

Probably is it not true that uncivilized man is naturally less selfish than his modern brother; but probably less selfishness is drilled into him. To the unlettered tribesman, the dugout canoe may be quite as wonderful as is a motor yacht to the sportsman of today; a wooden plow may seem as valuable as a gasoline-run tractor appears to the farmer of the twentieth century. Then why is the modern so much more apt than the primitive to use the personal pronoun?

1

II

The first men, so far as we can gather, were not concerned with property. They were without crafts, industries, herds, or agriculture; they lived in the trees, or in caves; they obtained their food as they could; they ate berries, nuts, roots, insects, and perhaps the carcasses of animals; and the findings of one were the possessions of all. Then gradually they evolved a few rude tools: a flint scraper, a flint knife, firestones, and in time no doubt a wooden club or spear. But the same principle still applied: the acquisitions of one belonged to all: if tribesman A speared a wild boar, he might kill it with a weapon made by the joint labors of tribesmen B and C, and the flesh of the slain beast would be enjoyed by the entire community in a common feast. If A sought to monopolize the weapon, or tried to keep the boar-meat for himself, he would find himself highly unpopular, and would be ostracized if not liquidated.

From this theoretical example let us turn to some known instances. What happens among the Eskimos of Greenland when one of the tribesmen has succeeded in harpooning a whale? Do the others all sit by while the hunter alone enjoys the fruits of success? Not at all! Everyone present receives his share of the meat. Here again the principle is that what belongs to you belongs to me. And the same rule governs some of the hunting tribes of northwest Asia: if a Chukchi wishes to use a boat which he finds lying on the beach, he simply uses it, regardless of the theoretical owner—and no question of payment is involved. Similarly, among the Iroquois tribesmen, the people not only lived in communal dwellings, but shared their possessions: if a man slew a deer, the venison belonged to everyone; if he raised some corn or pumpkins, everyone might partake of the food; if a woman cooked, everyone might dip into the pot. And if you were a stranger to the group, you would share in its hospitality—indeed, you might be fed though your host went hungry.

In much the same way, an Indian victor in warfare, returning laden with trophies, while he might theoretically keep everything, in practice had to prove his generosity by sharing his gains. Robert H. Lowie has this to say of the Crows: "A man who exercised his legal prerogative to the extent of actually retaining everything for his own use would certainly be flouted for his greed and would hardly succeed in recruiting followers for a second venture. To hoard the spoils in miserly fashion is so repugnant to Crow sentiment that probably no captain ever thus laid himself open to universal reprobation."[1]

Here the principle may indeed have been that "to the victor belong the spoils." But the victor knew better than to keep the spoils.

Obviously, the idea of private property in this case has developed to some extent; otherwise a successful brave would not retain the loot even in theory. Nevertheless, food and perishables are his only to the extent to which he needs them more than do his neighbors. The same state of mind is to be found among an African tribe, the Nuer: "Kinsmen must assist one another, and if one has a surplus of a good thing he must share it with his neighbors. Consequently no Nuer has a surplus. But the European has a surplus and if his possessions are of any use to the Nuer he ought, in their opinion, to share them with the people with whom he is living. . . . No Nuer is expected to part with his cattle or household property. . . . But were a man to possess several spears or hoes or other such objects he would inevitably lose them." [2]

E. E. Evans-Pritchard, in his book on the Nuer, tells us that the only way he could keep tobacco among this tribe was to deny that he had any and hide it well. "When I gave Deng a big lump of Anuak tobacco he managed to place a small piece of it in his pipe, but he had at once to distribute the rest of it. . . . Age-fellows do not even ask for snuff or tobacco, but, if they find it in a man's byre, they just take it. My own system was to give away at the first opportunity anything I possessed which Nuer might covet and to rest in poverty and peace." [3]

Even though claims of *me* and *me first* may have rent the air from the time of the earliest "durable goods," the principle that "What is yours is mine" has long co-existed with the idea of personal ownership. Take the case of the Samoans, who, according to Margaret Mead, extend the communal sharing to relatives even if not to more distant individuals. "From a relative one may demand food, clothing and shelter, or assistance in a feud. Refusal of such a demand brands one as stingy and lacking in human kindness, the virtue most esteemed among the Samoans. No definite repayment is made at the time the services are given, except in the case of the distribution of food to all those who share in a family enterprise." [4]

It is true that a return gift is "demanded at the earliest opportunity"; true also that there is no law other than that of custom and public opinion—which, however, may suffice. But contrast the system with our own, whereby men sometimes have to be haled into court before they will support mothers, wives, or children.

A further step may be seen among the Ba-Ila of Africa, who make

every man's elder relations the beneficiaries of his property. Thus, if
your chief grants you some land, it is not wholly yours; your older
brother or your uncle or your grandfather or any of your senior kinsmen have the right to help themselves. And they may take other
kinds of property also in the same free-handed way, so much so that
"a Ba-Ila who has gained large sums by his industry in working
for European settlers may be deprived of them all by his elder
relatives." [5]

Most uncivilized peoples, likewise, do not share our ideas of land
ownership. Some Australian tribes, such as the Kariera, wage war
without ever thinking of taking the territory of the foe; while those
fierce head-hunting warriors, the Jibaros of Ecuador, have a super-
stitious terror of enemy country, which they leave as soon as possible
after victory. Some other tribes, such as the Akikuyu of Africa, can
hardly conceive of the transfer of land by sale any more than of the
purchase of part of the sky. The difference in ideas regarding land
has been held responsible by historians for many of the quarrels between the whites and the American Indians: the former, in good
faith would believe that they were buying the land, whereas the latter,
in equally good faith, not having been taught that land could be sold,
would grant what they supposed to be the mere right to use the territory for a period, and would be infuriated when the newcomers in the
course of time refused to leave.

Among certain tribes in Africa, all land is regarded as the chief's—
which in effect puts up a perpetual "No sales!" sign. Among other
groups, as in Polynesia, the chief can make a bit of land *tabu*, and
therefore his own, by the mere act of passing over it and contaminat-
ing it with his powerful *mana*. And in the Andaman Islands, any
member of a group is privileged to use the hunting grounds of the
group. Though certain things such as food may be a man's own, all
that any tribesman need do is ask for what he wants, since "It is considered a breach of good manners ever to refuse the request of another.
Thus if a man be asked by another to give him anything that he
may possess, he will immediately do so. If the two men are equals
a return of about the same value will have to be made." [6]

Among those remarkable natives of New Zealand, the Maoris, communal sharing sometimes took the more striking form of authorized
robbery—which, however, the victim was not expected to resent, and
might even esteem as a compliment. Theoretically, the robbery was
a form of punishment, the penalty for an offense. But the crimes, in
western eyes, might not look like crimes at all. "A man's child fell in

the fire and was almost burnt to death. The father was immediately plundered to an extent that left him without the means of subsistence: fishing nets, canoes, pigs, provisions—all went. His canoe upset and all his family narrowly escaped drowning—some were, perhaps, drowned. He was immediately robbed, and well pummelled with a club into the bargain. . . . He might be clearing some land for potatoes, burning off the fern, and the fire spreads farther than he intended, and gets into a *wahi tapu* or burial-ground. No matter whether any one has been buried in it or not for the last hundred years, he is tremendously robbed." [7]

As the robberies were never resisted—resistance would have been regarded as a low-minded sort of trick, and, besides, would have deprived the offender of the right of robbing others—the practical effect was that under such a system personal property was, as F. E. Maning has observed, an evanescent sort of thing altogether. "The general effect," he points out, "was to keep personal property circulating from hand to hand pretty briskly, or indeed to convert it into public property; for no man could say who would be the owner of his canoe or blanket in a month's time. Indeed, in that space of time I once saw a nice coat, which a native had got from the captain of a trading schooner, and which was an article much coveted in those days, pass through the hands, and over the backs, of six different owners, and return, considerably the worse for wear, to the original purchaser. . . ." [8]

Among the Fiji Islanders a similar custom, *kerekere,* permitted a man to take another's property with such openhandedness that business as known to us was impossible. In the Fijis, again, the people in a sense shared all their belongings with the chief, since he was held to own everything; but the people in turn virtually owned all the property of the chief. If a famine arose, the leader might declare that the products of the fields were the common possession; if men were needed for planting, canoe-making, or some other public purpose, the chief might call upon his subjects in any region for the necessary labor; if a war broke out, he might exert absolute control over all property no less than over all lives. But even in peacetime, if any district needed some commodity, it might demand the goods of other districts, repaying the gifts in labor or in other things of value.

Thus we can see not only the autocratic rule of a warlike people, but strong survivals of the ancient doctrine that "What is my neighbor's is mine," and likewise, "I must share with my brother, and help him."

III

Let us proceed a few paces toward our own familiar world, and visit the property-holding Kalingas, a non-literate group in the Philippines. Among these people, the value of land—usually paid for in water buffaloes rather than in money—is determined not only by its intrinsic worth, but by the prestige it conveys. Thus rice lands have a high prestige value; and from this it follows that, "The prestige value of rice lands is so great a factor in boosting their price that the return is very low as compared with the interest rates on money." [9] This situation is not, indeed, without parallels in the west, where prestige may prompt the purchase of a handsome estate or conspicuous piece of business property, and where, in pre-industrial England, social and psychological elements made the price of land higher than its economic uses justified.

Turning to the islands north and east of New Guinea, we find a still more curious form of exchange, the *Kula*, which is involved also with prestige, and likewise with ideas of magic. In one direction bracelets of white shell called *mwali* pass continually; in the opposite direction necklaces of red shell, *soulava*, are carried incessantly over wide areas of sea. But all this is as far as you could imagine from modern business. For while *mwali* and *soulava* are constantly being exchanged, no possessor of either remains in possession for long; the recipient is merely entrusted with the article for a time and is in honor bound to return it at the proper moment. But the *Kula*, as Bronislaw Malinowski tells us, "is not done under stress of any need, since its main aim is to exchange articles which are of no practical value. . . . After all it only consists of an exchange, interminably repeated, of two articles intended for ornamentation, but not even used for that to any extent. Yet this simple action . . . has somehow succeeded in becoming the foundation of a big inter-tribal institution. . . . Myth, magic and tradition have built up around it definite ritual and ceremonial forms, have given it a halo of romance and value in the minds of the natives, have indeed created a passion in their hearts for this simple exchange." [10]

But this passion, though centering around a form of property, has little if anything in common with western acquisitive fury. It is not related to greed but to a creed; it is more of a religious ritual than a commercial transaction. And it has become a means for the transfusion and intermingling of cultures, and for friendly meetings and understandings between men separated by hundreds of miles of sea.

Ceremonial observances were likewise behind the seeming interest in property of a very different people, the Indians of the Pueblos of the American Southwest. Thus, among the Zunis, wealth may be important, but not for wealth's sake. The silver and turquoise of the mines and the sheep of the pastures are valued because they may enable a man to go through elaborate rituals and so bend the gods to his will: he may have a mask made, he may hold a feast for the tribal gods after building a house for them at great expense. But while you must have riches to be religious in the Zuni sense of the term, the people do not count possessions as such; he who merely accumulates will be less esteemed than he who comes from a family with permanent fetiches; and the ceremonial roles a man performs will earn him a prestige that no amount of hoarding could match. The situation in our own civilization would be remotely similar if men sought riches so as to build and endow churches and pay for expensive masses and religious festivals, but gained no repute by merely having money.

IV

If wealth among the Zunis is the stepdaughter of religion, in many regions it is the handmaiden of pride and display; pride and display that, strangely, arise not so much from possessions in themselves as from a sort of anti-possessiveness—the largesse, extravagance, or destructiveness with which possessions are abandoned. The same tendency has been observed in various parts of the world: for example, among the Melanesians of the Banks Islands, where wealth is the only stepping-stone to the highest degrees in the secret societies and to the resultant prestige, a man will make good his position not by keeping his riches but by distributing them abundantly at certain festivals.

But the most extraordinary case is that of certain Indians of the Pacific Northwest. Though the culture of many of the tribes has been lost to memory, we do have data enough in the case of the Kwakiutl of Vancouver Island. It is worth noting that this tribe on the whole was very well off as compared with most savages: the people had a never-failing source of food in the products of the sea; inexhaustible building materials in the great forests that covered their land; and a ready medium of transportation in the rivers and in the ocean channels. No man in their midst need go hungry; none need grapple for possessions in a last-ditch fight for survival.

Yet in one sense, their entire culture was built upon ownership.

Each family group or clan had its own hunting or berrying grounds; each held its own river preserves for catching the candlefish. But these were less treasured than possessions with no economic worth at all: houseposts and heraldic crests, songs, myths, privileges, names, and titles of nobility. The latter were prized above all else; and material goods were esteemed in the reflected light of the titles, because the man who acquired a title had to prove his right to it by the distribution of wealth. Both men and women, therefore, were much occupied with accumulating things of value: the latter wove mats and baskets, and blankets of cedar-bark; the men hoarded canoes, shell-money, etc. These possessions were lent out at interest, at a rate that might turn western usurers green with envy: an even hundred per cent. This usury was the easier in that the people had a form of inflated currency: one of their units of value was a "copper," a sheet of metal of little intrinsic worth, but rated as high as ten thousand blankets. Supported by such an artificial standard, it became simple to mount into the upper altitudes of finance.

In those ethereal heights, the air was not only rarefied, but so elevated as to be wholly out of sight of economic need. Wealth was important not for filling a man's pocket or stomach or gaining material enjoyments; wealth was important as a means to repute. It was a counter in a game, a means of shaming your rivals by showing your own greater generosity. In a sense, it was a method of warfare. " 'We do not fight with weapons,' " Ruth Benedict quotes the Kwakiutl as saying. " 'We fight with property.' " And the explanation is that, "A man who had given away a copper had overcome his rival as much as if he had overcome him in battle array." [11]

This is the fact that lies behind that distinctive institution, the *potlatch,* whereby the Indians of the Northwest made riches subserve the ends of glory.

It might be more accurate, however, to say that they made riches subserve the ends of vainglory. Here was no shrinking timidity, no deliberate self-abasement. On the contrary, the Kwakiutl believed in beating their own drums, loudly proclaiming their pre-eminent qualities and those of their forebears, while casting scorn upon the pretensions of their rivals. "I am the great chief who makes people ashamed," begins one of their chants, as reported by Miss Benedict—and here we see in epitome the megalomania behind the *potlatch,* the perverted traditions that used wealth as the instrument of a pathological self-exaltation. The *potlatches,* in short, were contests of the overstuffed and overriding ego; and they employed riches as the means of puffing out the ego by showing their contempt for riches.

From a far distance, and after long preparations, the tribesmen might convene for one of the festivals. There were two ways to prevail and prove that they were "great chiefs" and could "make people ashamed." One was by humiliating the enemy through outdoing him in a give-away. The other was by destroying property. Prized coppers were broken up; precious candlefish oil was poured into the flames; blankets were thrown away; houses were threatened with burning; canoes were demolished; slaves were clubbed to death, not because of animosity or out of plain ordinary cruelty, but because slaves were wealth and because slave-killing was an excellent way of proving scorn of wealth.

All this may seem absurd, but one wonders which is the more preposterous: the squandering of possessions in *potlatches*, or their accumulation in vast fortunes, far beyond the capacity of the owner to enjoy personally or employ for the general good, and yet prized and increased largely because of their prestige value.

Among the Kwakiutl, in any case, we observe acquisitiveness for non-acquisitive purposes, economic activity for anti-economic ends, and concrete and immaterial possessions that serve little purpose except exaltation of the ego. In all this there may be resemblances to the modern world. But the Kwakiutl, in their competitions of giving-away and destroying, have shown us a novel sort of acquisitiveness, well worth attention by the theorists who claim that it is human nature to get and to hold.

II

SHARING THE LOAF IN DAWN CIVILIZATIONS

Among uncivilized peoples, as we have seen, there is no hard-and-fast line between *Mine* and *Thine*; the land or the canoe or the tools belonging to John or Joe may equally well be taken over by Ed or Ted. Then are sharp-cut property lines in general the mark of the civilized? And does the lack of such lines indicate a state below civilization? Unluckily for theorists who like to pigeonhole all statements, no such conclusions can be reached.

We need only turn to our own ancestors to make sure that the rise of private property did not represent any necessity of nature nor even of human nature, but rather a twist of social evolution brought about by forces that could have led to a different end. In the view of one eminent authority, Sir Henry Maine, property originally belonged not to individuals nor even to small groups, but to a large social unit. And the evidence for this conclusion is to be seen in scores of directions. Even today, for example, the word "property" as applied to land does not mean the same to the native of Hindustan as to us; it includes the crops produced by the soil, but not the soil itself. Somewhat as in England before the exclusion of the poor man by the process of "enclosure," a strip of land is reserved for the common use, reaching as far as a watchman, on the edge of the arable section, can make his voice carry. The very use of so vague a method is eloquent of the gap between Hindustan and our own world, and suggests that property rights in our sense of the term are taken but lightly.

We might go on to observe ancient Ireland, in which most of the agricultural land belonged to the tribe and was redistributed among the individual farmers about every three or four years. Or we might consider the ancient Germans, whose freemen exercised rights in common over the land, while the meadows in springtime were divided among the families, but, after the harvesting of the hay, were opened to the cattle of all alike. Or we might note the old Slavic tribes, who did not privately own even furniture or other proceeds of labor, but possessed all property as a group, did all work as a group, and conceded every man a right to the food and other articles produced by his brothers. Or, again, we might turn to early Rome, in which the land was evidently held for the most part in common, until in time the

10

housefather, having been placed in temporary occupancy, began to acquire the idea of permanent possession, and so, thanks to the spur of a private acquisitiveness, gradually developed the notion of private property. But this thought seems to have been slow in arising; its basis, as Maine implies, appears to have been "not an instinctive bias toward the institution of Property, but a presumption arising out of the long continuance of that institution, that *everything ought to have an owner*." [1]

Another noteworthy example is that of the old Arab tribes, which held their flocks and herds in common. And other historic cases are those of the Essenes of Palestine, an ascetical group of males, which established complete community of property among its members; the early Christians, who, according to the *Acts of the Apostles*, sold their goods and divided them among all as the need of each demanded; the Aztecs of Mexico, whose system was based upon the communal ownership of productive property, so that a man took his land from the clan, more as a lessee than as a proprietor; the pre-industrial Japanese, among whom nothing that was a man's belonged to him exclusively, not even the house in which he lived unless he were a high lord, since his door must remain open to visitors; and the socialistic community established in Paraguay by the Jesuits early in the seventeenth century. The latter, a moneyless community, endured for a century and a half and left an afterglow that caused it to be remembered as a veritable paradise long after its destruction by a blast from without; it provided for a sharing of labor and of the products of labor on a basis of equal work and equal privileges for all.

In all these cases we see proof that the acquisitive impulse, as it is known to us moderns, is not a necessary feature of society. But there are examples of an even more striking nature.

A remarkable instance is that of ancient Egypt, where in theory the people and all they possessed belonged to the divine ruler or Pharaoh, despite the fact that private property actually did exist. A centralized control was, however, necessary, in order that the vital system of irrigation and canals might be regulated for public benefit without damage by private interests. The situation from the Middle Kingdom onward has been summarized by Alexander Moret: "The feudal princes and priesthood having been mastered and replaced by royal officials, the whole of society, nobles, priests and plebeians, became the helpers of the royal line. Every one, without distinction of birth or wealth, was called to play a part in the State, according to his capacity as priest, judge, militiaman, ploughman, or craftsman. . . ." [2]

In the documents of the Theban New Empire, we see the Vizier and his agents apportioning the land among the families of peasants, and from time to time making a redistribution of work among the family in response to the changing conditions brought on by sickness, old age, etc. Meanwhile the Pharaoh, through a vast bureaucracy of directors, inspectors, and other administrators, controlled the hosts of farmers, artisans, scribes, and others who were held to be in his service; taking part of the harvest of the peasants and part of the returns of the craftsmen and leaving them the rest as the wages of their labor, he allowed private possession to blossom forth in the bosom of State ownership.

Though forced labor and even slavery appear in Egypt as in other ancient lands, it is noteworthy that the greatest abuse of the theory of royal ownership did not occur during the thousands of years of many successive native dynasties; it occurred beneath Greek influence under the Ptolemies, who demonstrated that the doctrine of public ownership may in practice lead to flagrant evils. "By changing the intimate rule of the Pharaoh to his people to the rule of the State which owned everybody and everything," one commentator has phrased it, "the Greeks transformed the personal element of Pharaonic rule into the soulless domination of State control. It was a deliberate and well-thought-out policy, carried out with efficiency and ruthlessness. Centralization and exploitation were the two principles on which the Ptolemies acted." [3]

These results, obtained through a shrewd interpretation of the theory that the Pharaoh was the owner of Egypt and of everything Egyptian, showed how aggressiveness may take advantage of old tradition and belief to introduce communism of the most repressive type. All lands not already under the royal rod were now placed beneath State control; the farmer, reduced to virtual serfdom, had to remain where he was registered, yet might at any time be dispossessed. Even his house and the tools of his daily toil, though theoretically his, could be sold by the State in payment of overdue taxes. His labor was requisitioned for repairing canals and transporting State property; he was told not only what crops to raise, but in what quantity; most of his commonly used articles were bought from the king, or else from a private vender who paid so exorbitantly for his license that he could not undersell the king; and he was compelled to turn over to the State as much as it wished at a price fixed by the central authority. And not only agriculture—industry and trade were subject to the same severe regulation, accompanied by equally severe taxation; the State was the owner of all raw materials, and through the network of its inspection, its registrations, and its control of sales it placed such heavy pressure upon business that in the course of time free-trading was stamped out.

This tyrannical system, which was received by the people with apathetic and soul-crushing obedience, was continued by the Romans, since it fitted in well with the predatory plans of the Emperors and their Prefects. Under the Roman scheme, a large part of the country's wealth was drained off in taxes, without regard to ability to pay; and under the Romans, likewise, the way was opened for great landowners, who by the sixth century had mostly driven out the small holders; and these great landowners, who found their only serious rivalry in the growing strength and possessiveness of the Church, were able to turn economic power into political, and ruled over the villages with an independent baronial authority, against which the Emperors were powerless.

By this time, the original communistic concept had been lost in the raw and hideous power-hunger and acquisitiveness (the two being, as so often, hard to distinguish). But we can see here a curious evolution, first the doctrine of divine right, which denied private property in theory though not in practice, and then the manipulation of the theory so that private property largely disappeared in actuality, and then reappeared when powerful exploiters took advantage of the weakness, confusion, and impoverishment of the country to seize both

II

By contrast with Egypt of the Greek and Roman periods, in which the doctrine of State ownership was exploited with evils results not to be paralleled again for the better part of two thousand years, let us turn westward and southward beyond the Atlantic. In the great empire of Peru, during the period just preceding the explosive inrush of European gold-seekers, we find a communistic experiment of a different nature—one contrasting with that of the Ptolemies somewhat as the full moon contrasts with a shadow. Various opinions, ranging from laudation to outright condemnation, have been expressed in regard to the Incaic system; but the facts, it seems to me, speak for themselves, and the facts are startling and fantastic.

Despite their achievements in the arts and crafts, certainly the supreme accomplishment of the Incas is to be seen in the communistic organization and control which they established throughout their ter-

ritory. No closer to the Egyptian system of an earlier age than to the
Russian regime of coming centuries, this communistic order built upon
the proclivities of a people who had known communal sharing in their
tribal life, and whose traditions were therefore not violated by socialistic impositions from above. Nevertheless, the Incaic establishment
surely represents one of the most remarkable economic and social structures known to history.

An outstanding feature of the system is to been seen in one of its outstanding lacks: it had no money, nor anything corresponding to money.
Consider what this means: if you were a subject of the Inca, you
would be unable to make any purchase or sale, or to engage in any
speculating or investing; you would be unable to accumulate anything
for tomorrow or the day after; you could not shine nor think of shining through ostentation or display; you would have no hope of rising
to power by means of wealth; you would have no incentive to thrust,
scheme, and grapple in the marketplace, for there would be no marketplace in our sense of the term. Likewise, there would be no banks or
brokerage houses, no insurance offices or agents, no salesmen or adver-
tisers, no notaries or civil lawyers, no taxes or tax collectors. However, if you could not put anything aside for your old age, or provide
against accident or disease, neither would there be any need to provide
against accident, disease, or old age, since the State would care for
you at all times.

True, in delivering yourself over to a central all-protectiveness, you
would be surrendering your freedom. You would be told where you
must live, what work you must do, and perhaps even when and how
you must select your mate; you would not be free to travel, and you—
or rather, your family—would have to pay a stipulated tribute of labor
to the government. Even though this labor would be regulated in
quantity so that it would never appear oppressive, the restrictions
would be of a sort extremely galling to a free-born modern; but to the
Indian who had never known modern wants and desires, the burden
would seem comparatively light, if indeed it seemed a burden at all.
One does not rue the lack of what he has never had or imagined.

The Incaic administrative system was arranged with the mathe-
matical precision of an army. Over every group of ten families, there
was a government controller; over every fifty or a hundred families,
there was a higher controller; an official known as a *Curaca* super-
vised groups of one to five thousand families, while a still higher func-
tionary or *Hunu* was placed over ten thousand families, and an
Apocone had control of a province that included as many as forty

thousand families. It is noteworthy that such a graduated and neatly coordinated system could function efficiently, without the incentive of the acquisitive motive, and without payment of any salaries to the officials. However, one is tempted to add that perhaps the reason that the system did function efficiently was that there was no acquisitive motive, and that the officials were tempted by no emoluments outside the strict line of duty.

There appear to have been two measurements of value among the Incas: land, and the family. From the material point of view, to be sure, the only measurement was the land; and this, according to Philip Ainsworth Means, was never at any time subject to private ownership. The land actually was divided into three portions, though possibly not of equal size and quality: one for the Sun or state religion, one for the Inca, and one for the *ayllus* or tribes. But whatever the quantity, says Means, "the portion reserved to the ayllus was always sufficient to maintain the people belonging to the district." [4] When a man married, he received a *tupu* or strip of land of a specified size, deemed sufficient to maintain a childless couple; on the birth of a son, he was granted an additional *tupu*; but if his offspring were a daughter, he was allotted only half a *tupu*. One reason for this difference may have been that when the boy grew up and married, his *tupu* was turned over to him to provide for his needs, whereas the girl could not take the land with her to her husband's domains: her half *tupu*, if no longer required by her father, was turned back to the State. However, reapportionment of the land need not await events such as births and marriages: an annual distribution was made by the chiefs of the *ayllus*, who allowed each family as much as it was thought to require.

But there was, as already noted, a second measurement of value, the family—which should not be taken to imply that a man regarded his wife, his sons and daughters as chattels. However, the father of many children was relatively fortunate, since it was so much easier for him to discharge his duties to the State. Or, as the matter is phrased by Father Blas Valera, who has preserved the general laws of the Incas regarding tribute and labor: "Tribute was to consist solely of labor, time, or skill as a workman or artisan, or as a soldier. All men were equal in this respect, he being held to be rich who had children to aid him in making up his appointed amount of tribute, and he who had none being considered to be poor." [5]

Though all forced labor has to our minds a little of the evil aura of slavery, the subjects of the Inca apparently did not feel oppressed: we

have pictures of them going forth gaily to the fields, while singing their
tribal hymns. "In those times," says Father Valera, "there was such
a multitude of Indians, each man had very light work, because their
turns were regulated with great exactness, and one never had more to
do than another." ⁶ Even in the mines, the work was arranged so
that everyone would have sufficient rest. "The dignified position held
by manual labor in this Incaic polity," according to Mr. Means, "is
made apparent by the fact that everyone, from the Inca downward,
participated in it." Another notable fact is that any surplus of goods,
instead of being held for the aggrandizement, luxury, or power of a
small baronial group, was kept in reserve, "on deposit," as Father
Valera puts it, for the benefit of the people when needed.

But whatever one may think of the Incaic system, it is a far cry
from this paternalistic rule to the regime which followed. For the
Spaniards introduced the infamous *repartiementos,* whereby tribute of
the most onerous nature was exacted; multitudes of Indians were
worked to death, while others were driven to suicide or to slaying their
own children in order to spare them; Don Diego de Luna, Protector-
General of the Indians, could state that forced labor in the mines
threatened the native population with extinction. The difference between the ancient system and its successor is to be seen in the remark
of a Viceroy, Don Pedro de Toledo, who in the mid-seventeenth century declared that "the worst enemies of these poor Indians are the
greed of their Corregidores and the cupidity of their priests and
caciques (chiefs), who are all intent upon growing rich by the sweat
of the Indians." ⁷

The difference between the new system and the old, in other words,
was that the new was sharply acquisitive. And the acquisitive system
produced these results among others: it ripped down the fabric of the
Incaic life; it exploited the people so ruthlessly that the old arts and
accomplishments were lost; and it decimated and in places almost ex-
terminated the people themselves—so much so that, to take but one
example, no more than twenty thousand survivors were reported in
the eighteenth century in a region, between Lima and Paita, where two
million Indians had formerly flourished.

To say that the Incas must necessarily have given way before a
superior civilization is to beg the question. There was no necessity involved, nor was there any superior civilization; it is debatable whether,
from the point of view of civilization, the Spaniards were not inferior,
apart from the advantages given them by more powerful weapons, a
fanatical religion, and a devouring avarice. The fact that avarice won

the day must not be taken to mean that avarice was a superior civilizing force. The truth is that the invaders, under the goad of the acquisitive complex, had destroyed something precious, which money could neither buy nor replace. The Incas, despite their tragic end, had proved for all time that it is possible for human society, under certain circumstances, to function efficiently and beneficently without an acquisitive spur. And all that the Spaniards proved is that acquisitiveness is capable of destroying everything, including non-acquisitive institutions and ways of life.

III

THE RISE OF THE PRIVATE POSSESSOR

Since private property as we know it did not always exist, how did it come into being? When, in the course of the ages, did men develop the idea of personal possessions? When did thy first conceive of a title to land?

No historian, of course, was present to record these events, which in any case must have been ordinarily gradual and slow, and not everywhere the same. Several conclusions, however, are self-evident; and the first and most obvious is that man did not develop an acquisitive attitude of mind until he had something to acquire. But when he entered upon a settled existence; when he began to raise crops, domesticate farm animals, fashion pottery and fabrics, and dig in the soil for metals, he surrounded himself with possessions; and for the first time there was a wide cleavage between him and the beasts and birds of the woods and fields.

There seem to have been three main currents, which, along with a number of sub-currents, flowed in the direction of private property. And the first of the currents, and perhaps originally the more powerful, stemmed from religion and magic. It is necessary to bracket these words; to our remote ancestors, according to all the evidence, the two were not unlike in meaning. The universe, as they saw it, was permeated with unseen and uncanny forces that could be understood and appeased by magic only. And in the effort to appease those forces; in the effort to make sure, for example, that the wind-gods would grant the needed rain but would not send demons to smite with hail and lightning, early man would place his faith in specialists in wizardry and enchantment. And these specialists, who went by various names, such as shamans, medicine-men, and witch-doctors, were thought to be powerful in dealing with invisible spirits, and were regarded with much unquestioning reverence. It follows, accordingly, that these experts would be in a rare strategic position if they were unscrupulous, or covetous of wealth or power.

There is, as it happens, much evidence that the medicine-man (to use a generic term for all the priests of magic) did not always hesitate to use his alleged supernatural control for personal purposes. There is reason to believe that in many regions he employed his prestige, and his

18

supposed communion with unearthly forces, in order to further a quite earthly influence among his fellow tribesmen. And this influence might lift him to the chieftainship, by means of which he might control if not monopolize the tribal wealth. In many districts, indeed, the medicine-man appears to have been the first chief, the first leader of any kind aside from the tribal council.

Thus, in widely scattered regions—in Madagascar, in Liberia, in Australia, among the Chinooks and the Bolivian Indians, and sometimes in New Zealand and elsewhere—the medicine-man and the chief are one. Among the Dakotas, the chief leading a war-party was invariably a medicine man; and among many civilized people, such as the Incas of Peru and the ancient Sumerians and Assyrians, reputedly divine kings combined in their own persons the leadership of religion and the State. We cannot say just at what point magic became joined to acquisitiveness; but again we have considerable evidence.

For one thing, we may look at the fees demanded by the medicine-man. In some cases, but by no means always, these were small. In British Victoria, the medicine-man exacted an intangible and yet considerable price in his exemption from the work of the tribe. In the New Hebrides, where food was given to propitiate the gods believed responsible for sickness, the medicine-man not only prepared but in large part ate the food. In West Africa, a present such as a fowl, a goat, or a slave had to be given to the medicine-man. In the East Indian island of Nias, according to one authority, sickness is so costly that "one often meets people who have sold themselves into slavery in order to get the necessary funds." [1] And among the Tshi-speaking people of the Gold Coast of Africa, the priests "require compensation and make such extortionate demands afterwards that people, in order to secure their valuable aid, have been reduced to poverty and in some cases to slavery." [2]

An interesting story, illustrating the methods of some medicine-men, is told in regard to Hap-od-no, a famous wizard of the Indians of California, who had made his name and power known for two hundred miles north of his home. 1870 and 1871 were years of drought; and Hap-od-no, taking advantage of the emergency, "made a pilgrimage, . . . and at every centrally located village he made a pause, and . . . would . . . promise the people to bring rain to the dried-up earth, if they contributed liberally of their substance." [3] The people, not unnaturally, expressd their doubts; at which the sorcerer would angrily turn away, promising a still drier spell the next year. And when the next year also brought a drought, the people were convinced, and tremblingly brought offerings to the magician, and met his demands of fifty cents each. "Many," we are told, "gladly gave more. And he made rain."

True, Hap-od-no might have been in a predicament if, instead of a drought, the gods had brought down a deluge at the wrong time. But there have always been men willing to gamble on such contingencies. When they make bad guesses the complaisant human mind, which inclines to believe what it wants to, will offer excuses and tend to overlook the incident. But when they are right, they are miracle-workers.

In cases such as that of Hap-od-no, we may take it for granted that, even if the medicine-men had not set themselves up in business, eventually the thrust-and-grab of the exploiter would have made itself known. But in many if not all cases it seems evident that the rapacity of the magicians hastened even when it did not originate the process of private seizure. For the magicians moulded the world to their desire by means of two most terrible and potent weapons: man's dread of the unknown, and his awe before the alleged manipulator of the unknown.

A case in point, exemplifying one way in which the magic-workers may exert power, is to be seen among the Northern Maidu of California. Here a chief was elected on the basis of wealth (or, rather, of generosity in distributing wealth); but actually he was subordinate to the medicine-man, who dominated with a more-than-earthly authority by reading the wishes of the spirits, and so was able to decide when a chief should be chosen or demoted. Therefore, even if the chief had the wealth, he had to dance to the tune played by the medicine-man, who by controlling the possessor of riches could control the riches

II

An example on a much larger scale is that of ancient Babylonia, in which the priests took over the political and economic leadership. From the earliest times, the belief here prevailed that the priests were special intercessors between man and the gods; and one of their functions was to induce the celestial powers to give good crops. As a means of obtaining such a favor, the community must offer sacrifices; and after the gods had responded by providing the desired crops, the people must make further offerings. But not all these gifts were consumed by the gods themselves; part went to the priests for later use, and part was kept by them as the official trustees of the gods, with the result that the priests found themselves in possession of great quantities of grain and cattle, gold and silver, and other valuables.

At the same time, the priests loaned farm animals to the peasants, and may have taken the calves as a form of interest. They lent grain for seed, and received gifts after the harvest; and they dug irrigation ditches and claimed the irrigated fields on behalf of the gods. Thus they became capitalists controlling the country's agricultural life. Meanwhile they dominated trade through the temples which they built, since these centers grew to be the foci of community activity, in which the priests might aid by administering oaths in the name of the gods. Not only that, but the priests themselves might go into business as representatives of the divine powers; and might govern the land as the earthly agents of the divine.

A partially similar but much more flagrant case may be observed in ancient Egypt. During the days of the conquering Pharaohs, when spoils and plunder flowed into the land, the kings had dutifully acknowledged their success by rich donations to the gods who were supposedly responsible; and thus they laid the foundations of the power of the priests of Amon, whose share was disproportionately large, and who clung to their wealth and even increased it in the lean years when the public coffers were empty. Eventually, under Rameses IX, the right of collecting the temple revenues was surrendered to the priests, who thereupon replaced the Pharaoh in fact if not yet in name. Though the country meanwhile was falling into ruin, the priests engaged in gigantic building operations, erected a magnificent palace, restored the old temple of Amon at Karnak, and constructed a stone treasury in which to store their newly won revenues. No wonder that Ha-hor, high priest of Amon and commander-in-chief of the army, viceroy of Ethiopia, and overseer of the granaries, supplanted Rameses XII on the throne and became the founder of a new dynasty!

But even earlier, in the days of Rameses III (about 1200 B.C.), the wealth of the priesthood was a cancerous growth. As part of their endowment (according to the Great Harris Papyrus, the largest of ancient Egyptian documents), the priests held 169 towns in Egypt and Syria, 113,433 slaves, 493,386 heads of cattle, more than one-seventh of the country's land, and a fleet of 88 barques and galleys; they enjoyed an annual income of nearly half a million sacks of corn, over six million loaves of bread, a quarter of a million jars of wine, nearly half a million jugs of beer, and more than two million jars of incense, oil, and honey. And this at a time when workmen were denied the pittance necessary to keep them alive! at a time when some of them went on strike, complaining that they had no clothes and no oil, and were starving for lack of fifty sacks of grain.

In smaller ways also, the wizards and mystery-men of ancient Egypt found an easy path to self-aggrandizement in popular religious and magical beliefs. In matters of healing, and of protection against the fiends of misfortune and disease, magical prescriptions were followed about as frequently and as faithfully as the orders of physicians today—and with results not unrewarding to the practitioners. In every contingency of this life and the next, charms had to be employed, whether to drive out the demons that made a child sick, or to assure the deceased a smooth road in the hereafter. Obliging priests were able (for a fee) to provide the proper charm, which would enable the dead to arrive safely in the celestial realms, to ward off the monsters that threatened them, and to save themselves from forgetting their own names, and from losing their heads or hearts or mouths or their ability to eat or breathe.

More than that! the commercial-minded scribes and priests drew up the official papers of salvation—rolls depicting the scenes of judgment in the beyond, and declaring the innocence of the defendant. The name of the pleader, which was thoughtfully left blank, could be filled in by the purchaser; though his life had been one of thievery, rape, and murder, he would have the satisfaction of reading in the rolls that he had met the tests and was to be acquitted of all wrongdoing.

The method was simplicity itself. Luckily for the petitioner, there were no more than forty-two gods in the Judgment Hall; hence only forty-two denials had to be made, each by the barest statement. Therefore the list ran somewhat as follows (I repeat only the first few items, as reported in the late papyrus of Nebseni, about 1,600 B.C.):

"I have not done iniquity.
"I have not committed robbery with violence.
"I have done violence to no man.
"I have not committed theft.
"I have not slain man or woman.
"I have not made light the bushel.
"I have not acted deceitfully." ⁴

Surely, if you could escape punishment by such simple denials, you would find it worth while to reward the magician who had shown you how to hoodwink the gods.

III

There are reasons for believing that the faith in enchantments was connected with the rise of the power of gold. From our peculiar and biased vantage-point, in a world that for many centuries has looked upon gold with reverence and desire, we find it difficult if not impossible to see this substance in perspective. For what is gold? A metal, like any other—rarer than most, unique and pleasing in hue, and useful in certain arts and crafts. But instrinsically, what is it worth? Intrinsically, one has to admit, it is worth less for most purposes than stainless steel. Then how has it come to be so widely esteemed?

To begin with, it has not been universally prized. Among most savages in whose land it occurs, it is a stone like any other. Among more advanced peoples, such as the Mayas and Incas, gold was valued for its uses; its relative softness and perhaps also its color made it of interest for shaping objects of art, somewhat as we find interest in a richly grained marble. But it was in no way a standard of value. The last of the Incas, the Emperor Atahuallpa, must have been amazed when the plundering Pizarro required him to fill a large room with objects made of this precious substance.

The simple fact is that gold is not value; hence there must be a reason why it has come to represent value. But can we trace that reason amid the far distances of history and pre-history? There are grounds for holding that we can. For gold, it appears, was originally connected in men's minds with magic; it rose to prominence as a charm, an especially potent and sought-for charm, a favored method of control of the dread unseen world—and this at a time when a medium of exchange and a metallic currency were still unimagined and far-away.

The very color of gold, bringing reminders of the sun, would cause it to be esteemed as a magical metal. For the sun, to most early peoples, was an object of worship, as we may see in Egypt, Assyria, Peru, and many other lands; especial magic was connected with that great recurring daily marvel which was the source of light, heat, and fertility, and supposedly the fountain of life itself. Therefore any object that partook of the qualities of the sun might be expected to share in its magic, its life-perpetuating qualities; any such object would be eagerly sought. In this fact we can find an explanation of the abundance of rings, beads, necklaces, and other trinkets and jewelry of gold among early metal-working peoples. That gold was pleasing to look at was secondary; the important consideration was that it was connected with the sun-god, a divine substance that would provide a sort of automatic insurance against imps, devils, and demons, and guarantee the wearer good luck and long life. To procure its godly protection, men would make almost any sacrifice and undergo almost any risk.

A definite case, connecting gold with the gods and goddesses that gave life, has been traced by Wilfrid Jackson,[5] in a book wherein he shows that the cowrie shell of the Red Sea, perhaps because of its shape, came to be regarded as a token of the life-giving maternal powers, and so was prized as an amulet to ward off the danger of death from the living, and to prolong the existence of the dead. In time therefore, among the Egyptians, the cowrie shell came to be identified with the Great Mother, the divine cow Hathor. This in itself, of course, has no evident relationship to the exaltation of gold; nevertheless, the relationship is there, for natural shells were not abundant enough to meet the growing demand, and substitutes had to be found. I quote from G. Eliot Smith:

"The people of Egypt began to make models of these and other magical shells in clay, stone and any other material that came to hand. These were believed to have the magic of the real shells as life-giving amulets. In the course of these experiments people traveling between the Nile and the Red Sea . . . discovered that they could make durable and attractive models by using the soft plastic metal which was lying about unused and unappreciated in the Nubian desert (Hathor's special province). The lightness and beauty of the untarnishable yellow metal made an instant appeal. The gold models soon became more popular than the original shells, and the reputation for life-giving was then in large measure transferred from the mere form of the amulet to the metal itself."[6]

In this we see a plausible explanation of the apotheosis of gold. Once the Pharaohs had come to believe that the metal was connected with the prolongation of their lives and even with their immortality, they would spare no effort to obtain it; they would send expeditions into the desert to procure the enchanted metal. And if incidentally their followers had a brush or two with the natives whose land they invaded, and if a few lives were lost, this may be recorded as merely one of the first and least of the many wars that have centered about gold.

We know that the gold-seekers even in very early times, did not confine themselves to Egyptian territory; vast quantities of the yellow metal, more than thirteen hundred years before Christ, were being taken from the Sudan. And this gold was used with prodigality in the tombs of the monarchs, whose wellbeing in the hereafter was thus supposedly furthered. The best-known case is that of Tut-ankh-Amon, a minor monarch whose tomb somehow escaped the rifling that was the general lot; the coffin was of gold, a golden mask covered the face of the mummy, and golden rings, bracelets, and other jewelry occurred in great variety and abundance.

Certainly, it would not have occurred to the king and his advisers that their interest in gold and their zeal in obtaining it was putting an artificial value on the metal, and surrounding it with a halo that would remain through many centuries of trade and adventure, of plunder and pillage, of gold-rushes and gold-wars.

In a lesser way, copper too became coveted by the magic-seeker. The ore of this metal, malachite, was believed to share with gold the quality of an elixir of life, seemingly because of its green color, which brought to mind the vital green powers of nature. In early Egypt it became a common practice to daub the face with a mixture of this substance and resin; and eventually someone discovered that the malachite, in a charcoal fire, could be made to yield a metal with resemblances to gold. The resultant copper would, naturally, be regarded as sharing in the magical qualities both of the gold and of malachite. For these reasons, no less than because of its utility, copper was added to gold as a magnet of acquisitiveness.

To be sure, acquisitiveness had been possible even before gold and copper became standards of value. But avarice does not come easily when all negotiations are slowly and clumsily conducted by such means as the exchange of a hundred bushels of wheat for half a dozen cows, or of ten plowshares for twenty swords. It is hard to develop a plutocratic spirit when, as in early Athens, we find the relatively wealthy in the classifications of *hippeis* or "knights" (men rich enough to own a horse), and *zeugitae* (men whose possessions extended to a yoke of oxen). Large-scale capitalistic operations, besides, are under a handicap when the unit of value is an ox, as in early Greece; and when cumbrous iron money is used, as in Sparta. But when a magical value was placed upon gold and the metal rose in esteem until it could be accepted as the medium of exchange, the way was opened for a pride and fury and a competition in possessions such as men in simpler days could never have conceived.

The idea of money, however, did not evolve in a day. It entered the Western world from the East; in Egypt, after four centuries or more of foreign conquest had brought in great quantities of precious metals, it became the practice to use a prescribed number of *tabonu* of gold, silver, or copper to facilitate the exchange of goods; and the value of such goods was noted down in weighed metal in invoices and official receipts. Although still not in wide usage, this practice placed considerable masses of metal at the disposal of traders—in the form of bricks or ingots, or of rings or twists of wire.

More extensively, gold, copper, and silver (but particularly silver) was employed by the Chaldeans, who used the weight of small unstamped bars as the gauge of measurement in commercial transactions. These bars, which were weighed at the time of each new deal, were given various names, such as *shekel*, *mina*, and *talent*, and thus the earliest financial vocabulary came into existence. By the eighth century, B.C., the merchants of Assyria took a step nearer to true money by marking the ingots to announce their degree of purity; and in time this practice was imitated by their kings, and by the merchants and kings of Lydia, one of whom began stamping devices on the alloy electrum, to show weight as well as purity. Thus a true coinage came into being. And the system spread to the Greeks who, for lack of gold, made their money of silver and copper.

Now all this was, manifestly, a boon to the spreading trade of the early Mediterranean. Yet trade had, to some extent, proceeded in the early days even without money, as when, we are told, Agamemnon's army bought wine in Lesbos in exchange for prisoners of war, cattle, and other articles of sale.

It is hard to say whether acquisitiveness or adventure was more powerful in attracting the early trader forth from home. Remember that the pristine merchant did not live in a world where all was patterned and secure: the man beyond the nearest hill might be not only a stranger but a deadly enemy; and the man beyond the second hill might be unknown as the natives of Mars. In that uninformed universe, where superstition populated the land and sea with fabulous perils and monsters such as we find described in the *Odyssey*, it took a man of daring to venture forth. And if he wandered as a trader across unexplored waters, you may be sure that trade in many cases was as much a pretext as an incentive; the lure of the unknown and the zest for strange experience played a great part if not the main part. True, there was, there must have been a spur in rumors of the wealth of foreign parts; in fantastic dreams of get-rich-quick, and of a return home amid a proud panoply of gems and gold. True, also, more than one man may have rushed forth to trade abroad because his position at home was dubious. And, beyond that, many a one who nowadays would be considered no more than a brigand or a pirate, and whom any honest person might fear to meet on a lonely road, was honored as a legitimate trader.

Indeed, the distinction between merchant, brigand, and pirate, among the early Greeks, the Phoenicians, the Etruscans, and other ancient peoples, was often a little difficult to determine. It has been suggested by G. Maspero, in his voluminous history of the early Near East, that perhaps the men themselves hardly knew whether they were merchants or pirates, and acted as the one or the other as circumstances dictated. On the one hand, they were in danger from their intended customers, who might attempt to slay them when they landed, or might steal down upon them by night to rob them of their treasures. And, on the other hand, they themselves might behave with equal treachery, striking at unarmed throngs of would-be purchasers or sellers, slaying the old and useless, and bearing the women, children, and able-bodied men off to the slave market.

Leaving out of account the piratical forays, we may suppose the spirit of the early trading adventurers to have been not far from that of many of our own pathfinders, who pushed through the early West with the ostensible purpose of opening trading posts or laying down trapping lines, but actually were as eager to see new lands as to reap profit. The onward thrust of the explorer, much more than the commercial desire of the merchant, presumably accounts for the voyage of the Carthaginian navigator Hanno, who, if we can accept the supposed Greek translation of his *Periplus*, sailed south along the African coast as far as present-day Liberia. Exploration rather than trade, even if trade was the supposed reason, likewise explains the Phoenician voyage around the African continent, which, according to Herodotus, required two years.

In another revealing passage of Herodotus, we have an insight into the methods of early Carthaginian traders:

"There is a country in Libya, and a nation, beyond the Pillars of Hercules, which they are wont to visit, where they no sooner arrive than forthwith they unlade their wares, and, having disposed them in an orderly fashion along the beach, leave them, and returning aboard their ships, raise a great smoke. The natives, when they see the smoke, come down to the shore, and laying out to view so much gold as they think the worth of the wares, withdraw to a distance. The Carthaginians upon this come ashore and look. If they think the gold enough, they take it and go their way; but if it does not seem to them sufficient, they go aboard ship once more, and wait patiently. Then the others approach and add to their gold, till the Carthaginians are content.

Neither party deals unfairly by the other; for they themselves never touch the gold till it comes to the worth of their goods, nor do the natives ever carry off the goods till the gold is taken away." [7]

IV

Such simple faith and fair-dealing are as far as we can imgaine from the pillaging and plundering that too often flared from the acquisitive desire. And this brings us to the third of the main currents flowing in the direction of private property. The first, as we noted, was connected with religion and magic, and the second stemmed from the spirit of adventure and exploration. And the third, likewise, was related to the adventurous and exploring spirit, though with the addition of a ruthless, a ferocious element that does not necessarily go with mere wayfaring.

I have mentioned the brigand and the pirate, whose rise, according to all the evidence, synchronized with the growth of possessions. This, however, does not begin to express the facts: it would seem that as soon as rich settled agricultural communities began to be formed in fertile river valleys, in Mesopotamia and elsewhere, the cupidity of predatory groups was aroused. Such groups may have consisted of nomadic tribes, which, observing the wealth of the cities, were filled with envy and greed; but the ravagers may equally well have been reckless or degenerate offshoots of the very civilization on which they preyed—mercenary soldiers, or others trained in the craft of arms, and using their acquirements to grow rich at the expense of the parent country. Thus, in either case, arose the raid for booty, which is frequently mentioned in early Babylonia, whose cities could never be sure when they might not hear the scream of the fire-hurling barbarian and the crashing of swords as flying bands of plunderers stripped markets and temples and captured or slew the people.

From the raids for booty, which at first may have been small and half-organized, like the onslaughts of gangsters or highwaymen, full-scale wars in time took flame; the campaigns of the Assyrians, as of the Egyptians and many other ancient peoples, were really nothing but raids for booty on a large scale. The Assyrians, in fact, boasted of their loot; they conceded a share of it to each common soldier, so that he might be encouraged to participate in the plundering; and the quantities they took were enormous.

Consider, for example, the account of the incursion of the emperor Sargon (eighth century B.C.) into the Haldian empire north of

Assyria. The statements of the amount of booty, though doubtless exaggerated, are typical of Assyrian reports: 6,110 human captives, 525 cattle, 380 asses, 1,235 sheep, and 12 mules are listed, in addition to 34 talents of gold, 137 of silver, and a great variety of trophies of bronze, carnelian, lapis lazuli, ivory, ebony, and lead, including golden-handled caldrons, golden daggers, silver incense-burners, vases, lamps, colored cloths, golden bucklers, golden shields, and statues.

And why was this property of the Haldians taken by the Assyrians? There was one reason and one only: that the conquerors coveted the booty, and were strong enough to seize it. And no other excuse was deemed necessary. In that early world, in which the war-maker, the adventurer, the gold-seeker and the buccaneer might be one and the same, men were not ashamed of freebooting, and might be respected for it, take pride in it, and tell of it freely. This attitude of mind is shown repeatedly in Homer, as in this from the *Odyssey*:

> "For ere the Achaean host upon the land
> "Of Troy set foot, nine times I led a band
> "Of men and swift ships against alien folk
> "To war, and got much plunder to my hand.
> "Abundant spoil I gathered of my own,
> "And more thereafter when the lots were thrown;
> "And fast my substance grew, till I in Crete
> "A worshipful and honored man was grown."[8]

No reason is given for the warfare "against alien folk," nor is any implied, except the quest of "abundant spoil"; and nothing seems taken more for granted than that the marauder should become "a worshipful and honored man."

But not only private individuals or groups; even great communities, centuries after Homer, were not unwilling to enrich themselves by brigandage. Consider this passage from Herodotus: "After the blow struck at Marathon, Militiades . . . increased yet more in influence. Hence, when he told them that he wanted a fleet of seventy ships, with an armed force and money, without informing them what country he was going to attack, but only promising to enrich them if they would accompany him, seeing that it was a right wealthy land, where they might easily get as much gold as they dared to have—when he told them this, they were quite carried away, and gave him the whole armament which he required."[9]

But the profession of the pirate and despoiler, though sometimes

lucrative and though regarded with honor, was the scourge of the
ancient world. For one thing, piracy led directly to warfare. It was
organized Achaean pirates from Mycenae in Greece who, so far as
we can judge, destroyed the Cretan city of Knossos in warlike raids
sometime around the year 1400 B.C., and put an end to the island's
flourishing civilization. And it was the Achaean looters who made the
waters of the Aegean and of the eastern Mediterranean unsafe; it was
evidently they who were named in Hittite chronicles as the destroying
Ahhiyava, and it was they who spread terror to the settlements of the
lower Nile. During the many centuries when the business of preying
upon trade went merrily on, isolated private adventurers vied with
large groups for their share of the spoils, until in the last hundred years
or more of the Roman Republic a veritable pirate state was located in
Cicilia, with a fleet manned by offscourings of the entire Mediterranean world, and commanded by captains who rode with the pomp of
great lords. Like the robber barons of the Middle Ages, these buccaneering chiefs made legitimate trade almost impossible; they spread
their brigandage to the land, robbing cities and temples, and at times
threatening the food supply of Rome itself; in some regions, as in the
Aegean and Syria, they caused a serious economic decline. Yet Rome
made no full-scale effort against the ravagers until, in 67 B.C., the
tribune Gabinus proposed a law giving Pompey extraordinary powers.
After much opposition, the bill was passed; and Pompey soon proved
that piracy was not a necessary evil; in three months he swept the
seas clean of the raiders.

Piracy in the ancient world went arm in arm with the equally ill-
omened institution of slavery, and both had their roots in the same
lawlessness, the same war-making attitudes, the same insensitiveness
to human values, the same acquisitiveness. No one can say just
when and where the first slave was made, but it is certain that man
in his natural state does not enslave man: you will look in vain for
slavery among those simple primitives, from the Eskimos to the Pata-
gonians, who wage no organized warfare, and have no extensive possessions. But after possessions have incited raids for booty, and after
raids for booty have grown to the scale of wars, the idea would naturally arise that a live enemy is more valuable than a dead one, since
dead men do no work. And when live enemies had been found useful
to perform the menial labor of the camp, and to dig ditches and build
walls and plant the fields, there would inevitably be a demand for such
two-legged beasts of burden; and since they might have a costly urge
to run away whenever they could, and might die in great numbers be-

neath the whip, their ranks would have to be constantly renewed through man-hunts.

We find this to be the case in ancient Egypt, when the renowned Rameses II engaged each year in *razzias* or slave-raids, which were launched from Ethiopia, and brought in thousands of black men, women, and children, who dragged on their way in chains; the incidents of their capture were depicted on the temple walls as glorious episodes. In early Greece, warring cities rarely hesitated to seize not only one another's property but one another's citizens; in Assyria, as we have seen, the survivors of a conquered stronghold were regarded as items of booty; in Rome, slave-taking and warfare were so interwoven that Italy was flooded with captives from various lands—the historian Tenny Frank believes it seriously affected the country's racial constitution. That slaves might be the chief objective of the warmaker was proved time after time, and notably by the consul Marcus Popilius Laenas, who in 173 B.C. struck against a friendly Ligurian tribe; captured ten thousand prisoners to be sold into slavery (with the incidental loss of three thousand Romans); and defied a Senatorial order to release the captives.

The connection of slavery with warfare, and the kinship of both to brigandage, has rarely been illustrated more graphically than by the historian Diodorus of Agrium, who tells us how, after enjoying prosperity for sixty years following the overthrow of Carthage, Sicily fell a victim to the "Slave War," owing to "the great increase of affluence, leading to a corresponding accumulation of capital, which was invested in the wholesale purchase of slaves." [10] As a result, the island swarmed with unhappy wretches who were branded like cattle, were "shockingly overdriven," and were almost unprovided with food and clothing. The sequel is nearly incredible: "The wealthier Sicilians vied with their Italian neighbors in arrogance, avarice and brutality, and the big Italian slave-owners actually trained their cow-boys in criminal habits by refusing to serve out rations and then permitting them to live by brigandage." [11]

The inevitable result was that the country's life was disrupted: no man could travel on the highways without fear of being robbed or murdered; no man could live in the country without dread of attack by a bloodthirsty gang. Hardened to the life of brigands, the one-time cow-boys became more and more formidable; followed by bands of large dogs, robed in wolfskins or boarskins, and wielding bludgeons, spears, and heavy shepherds' crooks, they began ranging about the land. Worst of all, the authorities, "though they attempted punitive

measures, were afraid to inflict punishment on account of the power
and influence of the magnates whose property the brigands were."

The attitude of these magnates is illustrated by Diodorus in a telling passage regarding the great landowner Damophilus: "On one occasion, when some of his slaves presented themselves naked and broached
the question of new clothes, Damophilus refused to listen to them;
asked them angrily whether the travelers on the public highway went
naked and were not an obvious source of supply for anyone in want of
profit; ordered them to be bound to the pillars of his porch, and sent
them away with a whipping. . . ." [12]

Diodorus goes on to remark of Damophilus: "It was the old story
of an ill-bred and uncultivated character finding himself in possession
of irresponsible power and unearned riches, and the chain of excess
and pride duly terminated in the destruction of Damophilus himself
and in a great disaster for his country." [13]

That disaster was a slave-revolt. And Damophilus—even though
his case be an extreme one, and though the story be exaggerated—has
suggested that the laws of possession do not change greatly throughout
the ages, that the man bitten by the virus of acquisitiveness is apt to
view everything through a warping glass, and is unlikely to be deterred
by humane considerations or warning signs.

IV

THE RICH MAN IN THE EARLY NEAR EAST AND GREECE

The history of all countries, ancient and modern, suggests that when a people's attention is concentrated on material acquisition, art and literature and philosophy and all the finer flowers of civilizations either do not develop, or, if already developed, fall into a decline. In this fact, perhaps more than any other, we can see the reason for the comparative barrenness of civilization in most of the early Near East in contrast to that in the Greco-Roman tradition, in small Palestine, and in ancient India.

Consider briefly the case of Babylonia. Here, among flat-roofed cities in the uninspiring flat-lands of a great river valley, men developed a civilization of a material type, with distinct accomplishments in many practical crafts, but small contributions to the expansion of the mind and spirit. We have noted the rise of the priestly businessmen, for whom the temple was the center of commercial activity. And if we look a little deeper, we will find a world that seems to have grown sterile with the quest of gain.

On the surviving clay tablets, we find the records of multitudes of sales contracts, promissory notes, receipted accounts—the testimonials to minds absorbed by details of gain and loss, and exacting in draining every hair's breadth of advantage. Perhaps more important, we observe a predatory remorselessness, a denial of human values. We see how the usurer with his exorbitant rates of interest (20 and 25 per cent were commonplace) reached out long, greedy hands to clutch his debtor, in mose cases merely an average citizen, who had to borrow when his slim resources did not suffice for the needs of daily living. In return for the loan, the debtor might have to pledge his house, his fields, the slave who helped with essential work, or else some of his friends might pledge their all; and if he could not make payment, he might have to perform a certain number of days' work as a virtual slave. But if his labor was insufficient to discharge the debt, a fixed sum was added to the principal: for example, if the man had owed fifteen shekels, he might thenceforth owe twenty. And further additions to his liabilities were made in the same manner, so that a man who had once got entangled in debt might be sucked dry and enslaved.

Less complete records have come down to us from Babylonia's sister empire Assyria; but here too the hand of acquisitiveness bore down. Consider some actual cases. A certain Shamanash-nasir brings suit against Arbilu-hamat and his on Nabu-eriba, claiming that he has lent them a pound of silver, fifty ass loads of grain, a watering-machine, and an ox; and Arbilu-hamat and Nabu-eriba, acknowledging the debt, can only reply that they, along with three others, will serve Shaman-ash-nasir.

Or take the case of Salmu-sharra-iqbi, who has redeemed a man, his wife, and their daughter from one who had held them in slavery. But this redemption had cost money; the three released slaves were to work for Salmu-sharra-iqbi to defray the interest on his investment . . . until such time as someone could be found to pay the money and free them.

In a third case, that of a certain Nargi, we find a man surrendering his liberty and undertaking to work for one Bel-duri until return can be made for the loan of a bull and some grain. More startling yet! a man named Ishdi Ashur, who cannot pay the interest on thirty shekels of silver, must sell his daughter Ahat-abisha to the lender Zabdi, while still being obliged to repay the principal. Thus again personal freedom is subordinated to property, and the rights of man are subordinated to mere things.

A curious feature of the law may be seen in connection with woman, who was regarded as a form of property, and hence unable to share in her husband's possessions. Not only was she allowed no say in the disposition of property that we would now regard as communal; if she sold or pawned any of her husband's belongings, she was held to be a thief. Should her husband die, however, she might rise to be almost a man's equal—that is, unless she remarried and went to live in the home of her new spouse, which would cause her to lose title to everything. But if he, on the other hand, came to live with her, all his property would be hers. One takes it that men of property did not often marry widows and go to live in their homes.

But whatever the specific regulations—and in some ways the Assyrian provisions were milder than the Babylonian—we find that the preoccupation, in Assyria as in Babylonia, is with concrete things and material gain; and the rarer blooms of civilization, consequently, are not to be found. The same is true of Phoenicia, which was imitative in her arts, and won a place in history mainly through the seafaring of her wide-ranging traders. And something similar, again, may be said of Phoenicia's celebrated offshoot, Carthage.

The policy of the Carthaginians, in its concentration upon material ends, has been summarized by a writer on the economic life of the ancient world: "The qualities which they endeavored to develop in the young were, first and foremost, a love of undertakings in distant lands, smartness, if not roguery, in business, eagerness to make money, and a passionate love of wealth, versatility combined with tenacity, a political intelligence capable of profiting even by apparently unfavorable circumstances, obsequiousness to the powerful, and merciless arrogance toward the weak." [1]

These are not qualities calculated to make a people generally beloved. But many peoples have been disliked because of their prosperity; this would not be a damning indictment were it not that the city's commercialism was accompanied by certain huge lacks. For here was a state which, in its concentration upon getting and gaining, failed to rise far on the stairs of cultural values; no memorable thought, no memorable art, no memorable literature was added by her to the world's sum total. One is obliged to agree with Jules Toutain that the history of Carthage "shows the superficiality and weakness of a civilization in which the chief driving power of human activity is the conquest of riches, and there is no endeavor to achieve, by the side of and by means of economic power, political, intellectual, and moral progress." [2]

So thoroughly was the life of Carthage built upon commerce and possessions that even the army was bought—largely a mercenary army, which but followed in the footsteps of the Egyptians, the Carians, and others in carrying out the principle of murder for pay. However, the mercenaries, like their kind in all ages, exacted their price, and this not in money only. As was to be expected of men who would kill for a living, the mercenaries were a constant source of trouble; they resorted to intrigues and conspiracy, they indulged in strikes and fomented dissension against their employer. But perhaps still more sinister was the attitude of mind which they incited in their masters. Like most countries that exploit human material for commerical ends, Carthage hardly regarded her hirelings as creatures of flesh and blood. "The Carthaginian officer of the ordinary type," says Mommsen, "estimates his mercenaries . . . very much as men in modern warfare estimate cannonballs . . . war was converted into a vast pecuniary speculation, which was quite in keeping with the character and habits of the Phoenicians." [3]

This brings us to the deeper malady gnawing away at the heart of Carthage—the malady of that imperialism inspired by commerical greed, fed by the sweat and blood of the provincials, and preserved by

an army of mercenaries and of serfs. Carthage, trapped by her own
worldly ambitions, was following a one-way course: she must either
maintain the empire she had founded, or must sink to death amid its
ruins. But to maintain her empire, she must have regard for something beyond acquisitions—a fact which the Carthaginians, in their
lust for the loot of the moment, apparently overlooked. And so for a
while their coffers overflowed; they exacted a tribute of a quarter of
the produce of the soil from the subjugated farmers of Libya; they
established a great system of landed estates, whereon a single proprietor could command as many as 20,000 slaves; they imposed onerous tolls of men and money on subject cities; they permitted their
officials to pile up enormous fortunes as provincial tax-assessors. And
by these means and others, they made Carthage the leading financial
city of her day.

But, all the while, sharp teeth were gnawing away unseen. And
when the Mistress of Africa found herself at war with the Mistress of
Italy, the underpinnings sagged and the great edifice collapsed.

Yet we have reason to suppose that it need not have collapsed. A
comparison of the competitors indicates that they were not unequal in
power and resources—not unequal, except in one respect. The factor
that weighed most in favor of Rome was the difference in their colonial
policies. For Rome, at this stage, was comparatively youthful and
relatively uncorrupted; but Carthage was already old, and hardened in
the rites of Mammon. And the contrast showed itself in the fact that,
while Carthage was a dog in the manger with regard to her provinces,
Rome granted her colonies privileges both political and material:

"Carthage from the first maintained her exclusiveness, and did not
permit the dependent districts even to cherish the hope of some day
being placed on an equal footing. Rome granted to the communities
of kindred lineage a share in the fruits of victory, especially in the
acquired domains; and sought, by conferring material advantages on
the rich and noble, to gain over at least a party to her interests in the
other subject states. . . . Rome, as a rule, did not wholly take away
independence even from the subject communities, and imposed a fixed
tribute on none; Carthage dispatched her overseers everywhere, and
loaded even the old-Phoenician cities with a heavy tribute, while her
subject states were practically treated as slave-states. In this way
there was not in the Carthagino-African state a single community with
the exception of Utica, that would not have been politically and mate-
rially benefited by the fall of Carthage; in the Roman-Italic there was
not one which had not more to lose than to gain in rebelling . . ." [4]

The consequence was that the Roman structure, at the crucial moment, held together "like a wall of rock," while the Carthaginian "fell to pieces like a gossamer web." Just when their services were most needed, the Punic provinces deserted, and in her last tragic struggle the city had not the assistance that alone might have staved off destruction.

II

Acquisitiveness takes on new aspects when we leave the Near East and North Africa and turn to the Greeks. But here too the passion for gain was dominant; there are even reasons for believing it *the* dominant force leading to the decline of Hellenic civilization.

In the beginning, however, we see the private possessor largely subordinate to the community. We find a cross between private and public ownership; the tribal leaders divided the land into sections, for which the various families cast lots; and each family then became the owner of a particular territory which its head might supervise but could not sell, since it was the common possession of the group.

So prominent was the idea of clan and family that it was forbidden to dispose of property by will, while a daughter of the family did not, under Athenian law, necessarily deprive the family of her wealth when she married and went forth with a dowry; her husband had to give surety for the return of the property should death or divorce terminate the union. What this amounted to in practice was that the wife enjoyed the interest of her dowry but not the principal, which remained with her family. And this reflects the ancient belief that property belongs not to the individual, but to the group.

We can, however, see private property developing by the time of Homer—property not in land but in cattle, as when a retainer of Odysseus lists his wealth, which was greater than that of twenty other men: twelve herds of cattle, twelve flocks each of sheep and of swine, and eleven of goats, along with the necessary herdsmen. Since it is to be presumed that no one owner needed so many flocks and herds to support his family, we can already see something of that acquisitive spirit which, throughout the centuries, has prompted many a fox to seize a lion's share of the world's goods.

Nevertheless, the Greeks showed a disdain of the mere moneymaker. Traders were generally despised; politically they had little or no influence, and legally the State extended them small protection, and in fact often plundered them. This, however, could hardly have been the case if money and money-making had been exalted in the popular mind. On the contrary, as Alfred Zimmern reminds us, "The older Greeks did not want to be rich for the sake of riches. They were too sane and well-balanced to harbor such a desire. One of the central facts about their life, expressed over and over again, in their art and conduct and institutions, was their sense of harmony and proportion. They had overcome the wild passion of the child and the savage for 'too much.' " [5]

But what if some citizen had not overcome this "wild passion," and had grasped more than his share of the land? Then public opinion would cry out that the excess should be taken from him and redistributed. Here, undoubtedly, we observe a survival, even if a partially unconscious one, of the old communal sentiment.

We have seen, to be sure, that pirates and brigands in early Greece were common and even respected. And it is worth remarking that the "Heroes" of that same early Greece were prominent and esteemed largely because their wealth enabled them to surround themselves with military equipment impossible to poorer men, while this equipment in turn empowered them to thrust their way to political influence. Subsequently, something very similar was true of the oligarchies and the "tyrannies."

Certain characteristic effects of wealth, during the later centuries, are to be noted in Sparta. There was an ancient proverb that "Sparta will fall by weath, naught else"; the people, despite their frugal life, or perhaps because of their frugal life and the lack of any arts and graces to divert their interest, were notoriously covetous. And this was evidently why, though other Greek cities used coined money from about the seventh century onwards, Sparta prohibited any money not made of iron, thereby forestalling the base spirit of commerce—a man would not be over-greedy for money when he would require a cart to carry home the equivalent of a few dollars.

Yet the money-grabber had been thwarted for the time only. It was military victory which, as in many another land, eventually opened the golden flood-gates, and paved the way for decline. We have it on the authority of Plutarch that "The date at which Lacedaemon was first attacked by social disease and corruption practically coincides with the moment at which she overthrew the Athenian Empire and gorged herself with the precious metals." [6] Plutarch goes on to tell us that, so long as the old Lycurgean Constitution survived, this largely saved the country, until it was overturned by the actions of "an influential but headstrong and cross-grained individual named Epitadeus." Because of a quarrel with his son, this man drafted a bill per-

mitting the holder of family property to give it away during his lifetime, or to bequeath it by will as he chose, thereby abandoning the
immemorial tradition that made the land an inalienable family possession. Though Epitadeus acted out of personal vindictiveness, "the
acquisitive instinct," says the historian, "inspired his countrymen to
approve and ratify his legislation, to the ruin of the best social organization they ever had." The sequel is best told in Plutarch's own
words:

"Thenceforward, the men of influence threw off all restraint, and
began to add field to field by elbowing their next-of-kin out of their
inheritances. The rapid concentration of wealth in a few hands impoverished the country as a whole, and the penalties for this were the loss
of a liberal outlook and the closing of liberal careers, with a corresponding growth of envy and hostility toward the men of property. Not
more than seven hundred Spartiates survived, and of these perhaps a
hundred may have owned land and an allotment, while the remainder
were a destitute and disenfranchised mob sitting idly by in the town,
without any energy or enthusiasm to throw into the defense of the
country against the foreigner, but with eyes perpetually on the watch
for some opportunity of making a violent internal revolution." [7]

III

The degeneration produced by wealth may likewise be observed in
other parts of Greece. We can follow a long evolution in which, from
the earliest times, the idea of riches gradually, ruinously insinuated itself. We can see how the quest of wealth caused the olive and the
vine to be grown in place of the grain that had previously sustained the
people; and we can observe how, as a result, the country ceased to be
agriculturally self-sufficient, and had to rely upon foreign trade, which
led toward the spread of luxury, toward imperialism and war, while the
peasantry was impoverished and driven from the land. At the same
time, foreign trade produced a new aristocracy, an aristocracy of
money. And in this aristocracy of the *nouveaux riches*, ostentation
was the order of the day, and the key to political power. Banquets
and feasts for the people, lavish sacrifices, gifts of statues and temples,
a display of jewels in one's hair, and the wearing of mantles of purple
and snow-white—by such means a man might rise to a magistracy. By
such means power came to the few, and aristocratic groups or oligarchies arose to rule much of Greece.

Plato, in his *Republic*, refers to oligarchy as a form of government "which teems with evils," and further describes it as "A government resting on a valuation of property, in which the rich have power and the poor man is deprived of it." [8] No doubt, like many definitions, this is an oversimplification; yet it is true that, in the oligarchies, a superior class of citizen was recognized, with rights and privileges not enjoyed by the mass—privileges that might spring either from birth or from wealth.

One type of oligarchy is represented by the city of Colophon, in Asia Minor, where the ruling Thousand displayed themselves in the agora in fabulously expensive purple mantles, gold-diademed and perfumed. And a less lavish type of oligarchy was illustrated by the towns of the Boetian Confederation, in which a minimum wealth in land was a prerequisite to political rights. At Thebes, the class spirit was shown by a law denying the magistracy to anyone who had followed a trade within the preceding ten years; at Thespiae, if you had cultivated your own land or had learned any of the mechanical crafts, you would be debarred. And the lopsided nature of oligarchy was shown when, in Athens in the years 411-410, the detested Four Hundred ruled a city of thirty thousand freemen.

Another variety of government, also common in Greece, was the so-called tyranny that arose in many cities when usurpers snatched control by force of arms, and governed sometimes beneficently, and sometimes not. As in the case of the oligarchies, we see a close connection with wealth; Thucydides, indeed, assures us that the decisive factor was the growth of wealth. Everywhere except in Sicily, tyranny appeared only in towns where the old rural life had largely given way to trade and industry, and where privilege and poverty stood against one another in glowering opposition. In such cases, the masses needed no more than a strong leader to hurl them against the possessors; and such a leader, usually sprung of the very class he aimed to overturn, could be found in men with the means to buy support and to hire mercenary soldiers to spearhead their thrust for power. These tyrants were not always evil in their over-all influence, but by their very nature they were opposed to democracy, and inevitably they were despotic. But the essential point is that they could have arisen only in a land where wealth had caused disaffection and a sharp cleavage of classes.

IV

In other ways also we note the corrupting, disrupting influence of wealth. Some commentators, such as J. P. Mahaffy, see the same tendency throughout all Greek history: ". . . that love of overreaching, that ingrained shrewdness and intent watching of personal interests, which I have noticed all through the Greek civilization from Homer into the Attic times—these were an obstacle to all their perfection and not least in those branches of civilization which are their proper field." [9]

At the time of Demosthenes, for example, we find a situation not unknown to a later world. The great orator, as well as many other speakers, made indirect profits, some of them perhaps not unlike the modern lawyer's fee, but most of them appearing dubious because of their hidden nature. The phrase "conflict of interests," of course, had not yet been invented. Mahaffy significantly remarks: "If they all made indirect profits . . . the distinction between harmless presents and corrupt bribes was one which could not be easily established. . . . But the abuse of this indirect and underhanded method of payment was notorious enough, and contributed largely to the downfall of the independence of Athens." [10]

The reason is clear, for when the guardians of the State give more thought to their private moneybags than to their public duties, then the portals of the State stand neglected, and decay is certain to ensue. And that decay will be hastened by the force of example, since there is nothing that corrupts like a corrupt precedent.

In Aristotle, in Plato, and in most writers of the time, we read complaints as to the venality that pervades the body politic, making it impossible for a man to be both rich and honest, though the rich man was held up to honor no matter how he had gained his wealth, whereas the poor dragged out a miserable existence, depending upon the fees paid them as jurymen, or the two obols doled out to them for attending the theater, or joining the crowds before the temples on festive days for handouts of barley meal. While the number of indigents steadily increased—in Athens, by the mid-fourth century B.C., they constituted a majority of the citizens—the rich elbowed their way arrogantly forward, regarding politics as a profit-making business, and having little if any regard for the general welfare.

Still, there were two sides to the picture. There was a tradition, as in Rome, as to the public responsibility of the rich man whose contributions, in Athens at her prime, supported the theater, the navy, and other public enterprises. But the ancient system was to fail at the hour of need; after the adventure into imperialism, mere donations no longer sufficed, and, as a last resort, taxation was tried. And this last resort might have been efficacious if the people had not made every possible resistance. Deliberate evasion and fraudulent misrepresentation became the order of the day, so much so that a man who regularly paid his taxes might cite this as a virtue in a case at law.

Long before this time however, there had been a decay in the spirit of the people. The Athenians, having shoved their way abroad on a wave of imperialism, had shown their preoccupation with money in their dealings with the Delian League, which they had dominated and whose treasury they had taken over, monopolizing all but one-sixtieth of the tribute. And when little Samos had risen in revolt, Athens had struck back like a foreign conqueror, tearing down the walls of the city, confiscating its fleet, and exacting a heavy indemnity. By this time, the twin demons of riches and physical might had taken possession. By this time, Athens had fallen to such a state that Sir Henry Maine, in his *Early Institutions*, is able to classify it with those eastern imperialists who desire nothing of a colony other than taxes and soldiers.

Or consider the facts as another commentator has summarized them: "The power of money was spreading and corrupting morality. Those who had just enough to live on wished to be rich; the rich wished to be still richer. . . . There was no longer a profession which escaped the clutches of capitalism. . . . Agriculture was commercialized to such an extent that by the progressive eviction of small peasants and the concentration of estates in the same hands the system of large estates was recreated. Rhetoricians, advocates and artists, who had formerly reckoned it a dishonor to commercialize their talent, now felt no scruple in selling their goods as dearly as possible. Everything could be bought, everything had its price, and wealth was the measure of social values." [11]

It was one of the tragedies of Greece and of all mankind that this preoccupation with wealth was not only the accompaniment but a prime cause of the catastrophic wars. A single well-known case will serve to illustrate the part played by greed. The small Dorian island-state of Melos, which desired to remain neutral in the struggle between Athens and Sparta, was coveted by the warlords of the former, who saw in it a fruitful source of tribute. A dialogue between a native of Athens and a native of Melos, as recited by Thucydides, shows the trend of mind of the rulers. "We both alike know," says the Athenian, "that into the discussion of human affairs the question of justice only enters when there is equal power to enforce it, and that the powerful exact what they can, and the weak grant what they must." In accordance with this philosophy, the Athenian recommends the submission of Melos: "To you the gain will be that by submission you will avert the worst; and we shall be all the richer for your preservation."[12]

However, the Melians were not ready to avert the worst by submission. After an herioc resistance, they were overcome; and all their adult males were massacred, and their women and children were enslaved.

From the first, the Athenians had apparently been ruled by no motive better than self-aggrandizement. They had assailed the inoffensive Melians for the sake of tribute only; and having conquered them, they proceeded to suck the utmost profit from the victory. Indeed, one authority expresses the belief that the extermination of the men of Melos was "merely for the purpose of making way for a colony of Athenian citizens, who went out to occupy the houses and lands of their victims." [13]

This view is confirmed by Thucydides, who sees "the love of power, originating in avarice and ambition," behind many of the evils—the tumults, the conspiracies, the violent revenges—which characterized the Peloponnesian War. And the same diagnosis may be applied to the Athenian refusal to accept an honorable and even victorious settlement when, at one stage of the hostilities, the Spartans sued for peace. This diagnosis, likewise, may be extended to the fateful expedition to Syracuse, which was launched within six months of the sack of Melos. Drugged with power, and lured by the phantom of material gain; dazzled at the reports of Sicilian luxury, and covetous of the elegant linens and couches and plate of the Syracusan temples and homes, the Athenians delivered themselves over to the dream of conquest. We have reason to believe that the main support for the undertaking came from the commercial elements; and the records tell us that, among those voting in favor of the expedition, there were many who meant to accompany it as traders.

In essence, therefore, the expedition was little more than a great organized raid for booty. It was perhaps no more than a just nemesis that it should fail, that the fleet and army should be annihilated, and that thousands of the sons of Athens should be slain or enslaved. It was, similarly, perhaps no more than a just nemesis that the Sicilian adventure should mark the turning-point of the Athenian Empire, and the ebb-tide of Athenian culture.

V

The malady of acquisitiveness was not only a leading influence behind the disastrous wars; it was accompanied, as in many another land, by a lingering and bitter conflict of classes. Wherever we turn, we see this struggle. The people, during the period of disruption, clamored for cancellation of debts and redistribution of the land, they listened to spellbinders propnunding socialistic ideas, and ideas that went beyond socialism, and meanwhile there was an anti-intellectualism, a little like that in our own age; the supremacy and even the superiority of mediocrity was proclaimed by the demagogue Cleon and others.

Thus quality, in mind and in spirit, was being slashed to the level of the lowest common denominator—and this in part because of the false analogy provided by the doctrine that sought to make all men equal economically. The demoralizing effect upon the masses, living largely upon scraps and gratuities and seeking to share in the property of the more fortunate, has been stated by Polybius: "For the mob, livelihood in the property of its neighbors, as soon as it has got a leader sufficiently ambitious and daring, being excluded by poverty from the sweets of civil honors, produced a reign of mere violence. Then come tumultuous assemblies, massacres, banishments, redivisions of land."[14]

In various regions, such as Mitylene, Argos, and Syracuse, there were bloody revolts of the poor; while in Athens, which never went to such frenetic extremes, the opposition to the wealthy, following the Peloponnesian War, expressed itself in confiscations of property desired for the expenses of public administration. Meanwhile the needy were the objects of what we would call a "dole"; after the Sicilian misadventure, the State granted two obols per day to each of the poor; and thus not only the recipients were demoralized, but the State was corrupted by a concentration upon the people's fund to the neglect of more important aims such as defense. At the same time, every effort was made to increase the distributions, and, correspondingly, the means to enable the people to attend the theater. The comment of Aristotle is eloquent: "The avarice of mankind is insatiable; at one time two obols was enough, but now, when this sum has become customary, men still want more and more without end; for it of the nature of desire not to be satisfied, and most men live only for the gratification of it." [15]

Considering that the help was, as Aristotle further remarks, "like water poured into a leaky cask," it is no wonder that the city's re-

sources were dissipated, and that the orator Aeschines could speak of
the people meeting "not as deliberative assemblies, but rather as meetings of shareholders after a distribution of surpluses." The changing
attitudes may be illustrated by two contrasting incidents: in the year
483, the people followed the lead of Themistocles, put selfish inclina-
tions aside, and agreed to use the silver of Laurium to build a fleet,
even though ancient tradition permitted the revenues to be divided
among the people. (This, incidentally was the fleet which won the
victory of Salamis). But something under a century and a half later,
before the defeat of Chaeronaea, when a sentence of death and confiscation had been pronounced against a man who had heaped up riches by
illegal exploitation, the culprit's wealth was not devoted to any public
cause, but was divided among all citizens at the rate of fifty drachmas
each.

VI

It is a curious and contradictory fact that the poor and the underprivileged tend to propagate to the limits of subsistence, according to
Malthusian principles; whereas the privileged are inclined to have
few sons and daughters. This tendency of the well-to-do to commit
"race suicide" is conspicuous in the declining centuries of Greece, and
is itself a leading cause of the decline. That wealth should encourage
men to violate nature's strongest dictate, and to let their line die out,
is probably the strangest of all the strange results of acquisitiveness.
And yet the connection is visible enough, for riches bring self-indulgence, and self-indulgence brings an unwillingness to make sacrifices
even for one's closest kin; and such an unwillingness, carried to an
extreme, may involve a reluctance to have descendants, or, in any
case, many descendants.

And so, in Greece, a time came when one son was deemed sufficient,
whereas one daughter was held to be too many. With the sophistry
that flows so readily to the self-justifying, men would argue that this
restriction of the family was for the good of their children, since it
saved them from becoming paupers, or from having to divide their
estates after the death of their parents. Yet it is easy to trace less
altruistic motives. Polybius, in describing conditions in Boetia in the
third century, has some illumination to shed:

"People who had no children, in place of leaving their property to
their collaterals, as was formerly the custom, spent it on banquets and
drinking parties and bestowed it on their friends as common property;
a good number of those who had children reserved the major part of

their wealth for such convivial parties; so much so that many Boetians held more supper parties in a month than the month had days." [16]

The situation is further depicted by the same historian:

"We see in our time throughout the whole of Greece such a shrinkage of the birth rate, and, in a word, such depopulation that the towns are deserted, the fields lie waste although there are neither continual wars nor epidemics. . . . The cause of the evil is manifest. From vanity, from avarice, or from cowardice, men are unwilling either to marry, or bring up children without marrying." [17]

Anything that contributed to depopulation seemed to be favored. Abortion was permitted, unless opposed by the woman's husband or seducer; infanticide or exposure of the unwanted child was regarded as proper, and was even defended by the philosophers. Thus it came about that in Athens, in the fourth century, the voluntary loss of population was as great as all the losses caused in the third by pestilence and war. And in Sparta, because of laws forbidding citizens to engage in trade and making it impossible to divide the inherited strip of land, depopulation proceeded at an even faster rate.

In these facts we can see a leading reason why Greece withered and decayed. Wealth and its inheritance, and the luxuries and self-indulgence it encouraged, may not have been the only sources of the decline. Nevertheless, we may safely say that, except for the weakening effects of riches, Greece could not have declined so fast nor so far, nor have been so hollowed out by depopulation, nor have stood so helpless and unprepared when the Macedonian conqueror and later the Roman came marching in with clanking swords.

We may observe how, in Greece, by means of gradual seductions, the idea of enrichment worked its way into the confidence of the people. Holding forth an iridescent beverage, it offered them a poison; promising jewels and gold, it granted them a sword in the throat; inviting them to a banquet, it executed a death-dance above their mouldering bones. Treacherous as an assassin, it was like a fox that slays all the geese in a barnyard; and the desolated landscapes which it left behind, the deserted farms and emptied cities, the crumbling palaces and violated temples, remained as mute testimonials to the passage of a destroyer more powerful than storm or fire.

V

THE MONEY LORDS OF ROME

It is said of the Emperor Caligula that once at a banquet he served his guests with bread and other viands of gold. No man at this late day can vouch for this story; but true or false, it is symbolic of an age in which material things counted for all or almost all—an age of which Juvenal, in his third Satire, remarks that were one to produce a witness as virtuous as Numa himself, the first inquiry would be as to his property and the last as to his character.

If you could visit that Rome of the early Caesars, and wander among the gardens and villas of the wealthy, you would be dazzled by the opulence of your surroundings. You might stroll through miles of colonnaded walks, amid porticoes and basilicas, past fountains that gleamed from basins of silver, and beside mansions with walls of porphyry and delicate veined marble. Entering one of these private palaces, you might see a banqueting hall with columns of honey-colored Oriental alabaster; you might be regaled by a picture gallery or a museum of curios; you might observe elegant baths, where the white Carrara was varied by foreign marbles tinted with violet, russet, and green. You might step across floors of inlaid onyx or of glass, beneath walls coated with mother-of-pearl or with gem-studded silver leaf; you might rest your hand on a myrrhine vase or a citrus-wood table that had cost the equivalent of fifteen thousand dollars; while the very carpet beneath your feet might have been imported from Damascus at an expense of more than two hundred thousand dollars.

But if you were transported to the palace of the Emperor, you might see even these splendors eclipsed. In stories that seem straight from the Arabian Nights, we are told of draughts of melted pearls in the reign of Caligula, and of gemmed galleys bearing fruit-trees and gardens upon their decks; we are asked to believe that Nero would pay as much as a hundred and fifty thousand dollars for the Egyptian roses at a banquet; while Domitian, among other extravagances, is said to have poured out a sum mounting high into the millions merely in order to gild a temple on the Capitol.

It is not unlikely that some of these stories or all are exaggerated. But the truth behind them is clear enough, for the extravagance which they report is one of the outstanding facts of later Roman history.

Let us glance further at that extravagance. Suppose that you are a guest of the wealthy at one of the banquets that last from dawn to twilight. You and your fellow guests recline on couches, musicians play, dancers cavort, perhaps a tight-rope walker or a juggler entertains you, and slaves weave their way in and out carrying rare wines and even rarer victuals from the far corners of the Empire. You may not be served with nightingales' tongues (though such a dish has actually been mentioned), but the main dinner will probably contain ten courses or more, beginning with dainties made from as many as seventeen kinds of fish and game. All this will be served with the pomp and formality of a religious rite. As each dish is brought in, a *tricliniarch* will captain his *decuries* of slaves, a *structor* will arrange the dishes, an *analecta* will pick up the scraps dropped by the diners. There will be a special slave to carve the meats and fowls, a special slave to call out the name of each dish, a special footman to stand in attendance behind the couch of each guest. And the feasters may indulge in the disgusting, often mentioned habit of taking emetics in order to cheat nature.

In this degeneracy, you will of course see the Romans only after foreign aggrandizement and the wealth of empire have spread their softening, deleterious influence. But the full story is not expressed nor more than suggested by what you observe in the mansions and at the banqueting couches of the well-to-do. Before we look more closely at the imperial period, it may be well to go back through the centuries and glance at the rise of the money-god.

II

Early Italy was a land not of traders, but of farmers, who despised the merchant. And yet, in a way, the Romans were as greedy as tradesmen; their method of seeking profit was through the competition of war. Like the raiders of Assyria and many another land, they added to their property by taking that of their neighbors, though the particular property which they sought was land rather than merchandise. "This," as J. C. Stobart remarks, "was the Roman method of making agriculture pay. The spring of the year and the month which still bears the name of Mars was not only the season of returning life to nature, but it was also the time when the god and his worshippers buckled on their armor to seek fresh ploughlands, just as did the primitive Germans. It was Europe's first method of extensive farming, and the habit clung to the Romans long after they had ceased to be farmers." [1]

It is true that your neighbors, whose land you sought, might object to your "method of making agriculture pay." They might even be so churlish as to strike back, and try to take your land. But this would be one of your unavoidable little business risks.

Even after agriculture became relatively less important, the sword continued to be the symbol and the tool of Roman acquisitiveness. It was the sword that opened up the way to foreign lands, and laid the foundations of that empire which was to bring in streams of loot. An important distinction, however, must be made: the Romans did desire the loot, but not the burdens of empire. Somewhat like the British in India many centuries later, they were the rather confused and embarrassed recipients of empire. In some cases, it was literally wished upon them, as when Attalus III of Perganum, when he died in 133 B.C., left his kingdom by will to Rome—a bequest which was not only to provoke a scramble for the plunder of the new territory, but was to inspire similar bequests in Cyrenaica, in Bithynia, and elsewhere. But in 81 B.C., when Alexander II of Egypt offered the kingdom of Egypt itself, the Senators declined the gratuity. True, such refusals, in the long run, would have small effect. Without being able to foresee or avoid the consequences, Rome stumbled into empire in the course of her adventures abroad.

That her intentions were not commercial in the modern sense of the term, is proved by the fact that she destroyed the great seaports of Carthage and Corinth with all their docks and rich trading facilities, and permitted the former to lie waste for a full century until rebuilt by Julius Caesar, while the latter remained in ruins for well over a century before its reconstruction by Augustus. A nation of manufacturers and traders, ruled by the profit motive as we know it, would not have allowed the hundred-year obliteration of centers with such obvious possibilities for international business.

But it is the method of the warrior to destroy what he cannot carry off, and the warrior and not the tradesman prevailed in Carthage and Corinth, as in many another city devastated in Roman warfare. Fury against the enemy, desire for revenge, desire to put down a threat against the Roman commonwealth, were by no means the only incentives, nor even the leading incentives to the conquests. Think of the various kinds of valuable property to be acquired! And remember that a share of the booty would go to the general! First among the items of plunder, there were the people themselves—those who did not fall

beneath the sword or were not too old or infirm to be of any use. They
would all be herded off to the most available slave market, and could
be expected to bring a handsome price! Then the people's possessions!
their statutes and ornaments of gold and silver and bronze, their
swords and vases and fabrics, their furniture and gems, their oil and
wine and wheat! Truly, a treasury to which you could help yourself!

From the time of the Second Punic War, the booty brought to Rome
by her victorious generals was enough to upset the ancient economy;
as Pliny remarks, it introduced luxury into Italy. And now the
simple-hearted Roman, who of old had had no greater ambition than
to steal his neighbor's land, was fired with enthusiasm for theft overseas. Both an economic and a moral transformation took place. As
almost always in warfare, certain classes benefited, to the impoverishment of others; wealthy business men and capitalists arose; but the
peasants, who had gone forth to fight the wars, were only too likely
to find upon their return that they were forced into debt, were unable
to borrow what they needed, and must lose their farms.

Meanwhile those farms were being bought at a pittance by droves
of the *nouveaux riches*. And these upstarts, who in general felt no
allegiance except to the gods of the quick and large returns, took advantage of the new war-given supply of labor—the slave labor which more
and more replaced the free yeomen of former times, and transformed
the native economy by the creation of the hugh estates or *latifundia*,
in which the work was performed by rough and sometimes desperate
gangs of captives.

In the establishment of these great holdings, the land-greedy showed
no scruples. If they could not purchase a desired area legally, they
were content to take it illegally, through fraud, trickery, and even
direct seizure, often aided by the fact that the head of the family was
away on military duty. Thus the small farms disappeared, except for
a few scattered remnants. And the one-time farmers drifted about as
soldiers of fortune, at the command of factional leaders; or else they
joined the idling, publicly fed, publicly entertained, parasitic rabble.

Meanwhile the public wealth increased so rapidly that after 167 B.C.,
the Roman citizen paid no property taxes, nor any direct taxes at all.
Henceforth the common citizen would owe less and less in duties to
the State, and would expect more and more in gratuities; in this we
can see one phase of the social and moral degeneration which would
gradually become more conspicuous after the Punic Wars. And another
phase, and a still more obvious one, was concerned with individual self-
aggrandizement, as may be seen in many directions, but nowhere

more notoriously than in connection with the publicans, the "public business men," who received contracts for various public works, and notably for "tax-farming" in the colonies.

Ironically, it was Gaius Gracchus, one of the most public-minded of Roman reformers, who gave the movement its impetus. Evidently not foreseeing the road ahead in his zest to obtain cheap corn for the Roman populace, he introduced a law permitting prospective publicans to bid for tax-collecting rights aboard. In the beginning, remarkably enough, the system seemed to work not badly; but abuse was inevitable, since the rewards of abuse were enormous. The flaw lay in the honeyed inducement to the greedy: the tax-collector could make any levy whatever, and was obligated to return only a specified amount to the home government: the higher the taxes, the more his earnings; on all amounts above a specified minimum, these might be close to a hundred per cent! What, therefore, if the provincial had to sweat, strain, and groan for long, burdened hours? What if he had not food enough in his house, if his children cried out and he had hardly a scrap to clothe his nakedness?

One of the most scandalously corrupt of the publicans was Verres, at whom Cicero levelled some of his most scathing denunciations. This man, who had oppressed the fruitful province of Sicily, had made such profits that, after his days in office, he went about king-like in a litter carried by eight slaves, couched on a bed of Maltese rose-petals; during his trial he did his best to seduce his judges by a distribution of his ill-gotten gold. But even gold did not avail against the brilliance of the prosecutor; not even awaiting the judgment, Verres fled on the exile's obscure road. One must remember, however, that not every Verres had to face the lashing tongue of a Cicero.

And though not every publican was a Verres, the system itself was so bad that the honest man had a difficult time. For the publican ordinarily acted not only for himself but for a sort of stock company, whose income depended upon the revenues of the colonies; like the agent of a latter-day corporation, he had to consider the interests of the shareholders. F. Warde Fowler has well expressed the situation: "All honest provincial governors . . . found themselves in the same difficulty. They were continually beset by urgent appeals on behalf of the tax-companies and their agents—appeals made without a thought of the condition of a province or its tax-paying capacity—so completely had the idea of making money taken possession of the Roman mind." [2]

Even a man of such integrity as Cicero had so succumbed to the

impulses of the times that he could join in appeals for revenues wrung
from the backs of bleeding provincials. His letters have preserved
many such pleas, one of them to his son-in-law Furius Crassipides,
quaestor of Bithynia. Elsewhere, in his *pro lege Manilia*, he sheds
further light on an attitude apparently shared by the entire Roman
capitalistic class, who could speak unashamedly of war for the sake
of profits. Referring to the danger to the state if some of the citizens
lost their property and so dragged many down with them, he urges:
"Save the State from such a calamity . . . the whole system of credit
and finance which is carried on here at Rome in the Forum, is inextric-
ably bound up with the revenues of the Asiatic province. If these
revenues are destroyed, our whole system of credit will come down
with a crash. See that you do not hesitate for a moment to prosecute
with all your energies a war by which the glory of the Roman name,
the safety of our allies, our most valuable revenues, and the fortunes
of innumerable citizens, will be effectually preserved." [3]

Note how the "glory of the Roman name" and the safety of the
allies are bracketed with "fortunes of innumerable citizens."

Yet the maker of this plea was among the mildest of administrators
when for a year he was governor of Cilicia. One of his biographers
has summarized the case: "He contented himself with his legitimate
share of booty from the war—2,200,000 sesterces—with which he intended to defray the cost of the triumph of the Amaus. He left behind him a reputation far from usual, as a scrupulous, upright, and
equitable administrator—at least in so far as the customs of the time
permitted. He had tried to apply the principles of his *De Republica*,
and he was the first to attempt to introduce into Roman government
a conception of justice, fellowship and even of pity of which Rome
knew nothing." [4]

The fact that Cicero was comparatively moderate in his demands
upon Cilicia, and took no more than an ordinary fortune as the proceeds of his year's governorship, does not mean that he was not a man
of his age in his constant involvements in finance. His expenditures
were proportionate to his obligations: he not only maintained an elaborate mansion on the Palatine Hill, but had country villas at Pompeii,
Antium, Baiae, Astura, Caita, and Tusculum. The latter, his favorite,
was a palace of twenty rooms, which opened upon an ornamented and
columned gallery about three hundred feet long, with a view over forests, lakes, mountains, and valleys. He had equipped it, among other
things, with a library bedecked with Greek statues, and containing a

cedar table worth 50,000 sesterces; and he had built two gymnasia in gardens watered by their own aqueduct.

All this may have made a fitting retreat for a philosopher. But one remembers in contrast the squalid *insulae* of the commoners—the overcrowded several-storied tenements, waterless, without sanitary provisions, with no heating or lighting except of the most elementary, and in constant danger of collapse if not of destruction by fire. Also, one recalls that other men of wealth—for example, the financier Crassus—fattened on the returns from these "rabbit warrens."

To maintain his standard of living, unfortunately many another than Cicero had to go into debt. Cicero himself, in his *de Officiis*, tells us that at no time within his memory had the world fallen into such indebtedness; and in his second oration against Cataline he enumerates the types of debtors, including the men of wealth, who will not pay what they owe: the men who look for cancellation of debts by means of a revolution; and old debtors who, getting deeper and deeper "into the quagmire," are willing as a last resort to turn even to conspiracy.

Inevitably, where debt was common, the money-lenders or *argentarii* flocked. Some of these men gambled wildly, even as modern speculators. Take Rabirius Posthumus. Dealing in the stock of the tax companies, he lent money in several provinces, and in 54 B.C. was involved with Ptolemy Auletes, King of Egypt. After this monarch's expulsion from his dominions, Rabirius let himself get still more deeply implicated; acting through agents who might have been called "lobbyists" if that term had been invented, he sought to have the Senate restore the dethroned sovereign to power, and meanwhile he continued to lend to the ex-king, and induced his friends to lend. For he had his hands deep in one of those investments which one must either abandon as a total loss or keep alive with new funds; if he ceased his payments, Auletes would withdraw his friendship. But unhappily, the King was still not restored to his kingdom. After a time, the pressure of the creditors became so great that Gabinius, governor of Syria, yielded to it by marching into Egypt without Senatorial authorization; while he made Rabirius superintendent of the Egyptian revenues. But before the latter could obtain repayment, the fickle Auletes turned against him; and he lost all his money, and was hard pressed to escape with his life.

Here we have nothing more nor less than a huge gamble that failed. But Rabirius was not the only man who shuffled the cards for vast stakes: "There seemed indeed to have been a perfect passion for dealing with money in this wild way among the men of wealth and influence;

it was the fancy of the hour, and no disgrace attached to it if a man could escape ruin. Thus the vast capital accumulated—the sources of which were almost entirely in the provinces and the kingdoms of the frontier—were hardly ever used productively. It never returned to the region whence it came, to be used in developing its resources; the idea of using it even in Italy in industrial undertakings was absent from the mind of the gambler." [5]

Another notorious case was that of Scaptius, who sought out Cicero when the latter was governor of Cilicia, and asked the aid of the army on a bill-collecting mission against the citizens of Salamis in Cyprus. No wonder that the debt was hard to collect! Scaptius had been charging interest at 48 per cent! Cicero, upon investigation, found that Scaptius had used powerful influence at Rome to induce the Senate to legalize the loan; had obtained Roman cavalry to collect the interest; and had besieged the Salamanian Senate in their meeting-place, but had not obtained their acquiescence in the usurious payments until after five Senators had died of starvation. Almost equally strange! the lender of the money turned out to be none other than Brutus, one of the most respected of Roman citizens! Cicero, to his credit, refused to let the troops be used for a second time as a collection agency, and obtained from the Salamanians an offer to pay interest at a comparatively moderate and legal rate: 12 per cent, which Scaptius disdainfully rejected. The sequel is lost amid the mists of history. But one thing we know: that Cicero, upon returning to Rome, felt the heavy hand of retribution; Cato, the uncle of Brutus, prevailed upon the Senate to deny the orator the triumph he dearly desired. "The right to starve provincial senators who disliked paying 48 per cent interest to Roman aristocrats," drily remarks one historian, "seems to have been a fundamental aspect of that liberty upon which Brutus and Cato descanted so eloquently." [6]

In the following century, we find another case in which money-lending was connected with fighting, and involved another of Rome's celebrated sons: the philosopher Seneca, the tutor of Nero, and a stern critic of the morals of the age. Seneca was but following in the footsteps of other wealthy men when he made a large loan to Prasutagas, King of the Iceni, a British tribe. But it was his misfortune that the king died, and that when the loan was called in, the king's widow Boudicca (or Boaddicea) arose in revolt, and all Britain arose with her on the spur of various resentments against the Romans, and her troops engaged in sundry little acts of looting, destruction, and massacre. Eventually, however, at an estimated cost of seventy thousand

Roman lives, the rebellion was put down—a heavy price to pay for a war caused in part, even though only in part, by Seneca's money-lending.

In an eloquent passage, W. Warde Fowler has stated the effect upon the Roman Empire of the two chief classes of business men—the money-lenders and the tax-farmers: "It is hard to say which wrought the most mischief in the Empire. . . . Together too they did incalculable harm, morally and socially, among the upper strata of Roman soety at home. Economic maladies react upon the mental and moral condition of a State. Where the idea of making money for its own sake, or merely for the sake of pleasure derivable from excitement, is paramount in the minds of so large a section of society, moral perception quickly becomes warped. The sense of justice disappears, because when the fever is on a man he does not pause to ask whether his gains are ill-gotten; and in this age the only restriction on the plundering of the subjects of the Empire was a legal one, and that of no great efficacy. . . . There is lost also the sense of a duty arising out of the possession of wealth—the feeling that it should do some good in the world, or at least be in part applied to some useful purpose. Lastly, the exciting pursuit of wealth helps to produce a curious restlessness and instability of character." [7]

It is indicative of the moral insensitiveness of the times that a man such as Atticus, a friend of Cicero who has been regarded as a Roman of the highest type, could seek interest at rates running as high as 75 per cent, and could make a capital investment in slaves, and notably in gladiators, whom he rented at a profit. The incidental human agony, the mutilation, suffering, and death, seems to have meant nothing to investors such as Atticus.

Such callousness, one surmises, would not have been possible except for the tradition of cruelty and rapacity, the man-eat-man attitude visible all through the later Republic. Take the proscriptions under Sulla in 82 and 81 B.C., when the victorious general marched back to Rome and systematically began a massacre of his enemies. Not only did he slay several hundred on the day after his return to Rome; during the following eight months, he put to death an unknown number, which has been estimated as high as 4,700; he not only offered a reward for the assassination of the listed men, but confiscated their property. It is notable that many of the victims were of the wealthy equestrian class; and whether or not there is truth in the charge that some of the unfortunates were condemned simply because someone had coveted

their property, surely it was not altogether coincidental that many of
Sulla's friends were enriched by the confiscations.

But the proscriptions of Sulla were rivalled if not exceeded by those
of the Second Triumvirate. In this notorious episode, when Antony,
Lepidus, and Octavian sought to divide the world among them, political fear, hatred, and vindictiveness cost the lives of some of Rome's
most celebrated men, including Cicero. Here, intermingled with the
scarlet fabric of murder, we can see avarice lifting her leering face; we
can see murder for the sake of money, quite as distinctly as in the
crimes of the goriest bandits. The three conspirators, admittedly,
needed funds; and the easiest way to get funds was to rob men who
had them, particularly if the possessors happened to be political enemies—which they were not unlikely to be, as the friends of one of the
triumvirs were almost automatically opposed to the other two. And
the three, in their cynical game of power politics, were willing to sacrifice their friends. Thus, while eminent Senators fled to the shelter
of ditches or drains and ex-governors of provinces disguised themselves
as slaves or gladiators and implored their servants not to betray them,
the game of decapitation went on, and the triumvirs secured large
stretches of land for their veterans while filling their own treasuries.
What makes these proscriptions even ghastlier than those of Marius
and Sulla is the fact that, in the former instances, the confiscations
appear to have been more of an afterthought than a central design;
in the Second Triumvirate, the original design seems to have encom-
passed murder for the sake of enrichment. However, we must not forget that Antony, Lepidus, and Octavian had behind them the precedent of the earlier proscriptions and confiscations.

III

It is among the contradictions of Roman history that Octavian, one
of the cutthroat trio who usurped power and permitted widespread
depredations after the death of Caesar, became an emperor in many
ways notable for his attempts to halt depredations. In his efforts to
take some of the burden from the provincials, he imposed direct taxes
upon Roman citizens for the first time in generations, including a 5
per cent inheritance tax, a 4 per cent tax on the sale of slaves, and a
1 per cent tax covering goods sold at auction and by contracts of sale.
These impositions, not unnaturally, caused storms of protest, but were
among the factors enabling Augustus to introduce long-needed provincial reforms.

And so, during the early Empire, there was a marked improvement in some directions. The heyday of the publicans was over; a more stringent and honest administration sent abler and more enlightened men abroad, and for longer terms of office, and at salaries that reduced the temptation to suck the provincials dry. There were now, besides, more Roman citizens in the provinces, which made the practice of avarice more risky, as the extortions might be reported to Rome; and there were provincial councils that might check the exactions of the governor. Thus for a time the provinces enjoyed prosperity, and comparative freedom from exploitation.

To be sure, there were exceptions. We have observed one in the case of the Britons under Queen Boudicca. And Tacitus mentions another, concerning the Frisians, a people beyond the Rhine, who rebelled "rather from our rapacity than from their unwillingness to submit":

The tribute Drusus laid upon the Frisians, according to Tacitus, "was easy, and suited to their contracted means; namely, to furnish certain hides for military purposes. No one thought to insist on the particular size or thickness, till Olennius, the first centurian of a legion, being sent to govern them, picked out hides of some wild bulls, and demanded that according to their measure the tribute should be paid; a hard task even among other nations, and to the Germans the more intolerable, as their forests abound in beasts of mighty bulk, and their domestic animals are small. First they parted with the herds themselves, next they resigned the land, last of all they surrendered their wives and children to bondage. Hence their indignation and complaints: but as these brought no relaxation, they sought relief by war." [8]

At the very time when an outlying tribe such as the Frisians could be brought to such desperate straits, the moneyed lords of Rome were living in the marbled and retinued luxury that we have observed. There is, however, another side to the picture; the man of means, as in Greece, was expected not only to take but to give. It was held that wealth brought obligations toward the less privileged; and public opinion was a watchdog preventing evasion of such duties. The inscriptions of the early Empire show us a great number of public benefactors, who, it is true, often catered to a degenerate taste by providing gladiatorial shows, but sometimes donated monuments such as theaters, baths, aqueducts, roads, and markets.

Pliny the Younger, for example, though not one of Rome's wealthiest men, built and repaired temples, gave money for baths and communal feasts, offered to contribute one third for a school at Como, and showered forth many other benefactions. Agrippa, a friend of Augustus, constructed the Pantheon at his own expense. And Augustus made donations on a magnificent scale; more than once he balanced the imperial budget by meeting the deficit out of his private funds; on one occasion, he defrayed the cost of repairing the Italian roads; and in other instances, he gave liberally for famine relief, public amusements, and public works.

Not that political foresight may not here have mingled with philanthropy. "It would be in accord with the facts," remarks Ferrero, "to say that these striking largesses were one of the means by which the imperial authority was gradually concentrated in the heart of the Roman State, and surrounded itself with so much gratitude, so many interests, and so many hopes as to be able definitely to secure the principal position against all the organs of the State." [9]

And if Augustus was but taking the oath expected of the wealthy, some of his successors followed in his footsteps, though with notable variations. Domitian, when he spent the equivalent of 2,400,000 pounds for gilding a temple, was not himself the real beneficiary; the actual if involuntary donors were the well-to-do men robbed or slain beneath his dictatorship. Having made himself censor for life, he proceeded to take what he would, like the super-brigand that he was. Let a man have a fortune that stood out above the majority, or let him possess a rich villa, and he might expect to pay for the ruler's extravagance with his plundered lands if not with his life.

Nor was Domitian the only emperor who maintained his pomp and display by methods of banditry. Under Tiberius, under Caligula, under Nero, and under Commodus and other self-indulgent sovereigns, similar means prevailed. Caligula even introduced torture, which was employed in his presence to exact confessions justifying confiscation of property; among those on whom he applied such methods were his adopted son Tiberius Gemellus, and the Praetorian Prefect Macro and his wife.

IV

Beginning with Tiberius, the emperors were assisted in their raids on private property by the tool known as *delation*—one of those iniquitous devices which, under other names and with partially different features, was revived by the Inquisition and by the totalitarians of the twentieth century. A *delator* was an informer; he was a man who, out of malice or avarice or a combination of the two, acted as a sort of private spy, and notified the emperor of any word or act of a subject that could be construed as in the remotest way treasonous. As the condemned man's property would be confiscated and the *delator* would receive a share—usually one fourth—the business of *delation* might be highly remunerative. Tacitus gloomily refers to a whole year being "an uninterrupted series of accusations," and remarks, "For myself, I have only to record the mandates of despotism, incessant accusations, faithless friendships, the ruin of innocence; one unvarying repetition of cases terminating in the same event." [10] Toward the end of the reign of Tiberius, according to the historian, all classes in Rome were overshadowed by the terror; all men, even foremost senators, might turn informers; no man could be sure that a chance word or a careless deed might not serve as his death sentence.

Take the case of Clutorius Priscus, who had had the poor discretion to write an elegy on the Emperor's son Drusus. Drusus, contrary to expectations, recovered; and so Priscus had to die. Or consider the crime of Cremutius Cordus, who had written a history in which he referred to Caesar's murderer Cassius as "the last of the Romans." For this ill-advised historical judgment, Cordus was forced to take his own life. In most cases, it is true, the condemnations cannot be ascribed wholly to the emperor's cupidity; political animosity, political antagonism, and sheer fear were important elements. But this was not necessarily true of the *delators* themselves. Moreover, the avarice of the rulers may be judged by these remarks of a modern commenator: "The slightest suspicion of disloyalty or discontent, the most insignificant act or word, which a depraved ingenuity could misinterpret, was worked up into a formidable indictment by men eager for their share of the plunder. To have written the memoir of a Stoic saint or kept the birthday of a dead emperor, to possess an imperial horoscope or a map of the world, to call a slave by the name of Hannibal or a dish by that of Lucullus, might become a fatal charge." [11]

So deeply entrenched was the profiteering motive that no prudent man failed to remember the Emperor in his will. But this was perhaps to be expected in a land where heritage-hunting was almost a recognized institution. To ingratiate one's self with the childless rich—to feign friendship for the sake of rewards—seems to have been considered an honorable form of business activity. On the other hand, if a man were not a legacy-chaser, he might be afraid to make a gift to a childless acquaintance, lest he be suspected of having his eyes on a bequest. It is possible to read more than an ironic meaning in Juvenal's remark when, celebrating a friend's escape from shipwreck, he notes that no one would waste a sick hen or a crow on him, as he had three children.

True, one cannot suppose that the wealthy testators never saw through the fawnings of the carrion-seekers. But they exacted their price, as Samuel Dill puts it, by gathering an army of dependents in old age, "such as a career of great achievement could hardly attract." More than that! since no head of a family could expect to be so attended, they placed a special value upon childlessness. And this sordid consideration would appear to have contributed to that decline of the birth rate which depleted the old Roman stock.

A similar groveling of the human spirit can be seen in another institution, that of host and client. As a rich man needed attendants to maintain his place in society, he might be willing to fling out a cast-off garment disdainfully, throw a few coins, or extend a patronizing last-minute dinner invitation to one of the wretches who trailed after his chair in the street, ran his errands like a busboy, and minced at his morning receptions. Not that the client was necessarily an undistinguished man; no less a personage than the renowned epigramatist Martial had had to submit to this form of humiliation. One can only surmise how many bright spirits were dimmed if not crushed beneath the ignominious system.

"In this materialized society," Samuel Dill points out, "all the prizes go to the coarser qualities; there is nothing but neglect and starvation before taste and intellect. . . . The man who will expend a fortune on his baths and colonnades, can spare a Quintilian only a fraction of what he will give for a pastry cook. The grammarian, who is expected to be the master of all literature, will be lucky if he receives as much for a year as a charioteer gains by a single victory." [12]

Before we throw any stones at the ancient Romans, let us ask if these words would not have a familiar tone if, for "grammarian," we were to substitute "artist, author, or musician," while instead of "charioteer," we were to say "champion of the prize ring."

In a land where wealth was mistaken for quality and where acquisition was regarded as synonymous with merit, we must not be startled to see the ethics of buy-and-sell extended to politics, and even to the highest officials of the Emperor. We must not be surprised, for example, at Gibbon's statement concerning Cleander, minister of the worthless Commodus: "Avarice was the reigning passion of his soul, and the principle of his administration. The rank of consul, of patrician, of senator, was exposed to public sale; and it would have been considered as disaffection if any one had refused to purchase these empty and disgraceful honors with the greatest part of his fortune. In the lucrative provincial employments the minister shared with the governor the spoils of the people. The execution of the laws was venal and arbitrary. A wealthy criminal might obtain not only the reversal of the sentence by which he was justly condemned, but might likewise inflict whatever punishment he wished on the accuser, the witnesses, and the judge." [13]

Under such a regime, one may be sure, an accuser would think twice before bringing a rich man to the bar on any charge however merited. And a witness would think twice before testifying against a rich man, and a judge before condemning him.

All this, however, apparently mattered little to Cleander, who within three years "had accumulated more wealth than had ever yet been possessed by any freedman."

But if Cleander may have seemed to have reached the lowest extreme in putting the office of consul or of senator up for public sale, he was to be far outdone a few years later. In 193 A.D., after the murder of the Emperor Pertinax, some of the Praetorian guards ran out on the ramparts of Rome, and let it be known that the Roman world would be sold by public auction to the highest bidder. One would not suppose that so preposterous a proposal would be taken seriously; but though many heard it with shame and fury, there was at least one—the wealthy old senator Didius Julianus—who evidently regarded it as a good business proposition. Having listened to the cooings of flatterers, he rushed to the ramparts, and began to bid for the throne against Sulpicianus, the father-in-law of the beheaded Pertinax. The contest must have been most exciting: Sulpicianus promised each soldier a gift of five thousand drachmas, but Julianus surpassed this by offering six thousand, and consequently was declared Emperor, and marched amid the swords and shields of the troops to the Senate-house, where his election was acknowledged. Not that he had much cause to exult: after a troubled reign of sixty-two days, he was to lose his head in the literal sense of the term.

V

Though avarice here reached one of its climaxes, greed in the Roman world did not ordinarily follow the commercial channels familiar to later centuries. And in part this was because trade, in the Roman world as in the Greek, was slow, uncertain, and precarious, while industry on the modern scale was unknown. And in part the

reason was the low repute of the trader. "Unlike the Greeks of the
Athenian and the Hellenistic period," says one commentator, the
Romans "were not deeply or for a long time interested in trade." [14]
Many of their traders were mere adventurers who sought quick fortunes in the colonies, and cared more about the speed than the method
of their enrichment. To men of the senatorial order, besides, trade
was forbidden. The specific regulation, beginning with the Claudian
Law first proposed in 219 B.C. and reaffirmed by Julius Caesar, forbade senators and their sons to own ships of more than 300 amphores
capacity (less than 1,760 gallons). Since this made trading by sea
virtually impossible, agriculture rather than commerce formed the
great source of wealth, and notably so in the final period of the Empire.

Nevertheless, the life of Rome's declining centuries was crisscrossed
by avarice, which was itself a large factor in the decline.

One direction in which this avarice erupted was in the army. While
the other armed forces may not have gone quite to the extreme of the
Praetorian Guard in auctioning off the Empire, they approached it in
the pocketbook control which they exercised over the State. "Make
the soldiers rich and do not trouble about the rest," was a principle
announced by the Emperor Septimus Severus, whose troops had been
paid 20,000 sesterces each for crowning him (the funds having been
obtained by confiscations in the provinces). . . . "The soldier must
have a full purse."

But the soldier's purse, it would appear, was a bottomless cavern.
And this perhaps was only to be expected, since the legionaires but
followed the universal law of greed: the more they received, the more
they wanted. Thus various emperors, such as Maximian (235-238)
glutted the army with gold; while, four decades later, the Senator
Tacitus was put into office because of his wealth although he was
seventy-five years old and protested against his elevation.

When the first consideration in any army's mind is its pay, the last
consideration is likely to be the country's welfare. A connection can
be traced between the increasing rapacity of the Roman army and its
declining quality and defensive ability. One fact instantly strikes us:
with the waning Roman economy, the troops came to be paid in goods
or land rather than in money; and this made it too costly to maintain
a native army—which brought about the wide acceptance of barbarians, who fought under their own chiefs and were content to take land
in payment. This, manifestly, led toward the feudal system; and
quite as manifestly, it pointed toward the day when Rome would be
too weak to stem the floods of invasion from the forests and steppes.

Just as the army was one of the focal points of avarice, so the slave system was another. In order to understand this statement, we must range both backward and forward in time, for it would not be incorrect to say that the Roman Empire began and ended in slavery—that is, it ended with the rise of a serfdom so near to slavery that the difference lay as much in nomenclature as in fact. From the time of the Punic wars and onward, droves of slaves were driven by the warmakers to the markets of the Mediterranean, and to Rome itself—the captured men, women, and children of overrun cities and provinces. Some of these were no doubt comparatively well treated; but others, many others, were handled with the utmost brutality—so reputable a Roman as Cato the Censor could argue that it was cheaper to work them to death than to treat them kindly. And there were many Catos in the Roman world—men who dealt with slaves as with cattle in the slaughter pen, who drove them to the limits of endurance on the vast ranches, lodged them at night in fetid dungeons or *ergastula*, beat and abased them as domestic servants, or trained them as gladiators to murder and be murdered. Under the Empire, however, when the *pax Romana* cut off the spoils of foreign conquest including human booty, the slave came to be treated with a new consideration, not only as an item of property but as a man; many slaves found the way open to manumission and even to posts of responsibility and fortune as freedmen.

But this does not mean that the freeing of the slaves was necessarily an act of pure benevolence. On the farms it had been found that slave labor was more expensive than free, since slaves would not work except under compulsion, and then would give forth no more than a begrudging minimum of effort. And in the cities it was becoming too expensive to maintain establishments for slaves, and to provide them with the family life that had grown to be the custom. Under these circumstances, many masters found it cheaper to set their slaves free.

In any case, the Roman world was drifting away from slavery, which was becoming obsolete or almost so. But just at the turning point, new social changes and new acquisitive forces introduced a new and more enduring servitude.

Most conspicuously, those acquisitive forces are to be seen operating in the breakdown of the civil administration and in the growth of the great landed estates. To be sure, other forces than cupidity were in action; but private greed was a powerful element in the collapse of the ancient system.

The trouble, from the point of view of the civil administration, was not that the government did not perceive and make strenuous efforts to correct the evils; a succession of enlightened leaders—Aurelian, Diocletian, and others—struggled mightily against the forces of ruin. But they battled gigantic odds. And some of their best-intended efforts led only to frustration. Thus, in its attempts to collect the taxes necessary to carry out its paternalistic and often grandiose projects for public relief and improvement, the government clamped down a servitude in some ways comparable with that of Egypt under the Ptolemies, binding the farm workers to the land, and the city workers to hereditary guilds, while the property owner was in danger of being drained dry. Here, of course, was a situation ideal for the corrupt official. It is not surprising, therefore, that the venality of Rome's under-agents, along with the dishonesty of the landed proprietors, proved too much for the rulers, while provincial administration became, as Samuel Dill describes it, "a synonym for organized brigandage."

As a root of the many-branching evil, consider the institution of patronage, whereby the small received illicit favors from the great. "Entire villages entered into it," says J. W. Thompson. "The effect was to estop the imperial authority, to arrest the administration of justice, and collection of taxes, and to bring the government to naught. In spite of imperial endeavors to restrain the spread of the practice, it continued to flourish in both East and West. It is found in Asia Minor and in Spain, in Egypt and in Gaul." [15]

Closely related to patronage, we can see the "conflict of interests," a disruptive influence that bit deep—there were even instances in which Emperors profited from the gifts of interested parties. On a somewhat lower level, we may note the prohibition against a governor's taking a second term of office in the same province, lest he form too strong or tempting connections. And there were the regulations forbidding anyone to interview the governor after the closing of his court at midday; while he is ordered not to accept invitations to the "luxurious quarters" of the wealthy.

Meanwhile other evils were almost too numerous to mention: the evils of raids upon unprotected property, and particularly that of the persons least able to strike back, such as orphans and widows; the evils of a debased currency, which sometimes became so bad that the government refused to accept payment in the very coin it had meted out; the evils of the land-tax, a leading factor in the decay of agriculture and the overgrowth of cities; and the fraud in army supplies, which became so serious that we hear Diocletian lamenting his inability to supply the armies, owing to prices which had leapt to four and even eight times the value of the commodities.

At the same time the great proprietors, aided by purchasable tax-collectors, were largely able to evade their share of the tax upon the land, or else contrived to harness the burden about the shoulders of men less able to pay. They bribed the assessors to falsify entries of taxable property; they bribed bookkeepers to color the records; and they took advantage of the rise of men who bought their way to high office.

Thus we can see the fraud in the case of the *susceptores,* who received the tribute necessary to support the army and the government functions. These rogues employed all methods of chicanery: they used false weights and measures; they tampered with treasury lists; they withheld receipts, or granted invalid receipts; they profiteered by means of a law which denied the validity of receipts and so made it possible to exact double payment; they applied actual terrorism. Conditions grew so bad that more than once the Emperor felt obliged to remove these vicious officials from an entire province.

But if the *susceptores* were little more than freebooters, nothing better can be said of another class of officials, the *discussores,* who were appointed to ferret out and collect delinquent payments. Their activities during the dying years of the Empire, have been vividly described by Samuel Dill:

"Their object, of course, was mere plunder. . . . Estates were frequently changing hands, and, in the confusion of a time of invasion and panic, documents would be lost or purchases would be made without full knowledge of the liabilities of the vendor. The discussor, who had obtained his office by intrigue, came down with a powerful retinue, obtained doubtless in the same way, demanding old receipts, presenting a mass of cooked accounts, which no one could check, least of all the simple farmer. What followed, as described by the emperor, resembles the worst scenes in Turkish provincial government, outrage, torture, imprisonment, murder; and all these enormities were countenanced, and actively supported, by officers of the palace and the praetorium, with the aid of the soldiers of the neighboring garrison. Who can wonder that people exposed to such brutality . . . should welcome the rude justice of the Gothic chief?" [16]

In the avarice, fraud, and banditry of hosts of small officials, therefore, we can see one root of the evil which was undermining the Empire. And a second root, as already suggested, is to be noted in the great landed estates.

Here we have a force that goes back more than half a dozen centuries, to the great wars of the Republic, which brought in hordes of captives and transformed agriculture by largely substituting slave-gangs for the small farmers. From these movements, a multitude of evils arose to afflict both country and city. In many regions, pasturelands replaced cultivated areas; while the production of grain, as in Greece in earlier centuries, was vitally reduced, giving place to less essential crops, and particularly to the vine. As a result, famines occurred, particularly in the Greek and Asiatic provinces. The Emperor Domitian, according to Suetonius, tried to combat this condition by an edict forbidding the planting of any more vines in Italy, and ordering the destruction of half the vineyards in the provinces—but apparently all he accomplished was to evoke a great cry of protest.

Meanwhile the large landholder, in the course of the centuries, grew to be a veritable lord, whose word was a command to slaves and free men alike. By the fifth century, he had his own armed force, kept his own prisoners, was his own law-making and law-enforcement agency, and collected his debts by the simple procedure of sending soldiers to seize the debtor.

And what the landowner did not grasp by armed might, he was more likely than not to obtain by collusion or fraud. Sometimes he maneuvered to obtain property at trifling prices; sometimes he appropriated the better lands of small holders, leaving them only the worthless tracts; frequently he caught the small proprietor in hopeless coils of debt. Then, due to arrears in interest, the poor man might be forced to part with his land at much less than its value.

Thus, by devious methods, the small holder was more and more forced out, the great estates became greater, and medievalism drew nearer. Indeed, medievalism was actually at hand; the poor freeman, uprooted from his land, helpless amid the armed violence of the times, and in need of a shield against the brutal blasts of invasion, was driven more and more to rely for protection upon the landed great, who would sometimes indeed give him protection—though at what a price! The beneficiary was free no longer; he must serve his benefactor; he was attached to the land, a serf who could not leave his district nor even marry outside it. Singly and in groups, men surrendered to the seemingly inevitable, and gave themselves up to the lords of the land. And thus they signallized the end of the long centuries of Roman rule.

VI

THE MIDDLE AGES: BRIGANDS, BARONS, AND BANKERS

In the tragedy of the distintegration of the Roman Empire, and in the dreary phantasmagoria of the Dark Ages, we see proof that the forces of avarice are a little like disease germs, always lurking in hidden places, ready to attack and multiply. When the body politic is sound, they may be kept in relative control; but once illness has attacked the people's moral fibre and their administrative and political system, the microbes of catch-and-grab and get-and-gain will win control, with weakening if not disastrous effects. And the malady will not be cured, or even held in check, until a strong administrative system is once more established, and exerts a new spiritual and moral suasion.

Here, in epitome, is the story of Western Europe during the period of Rome's downfall and for half a dozen succeeding centuries. Almost everywhere in the secular world, we see ascendant predatory forces; almost everywhere we observe greed unleashed. Europe is a little like a forest in which wolf preys upon wolf.

We can observe this in the barbarian invasions, wherein loot and pillage ride with the inrushing hordes. To be sure, we have here a wide variety of peoples, some far more savage than others. There were some who, like the ancient Slavs, were cattle-breeders and agriculturists of a sort and had made a start toward civilization, though they still confused the merchant and the marauder. Then there were the vast German hordes who, while they too had made a certain progress, did not hold either the life or the property of a visiting trader to be sacred, and augmented their often scanty existence by piratical raids: witness the incursions of the Vikings, sometimes made with fleets of hundreds of ships, whose crews were not only gluttonous and blood-thirsty but avid for gold. Beyond these, there were the still wilder tribes that swept in successive waves from the far distances of Asia—Avars, Huns, Bulgars, Magyars, Mongols, etc.—"peoples of prey," nomadic horsemen with few possessions, who revelled in warfare and murder, and plundered with no compunction.

But all these peoples were more or less alike in one respect: their desires were aroused by sight of the wealth of the Roman Empire, or by fabulous reports of that wealth. Example after example could be cited. In the region of the Rhine and Danube, the Germans seized not only the state lands but all private property. In Gaul, in Spain, in Italy and elsewhere, various tribes such as the Burgundians, Visigoths, and Ostrogoths, by reason of acting as military defenders, demanded a share in all properties and their fruits. The first two of these tribes were not content with less than two thirds of the vineyards, gardens, houses, cattle, and slaves. But their exactions were mild beside those of the Lombards, who not only occupied the land, slew the landowners, and looted the churches, but compelled the surviving Romans to pay a tribute of one third of everything produced by the country.

The pillagings of the Vandals under Gaiseric, who ravaged like a whirlwind and set up a pirates' stronghold at Carthage, are of course legendary. But hardly less rapacious were the Visigoths, who, according to St. Jerome, stripped every sign of civilization from the vast territory between the Alps and the Pyrenees and between the Atlantic and the Rhine; sacked the churches and monasteries; carried away the sacred vessels; and bore off the furniture, jewelry, and cattle of the Roman villas, while drinking the wine. We have pictures of the still more barbarous Almanni loading their chariots not only with clothes and furniture but with the very stones of the demolished mansions. Worse still! many of the raiders, in the senseless way of brigands, ruined everything they could not cart off—hacked down fruit trees, set fire to harvests and houses, and did their best to make a desert of the land.

A vivid picture of the greed-driven invaders is presented by Gibbon in describing the sack of Rome by Alaric, king of the Goths, in 410 A.D. (and Alaric was far from the most terrible of the barbarian leaders): "In the pillage of Rome a just preference was given to gold and jewels, which contain the greatest value in the smallest compass and weight; but after these portable riches had been removed by the more diligent robbers, the palaces of Rome were rudely stripped of their splendid and costly furniture. The sideboards of massy plate, and the variegated wardrobes of silk and purple, were irregularly piled in the wagons that always followed the march of a Gothic army. The most exquisite works of art were roughly handled or wantonly destroyed. Many a statue was melted for the sake of the precious materials; and many a vase, in the division of the spoil, was shivered into fragments by the stroke of the battleaxe. The acquisition of riches served only to stimulate the avarice of the rapacious barbarians, who proceeded by threats, by blows, and by tortures to force from the prisoners the confession of hidden treasure."[1]

II

Since the barbarians in their raids and wars were kindled with the brigand's lust for riches, what shall we expect of them when the power of the Western Empire has finally broken down and they themselves are the rulers and law-makers?

For our answer, we need merely glance at the history of the next several centuries. First let us observe the Merovingian monarchy of the Franks, founded on the ruins of the old Roman authority. Here, as historians agree, we see civilization ringed about by heavy shadows. We see a sharp, a catastrophic decline from the systematic regime of the Romans; we see commerce withering away, industry reduced to a local level, cities depopulated, public buildings falling into decay, literacy among laymen almost a forgotten art. And now, as usually when culture dwindles, the restraints to rapacity are discarded; government is virtually founded upon plunder.

Among the Merovingian kings, the sense of public responsibility was absent. Each of these rulers saw the world's end and beginning in himself. His kingdom, as one historian has phrased it, "was for him only a soil for exploitation."[2] He fought as did any pirate chief. He sent expeditions abroad—to Germany, to Italy, to Spain—for reasons that any pirate chief would have approved: to capture booty and levy a tribute. And not content to plunder foreigners only, he made raids upon his own subjects by demanding payments and services, in return for which he gave nothing at all, while he helped himself to all the gold and silver of the realm and stored them in his coffers.

The same covetousness, meanwhile, pervaded the whole administration. The monarchs appeased their retainers by handing them large shares of the wealth filched from the people; and their followers, in turn, greedy for gold, fought one another in rival groups, wherein bribery was the chief weapon, since "The last word in politics was to bribe a rival's 'faithful' followers."[3] Upon many of these schemers—who attached themselves to the ruler by a bond known as the *Commendatio*—grants of money or of land known as *benefices* were bestowed, and these grants were soon extended to cover exemptions from taxation, the gifts of public posts, and other favors. Unless some such reward was in sight, the king could expect no obedience, for nothing was done except for pay.

Manifestly the Merovingian monarchy, termite-ridden with avarice, could not endure. But whenever we look during those dim centuries following the fall of Rome, we see a somewhat similar story of trampling lords; we observe the virtual fragmentation of civilization, if the term civilization applies to the wolf-pack existence of those days. In forest hideouts or in rude wooden castles in mountains or on river heights, a multitude of petty leaders claim control over minor dominions, wrestle with fellow princelings for what they can get, and show no more regard for the weaponless commoner than for the wild boar of the woods. Now we enter the period of the robber barons, noblemen in name and bandits in reality, whose chief if not only means of subsistence is robbery, and who make the few straggling roads and the river highways unsafe and terrible and forestall or paralyze what little commerce might otherwise flow. Now, too, we encounter pirates so dread that they set decoys on the shore in order to lure ships to destruction. Now, again, we come face to face with the private wars, wherein Baron A sends his armed men against Baron B because of some personal feud, or because he is jealous, or because he covets land or castles. Now, except for the authority of the Church, which is uncertain and partial at best, there is no power to restrain the murderous hand or hold back the lunge and thrust of freebooting lords. As always when a central control is lacking, acquisitiveness has free rein. And acquisitiveness, attended by bigotry, ignorance, arrogance, and terror, leaves most of Europe near the barbarian level throughout several of the most miserable centuries on record.

Just what has to be endured, is shown by some of the stories coming down to us out of the mists of those dismal days. In one incident we observe the sons of a high official named Waddo, who make a trade of highway robbery, and number not only merchants but even officers of the king among their victims. When the count of Potiers takes up arms against these brigands, what should they do but appeal to the king himself, striving—fortunately, without success—to win him to their side by a jewelled bribe?

Another incident, described by St. Gregory, is characterized by a modern commentator as "probably typical of many."[4] It concerns a Guntram Boso, who, along with his daughters, was proceeding with an armed party from Potiers. Somewhere on the road he had the ill fortune to encounter a second armed party, led by Duke Dragolenus, and apparently decided to make the best of a bad situation; he sent a friend forward with a peace offer: Dragolenus might have what he wished of Boso's treasures, as long as he let the daughters pass unmolested. But he met this concession with a jeer; and pointed to the rope by which he had dragged many a victim before the king. As a result, a conflict-at-arms ensued—in which, one is glad to report, the haughty Dragolenus was dragged down. But it can hardly be supposed that every Dragolenus met a similar fate.

If even the affluent and the nobly born could not venture abroad without fear of desperadoes, what of the common man? Naturally, he could not venture abroad at all. The perilous, brigand-infested state of the country gave him good reason for staying at home; as a worker bound to the land, under the nominal protection of the lord of the domain, he had at least some hope of security against the armed raiders. This hope, it is true, often proved illusory; he and his family might be attacked, abused, or even torn limb from limb by some marauding party. But even in the absence of any such misfortune, his kinsmen and he were regarded in much the same light as the mule and the ox. So who was he to protest if the seigneur and his huntsmen trampled the sprouting fields, or if sackers and looters in the private wars fired his haystacks and barns, drove off his livestock, or hewed down his orchard trees? His cries of rage—and there is no knowing how many times he wrung his calloused hands, and called out to deaf heaven—were certain to pass unheard by the freebooters, as by the ears of history.

But this does not begin to express the means or extent to which the poor man was victimized. He was vicitimized in the first place, of course, by the seizure of the land by the great and powerful, including vast domains originally regarded as the common possessions of all, which had been taken over by the Church if not by the armed barons. And beyond this, the serfs were compelled to render services and pay fees for the use of what had formerly been theirs.

These fees and services were by no means slight. In many cases, the only apparent limits were in the lord's ability to drain another ounce of blood. While attached to the land in the way of cattle, the serf had to pay the price of servitude in multiple ways. There was the *chevage* or capitation tax, a small yearly sum that by its very nature was a mark of servitude. There was the *taille*, another personal tax, whose amount could be fixed by the lord, even to the extent of taking anything possessed by the serf. There were the payments in money, or in commodities such as grain, cattle, poultry, or wine; there were the fees, also in commodities, which the serf had to pay for the use of the oven, the winepress, or the mill of the lord; there were the taxes in commutation of military services, and for the lord's enterprises such as crusading expeditions or the marriage of his children or even his ransom from captivity; and there were the tolls for the use of the roads, and the fines exacted by the siegniorial courts. There was, on occasion, the onerous fee paid by the peasant for sending his son to school (a fee which, one may be sure, there was rarely occasion to pay).

And there was the *merchet* or marriage fine, and the *heriot* or mortuary: "In most manors, though apparently not in all, the lord claimed by this custom the best possession left by his dead tenant; and (so long as he had left not less than three heads of livestock) the parish clergyman claimed the second best. The case of a widow and orphans in a struggling household is one in which no charity can ever be misplaced; yet here their natural protectors were precisely those who joined hands to plunder them; and every parish had its two licensed wreckers, who picked their perquisites from the deathbeds of the poor." [5]

But beyond all the above, and still more important, there were the services performed for the lord, which might be for a specific number of days a week, but might cover anything at all and for any period of time that the lord demanded, from cultivation of the fields to renovation or defense of the castle, and from upkeep of the roads to transmission of messages across those same dangerous and robber-haunted thoroughfares.

All the evidence goes to show that the lords were overreaching themselves. They did indeed get the objective of the moment; but the long-range objectives were lost to their vision. It was not only that they produced a deep, smoldering sense of injustice that led to the bloodthirsty fury of the *jacqueries* or peasants' rebellions and would break out hundreds of years later in the French Revolution. It was that, even from the point of view of efficient agriculture, the landlords were defeating their own ends. Few of them, aside from some of the kings and clergy, could see that land could be made to yield properly only when one gave thought to the producers; that men, treated like "dumb driven cattle," were like dumb driven cattle in lacking the will and the ability to obtain the best results. Hence production proceeded haphazard, by wasteful methods; the soil no less than the workers was neglected; and frequently famine was the result (in France alone, in the years between 970 and 1100, no less than sixty years were famine years).

But this often-repeated terror need not have occurred. It was the bitter fruit of exploitation. As one writer has expressed it, "Far from being the co-partner of the farmer, the landowner under the feudal regime was, so far as the peasant was concerned, a mere parasite. . . . He discouraged initiative and dried up all energy at its source, by taking from the villein an exorbitant part of the fruits of his work, so that labor was half sterile. Indeed, the initial error of the feudal lords was that they exploited the peasant, instead of assisting him to exploit the land." [6]

Little wonder, then, that the serf had small value, not only as a worker but as a man. Little wonder that, in the eleventh century, a French serf was valued only at 38 sous, whereas a horse was worth 100. We need not be surprised if the farm population, brutalized, repressed, and exploited, had little to bequeath to the coming age but ignorance, coarseness, and brutality.

III

Toward the close of the Middle Ages, we witness the emergence of a new social order. The great feudal estates, unable to endure the strain of their own parasitism and the drain of continual predatory warfare, are splitting apart like overripe fruit. Free laborers are arising, enjoying for a period a prosperity unknown since the ancient world; cities are developing, and a wealthy bourgeoisie is growing to influence and leadership; commerce with the East is flourishing, and the dormant intellect of Western Europe is stimulated to a new power and brilliance. In a word, the world is being regenerated; dawn has arrived after the centuries of darkness.

But in this revivified world, the forces of acquisitiveness remain, in some respects gaining strength, since fresh opportunities for gain appear, and fresh incentives to the gold-seeker. This is particularly true of the teeming ports of trade, and not least in that center of magnificence, the city of Venice. Here we see how avarice, as so often, incurs its own nemesis. There is an irony in the fact that the capture of Constantinople in 1204, instigated by Venice largely owing to the unbridled possessiveness of her citizens, resulted in such enfeeblement of the Eastern Empire as to make possible the eventual triumph of the Turks, which in turn produced a rapid eclipse of the trade and wealth of Venice.

As a segment of the same picture, we may note a further fact; the part played by the commercial spirit in obscuring or obliterating noncommercial genius. As throughout history, the law seems to be that when men's minds are given to accumulation, little energy remains for

more liberal talents. C. F. Young, in his study of the Medici, draws an
interesting comparison between Venice and her rival, Florence: "...
the root of the reason why Venice produced no prominent men was the
inordinate love of money. A race with whom money-making and
money-spending is the one serious interest cannot penetrate to those
'avenues by which the mind soars to its highest limits.' Florence also
loved money, but it was not her chief interest. And so we have this
significant result: Florence, with Art and Learning as her passion, and
with her long line of immortal names in every branch of these, the
city which led in producing the civilization of Europe; and, on the other
hand, Venice, producing next to nothing of the kind—no great poet, no
great scholar, no great sculptor, no great statesman known to all the
world, no great painter, even, until her rival had been leading the way
in that particular for a hundred and fifty years . . ." [7]

It is true that, even in Florence, the power of wealth imposed itself
strikingly toward the close of the Middle Ages; the Medici family,
which elevated its members to the Papacy and to the most important
thrones of Europe, had built its authority upon the cornerstone of riches acquired in commerce and banking. But the early Medici did not
embody the spirit either of the feudal suzerain or of the typical modern
multi-millionaire; like the ancient moneyed lords of Greece and Rome,
they felt that wealth involved public responsibility no less than private gratification; and their donations for art, learning, and charity
were enormous. One of the founders of the family, Cosimo de Medici,
is known to have bestowed more than four hundred thousand gold
florins for various benefactions; and similar sums were ladled out by
Lorenzo the Magnificent and others.

Nevertheless, in many ways, the rise of such financial potentates was
far from wholesome. While some of them may have been honest
enough, still as a group they represented an unhealthy concentration of
power; and concentration of power, as in most cases, led to abuse and
corruption, and the corruption in its turn was fast sapping the liber-
ties of Europe in favor of a morbid and often bloodthirsty despotism.
Even though the Medici, in the beginning, were far from the worst of
the reigning powers of the land, they certainly were not philanthro-
pists pure and simple. By the power of money they bought a large
part of the land of Florence, and gained control over popes and kings.
Hence they would have been more than human had they neglected the
power of money. It was unfortunate, but not unnatural that the most
illustrious of them were unable to keep their fingers free of stain.
Here is a statement regarding Lorenzo the Magnificent: "Lorenzo had

so confused his own business with state business that when he had
involved his private fortune in unfortunate speculations it was the
state that went bankrupt to save its 'prince'; the interest on the public debt was reduced, dowries deposited in the *monti* were confiscated,
even the coinage was debased. The credit of Florence never recovered. . . ." [8]

Like later financiers, the Medici created exclusive rights, more for
personal advantage than for the general good; their restrictions tended to hamstring economic life, as in the case of the monopoly upon
corn, in the customs duties between town and town that lasted until
1737, in prohibitions that forbade private citizens to buy anything for
resale, and in the controls making it difficult for shopkeepers to stay
open during the fifty holidays. Worse still! the taxes upon import and
export trade, at a time when Mediterranean commerce was already
waning, was a heavy burden upon the people. And as if legalized parasitism were not enough, corruption entered with her foul claws: "The
Medici in effect bought and sold the honor of the public officials, lent
money, jobbed posts at a profit, and winked at peculation, until they
had created a sufficient body of amês damnées, men who had everything to gain by a continuance of their corrupt authority." [9]

This is the more significant, since the Medici were not mere isolated
types. Although richer than most of their contemporaries, they were
representatives of the growing class of bourgeois leaders. They were
but one group out of the thousands who, throughout Europe, were rising by means of trade and finance and causing a redistribution of
wealth and power in the hands of the few. Numerically, these self-
made patricians were but a minute fraction of the population: in Venice, the wealthiest city in Western Europe, they numbered but two
thousand; and in Basle they comprised but 4 per cent of the thirty
thousand inhabitants. Yet the small minority succeeded in buying the
greater part of the urban property: in Frieburg, for example, thirty-
seven burgesses owned 50 percent of the city's wealth. They purchased
country lands and baronies; they conspired with princes to strengthen
absolute monarchy; they squandered public resources and produced
wars for their own advantage; they violently prohibited the workers
from organizing or striking; and they fostered an oppression that often
kindled insurrection. "Into medieval economic organization"' P. Boissonade charges, "they brought unrest and pernicious ways; reckless
speculation, the practice of rings and monopolies, even of Cartels, the
most complete absence of scruples and a contempt for every law of
morality." [10] They were charged by contemporaries with destroying

all chance of work for small trades, and impoverishing a thousand
worthy merchants for the enrichment of one.

IV

A particularly sinister turn involved the working classes. After the
advances from the servitude of the Dark Ages; after the emancipation
of the serf and the rise of self-respecting free labor, a considerable part
of the people was sinking back toward misery and destitution. The
trouble, to be sure, was due in part to ecclesiastical exactions; but more
largely yet, it arose from money-hunger among the laity. Simultaneous
with the growth of the new capitalism, we may observe the establishment of guilds wherein for a time the craftsman and the artisan enjoyed
a rare felicity, while the journeyman was almost equal to the master.
But this benign period was all too brief. Avarice insidiously crept in,
the old greedy "All that I can get for myself!" And large elements of
the workers came to be oppressed by the very guilds designed for their
protection. Those guilds, to a great extent, fell under the control of
the well-to-do, who converted them into exclusive corporations regulating not only capital but prices, wages, and hours of work.

At the same time, restrictive forces were operating within the guilds
in favor of the privileged workers or masters, who built the organizations upon the aristocratic basis of heredity rather than upon plebeian
equality or merit; even the public offices which they controlled came to
be hereditary. To debar the have-nots among the workers, they imposed exorbitant fees upon the applicant for membership, or asked him
to bear the burden of banquets beyond his means; unless he happened
to be the son of a master, he was required to pursue an inordinately long
training as apprentice or journeyman, sometimes as much as twelve
years.

Thus the apprentice system, originally intended to enable the
artisan to learn his craft, became converted into a form of repression—
and of oppression. To the poor boy trying to learn a trade, it might
be nothing more than a specialized form of slavery, as we see in a case
dating from England of the fifteenth century, when "One petition
declares that William Ingland sold John Calker 'oon Richard Dugdale
... for terms of ten years to do him service in his craft.' "[11] This, says
a modern commentator, "appears to be a very extraordinary arrangement, but it is not the only instance of the sale of workmen of which
we have knowledge." [12] Such disposition of labor, even though rare,
speaks eloquently by the very fact that it could occur at all.

The result of this exploitation, not only in England but on the Continent, was that a great mass of laborers, permanently cut off from their fair share in the fruits of industry, lived out their lives on shifting sands of insecurity. Sometimes they were compelled to accept the wages dictated by the guilds or municipal authorities (and how low these might be, can be gauged from the fact that in Norwich many workers served for a penny a day). Sometimes, again, they were forced to receive part payment in commodities—and, worse still, in commodities arbitrarily priced from above. And sometimes they were drawn into tangles of debt by a spidery system of loans, while at all times they were in danger of unemployment and consequent starvation.

The effects have been well summarized by James Westfall Thompson: "The working classes thus became mere wage-earners, employees hired and discharged at will, subject to the vicissitudes of market conditions, in slack times out of work, and continually liable to the imposition of lengthened hours of labor or a lowering of wages. The problems of capital and labor as they exist today have their origin, not in the industrial revolution of the eighteenth and nineteenth centuries, but in the industrial revolution of the fourteenth. Machinery and 'big business' have only aggravated and magnified conditions that were in existence before the 'industrial revolution.' " [13]

At the same time as they bequeathed oppression to the future, the acquisitive forces of the late Middle Ages brought down an epidemic of begging and vagabondage, Swarms of the jobless poor crowded the roads and the outskirts of the cities, in such numbers that in Florence alone there were at one time about 22,000 beggars. As elements of social unrest, fomenters of strife, and breeders of vice, crime, and disease, such rabbles of the unemployed could hardly be otherwise than an infection in the state. But still more portentous than vagabondage itself were the upflarings of discontent sprung of the same general sources—the strikes, the boycotts, the insurrections, the *jacqueries* or peasants' revolts, which, surpassing the outbreaks of an earlier date, erupted in many lands throughout the fourteenth, fifteenth, and sixteenth centuries.

In some of these rebellions we can see forewarnings of the coming "class war," the "revolt of the proletariat." Take the disturbance originating in Ghent in 1378, when the insurgents sought to bring the wage-earners into conflict with the industrialists, and to hurl journeymen against masters, and peasants against clergy and noblemen, with the object of setting up a dictatorship of the working class. That the leaders followed the principles of certain later revolutionaries, *The end justifies the means*, and *Humanity last!*, is shown by their aim to exterminate all the bourgeoisie and all the lords, aside from very young children. Fortunately, the rebels were put down in the battle of Roosebecque in 1382, though at the cost of 26,000 lives. But had they come just a little nearer to success, they might well have set all Europe on fire.

A better known uprising was the one led in England at exactly the same period (1381) by the celebrated Wat Tyler. This outbreak can be traced to a variety of economic sources, including the suppression of workers by wealthy employers, the demand for the end of serfdom, and laws attempting to regulate labor and prescribe a minimum wage. Fanned by a graduated poll tax, which had been adopted in lieu of taxes on merchants or landowners and fell most heavily on those least able to bear it, this revolt had such success that the rudely arm fighters had soon taken the city of London and surrounded the king in his castle. But after the orgies of victory, whose chief results were the looting and destruction of many fine houses and the beheading of numerous citizens, the insurrection was suppressed and left no enduring fruits of good. The lords still clung to their privileges; if anything, they tried to draw the bands tighter about the wrists of the workers, while struggling harder than ever to retain their prerogatives. As is so frequently the case, violence had not obtained its objective.

A somewhat similar story is told by the German Social Revolution of 1525. Here we can see how the people had been goaded alike by the rapacity of the clergy, the extortions of the usurers, and the exploitation of the wealthy burghers and nobles, who wallowed in luxuries while they artificially raised the price of necessities, adulterated the food and clothing of the commoner, stamped out the small shops and handicrafts, and kept wages down to starvation level. The explosion, therefore, in spite of large religious elements, can be traced in good part to the resentment and desperation of the exploited masses, who could not obtain recognition of reasonable demands, such as the establishment of a uniform coinage, and the elimination of crushing monopolies.

It is worth noting that this age, when the populace was bled and degraded, was an age in which cultural values sank and withered. As Johannes Janssen remarks in his history of Germany at the close of the Middle Ages: "In proportion as the materialistic spirit and the love of money-making gained ground, with the concomitant distaste for the higher pursuits of life, an increasing number of young people devoted themselves to commerce and remunerative trades.[14]

It followed that the work of artists and artizans ceased to be in demand, and that no less a painter than Hans Holbein the Younger, now recognized as one of the world's greatest, was compelled to eke out a living by house painting, and by dabbing coats of arms at two guilders each.

It was not for the sake of the Holbeins, of course, that the enraged multitudes struck out in the Social Revolution. But, unfortunately, the results were much what they have been in all peasants' rebellions. Wherever the conflict had raged, the country was scarred by the ashes of burnt villages, the smoldering ruins of cloisters and castles, the graves of thousands of slain peasants. Cattle had been driven off, and all movable property carted away; utter destitution had stricken multitudes of orphans and widows. And the returns for all this sacrifice were just as after the rebellion of Wat Tyler. The exploiters had learned nothing, had conceded nothing, had relaxed in nothing; instead of seeking to ameliorate the evils that had ignited the revolution, they clamped down with the jaws of a tighter vise.

The French Revolution still lay far in the future. And if the German outbreak of 1525 cannot be named as one of its direct ancestors, certainly the attitude of mind that sparked the German uprising was in the background of the monster outbreak of the late eighteenth century.

VII

THE MIDDLE AGES: PIETY AND THE POT OF FLESH

Few of the great religions have been more antagonistic to Mammon than early Christianity. Like the followers of Gautama, who preached "desirelessness" and worldly renunciation, the original Christians were wedded to meekness, humility, and poverty. "Jesus said unto them, If thou wilt be perfect, go and sell that thou hast and give to the poor," we read in Matthew, 19; and, again, this celebrated pronouncement, "It is easier for a camel to go through the eye of a needle than for a rich man to enter into the kingdom of God." Manifestly, we have not here the ethics of capitalism. Yet by one of history's tragic ironies, the institution founded by the Mammon-hating Jesus was to become one of the great capitalistic establishments of all time.

It may be that, considering the state of man and his precedent of acquisitiveness, no religious organization could have taken permanent control without becoming a temporal power. In the simple days before her ascendancy, the Church was indeed faithful to the goal of her founder. So long as her followers remained poverty-stricken, she exalted poverty and railed at the curse of worldly riches. But perhaps the germs of a fatal malady already slumbered in her breast: witness, for example, her pictures of the greater riches that awaited the devout in heaven, her visions of the celestial city with the streets of gold. What was this, after all, but postponement of the rewards of acquisitiveness from the here to the hereafter? One suspects that Mammon had crept in unobserved. While wealth remained as far out of reach as the ivory portals of the beyond, the Christian leaders maintained a stoical resistance to all the seductions of this world; but as soon as temptation flashed in their path with a golden enchantment, piety proved unequal to the strain, and the would-be followers of Christ showed themselves to be but human in the fickleness of their judgment and the frailty of their will.

"Passing rapidly from a condition of distress and persecution to the summit of prosperity, the Church degenerated as rapidly from her ancient purity, and forfeited the respect of future generations in the same proportion as she acquired the blind veneration of her own. Covetousness, especially, became a characteristic vice." [1]—Such is the verdict of the celebrated historian Henry Hallam; and few who have studied the facts will disagree. Still theoretically devoted to simplicity and humility, the Church became bureaucratic in her organization and resplendent in her trappings. Still preaching against the iniquities of Mammon, she bedecked herself in gorgeous vestments, erected majestic basilicas, and equipped her bishops to live a life of royalty, in palaces like those of princes and with the retinues of potentates. In no time at all, she was invaded by most of the evils of what would now be called "corrupt politics"; she became the prey of nepotism and bribery, she was afflicted with gnat-like swarms of office seekers, she let herself be imposed upon by charlatans, beggers, and parasites, who fattened upon her bounty while the honest poor man starved.

The extent of her wealth is almost incredible. In the Eastern Empire, where the monks owned one fifth of Chios and the entire island of Patmos in addition to many other possessions, the process is hardly less visible than in the West; but it is the West that shows its most glaring aspects. "There are plain indications," one commentator reports, "that about a third of the soil of Western Christendom belonged to the Church in the ninth century, although it suffered from the policy of secularization pursued by the first Carolingians, and from the frequent usurpations of powerful laymen." [2] In England, the kings endowed as many as forty abbeys at a time; in Augsburg, Salsburg, and Freisingen, the bishoprics laid claim to no less than a thousand to sixteen hundred manses or domains. Twenty thousand serfs were subject to the Abbey of Saint-Martin in Tours; while, also in France, by the twelfth century, some of the abbeys held title to as many as 100,000 hectares of land, and the Bishop of Langres held an entire county. In Spain, one would have had to travel twenty-four miles to circumnavigate the estates of the Archbishop of Santiago; in Florence, two hundred castles were claimed by the bishopric; in Bologna, the ecclesiastical property comprised two thousand manses; in Germany, half of the soil was held by the Church. Many churches possessed from seven to eight thousand manses each; those with a mere thousand were, as Hallam puts it, "only indifferently rich.' And as if this did not suffice, the churchly wealth in many districts had grown even further by the close of the Middle Ages. In France of the fifteenth century, the religious revenue surpassed that of the State; in England, the returns were twelve times those of the king; in Italy and the two Sicilies the Church monopolized from two thirds to four fifths of the land.

Hence it has been plausibly suggested that, except for the antagonism and usurpations of the lay lords and sovereigns, the Church would have become the sole owner of all Europe. The extreme possessive attitude of some of the religious leaders stands forth in the case of Pope Gregory VII (1073-1085), who claimed lordship not only over the Christian countries of Europe, but also over those still to be conquered from the non-Christians, and further asserted that no territories once annexed to the Church could be withdrawn by any act of man or circumstance.

It is true that not all the accumulated wrath was used for unworthy or merely gainful purposes; the Church was a vast charitable and humanitarian organization, which needed great sums for maintenance of its proper functions and for succoring the poor; it was mainly the Church which, in its monasteries, kept the light of knowledge burning, even though feebly, throughout the Dark Ages. Nevertheless, the wealth acquired was far in excess of that required. And the effects were much what they have often been among lay possessors: an aloofness, an arrogance, a disconnection from the root sources of humanity and from the simple realities of human life and human feeling. "The Church," says James Westfall Thompson "forgot the poor and the lowly in its ambition to build up power and to accumulate riches." [*]

In other words, the Church turned its back on its own parentage.

II

What were the means by which it rose to be a landed power of unexampled magnitude? They were many and various, and the worst part of the sad story is that the Church, as has been truly stated, "in addition to its temporal revenues, had enormously added to them by capitalizing its spiritual prerogatives. It was a system of venality and extortion unparalleled in history." [*] For it was a system designed to reap a price from every superstition, every religious belief and observance, every aspiration of the devout mind, every phantom of the terror-ridden. Hence it brings us a reminder, though on a far vaster scale, of the methods employed by the medicine-men of savage communities when they wax rich and powerful.

One bountiful source of churchly wealth was the gifts of the believers— gifts donated not only out of overflowing liberality, but often as an expected offering, a duty, somewhat in the spirit of a pagan sacrifice to some fearsome divinity. If a man entered a monastery, his lands and personal possessions would be an assumed part of the price; if he set forth on a military expedition from which he might not return, he might further his welfare in the next world by adding to the property of the Church in this. Or one who clung to his possessions while alive might bequeath them to the Church upon his death, and thus achieve the double end of enjoying them while he lived and using them to pave his pathway to bliss in an otherwise uncertain future. And if a testator had any doubts, he might be helped by the promises of the priests as to Heaven's gratitude. "To die without alloting a portion of worldly wealth to pious uses," remarks Hallam, "was accounted almost like suicide, or a refusal of the last sacraments." [5]

The situation with regard to wills has been graphically portrayed by G. G. Coulton—who is writing, indeed, of England, but whose words might equally apply to the Continent. After reminding us that the Church had exclusive jurisdiction over the probating of wills and that the feeling arose that "intestacy, except in the case of sudden death, was disgraceful," this authority goes on to diagnose:

"Let us put ourselves for the moment in the dying man's place. Whatever else the poor wretch may believe or disbelieve, of hell and purgatory he has never been allowed to doubt. Whenever he entered his parish church, there stood the great ghastly picture of the Last Judgment staring down on him from the walls—blood and fire and devils in such pitiless realism that, when they come to light nowadays, even sympathetic restorers are fain to cover them again under decent whitewash. A picture of that kind, seen once or twice a week for fifty years, is indelibly branded upon the soul of the dying man; and . . . here on his deathbed he has at least the faith of a devil—he believes and trembles. He knows that gifts to the Church are universally held to be one of the purest preservatives against the pains of purgatory; he has perhaps even seen men burned at the stake for denying a truth so essential to the Roman creed. What wonder, then, that deathbed legacies to the clergy and to the churches became so customary that the absence of such pious gifts was sometimes taken for proof presumptive of heresy . . ." [6]

All lands received by the Church, in medieval times as in modern, were exempt from taxation by the State; and some lands were exempt also from military service—a fact which the bishops took advantage of, by means of collusion with lords who granted their property to the Church, only to take them back again shorn of their previous obligations. And if this was fraud, it was certainly no more so than the forgeries by which certain monks, and even some of the popes, profiting from the fact that few could read or write, manufactured documents giving them the title to land. Among these was the audacious

Pactum Ottonis, a forgery which, based in part upon a previous forged charter, laid claim to lands not even included in the Western Empire.

A more regular and permanent source of income was through the tithes, a sort of ecclesiastical tax, which at first covered only the products of the earth, but sometime around the year 1200 was extended to include every form of income. When we consider that in England of the late Middle Ages, a laborer who earned no more than two pounds and eleven shillings a week would have to pay more than a week's wages each year as a tithe to his rector, we can see that this tax was nothing to take lightly.

At the same time, while the Church struggled against the usurpations of powerful laymen who stripped her of much of the proceeds from tithes and other sources, her bishops devised new methods of pillaging. One of these is to be seen in a practice not less corrupt than the auctioning of the Roman Empire centuries before by the Praetorian Guard: simony, the placing of spiritual benefices upon the sales counter, with results sometimes as preposterous as they were vile, as when the see of Narbonne was purchased for a child of ten, and when an infant of five was dignified with the title of Archbishop of Rheims. Even when the results were not quite so extreme, corrupt agreements and purchase by bribery became so common by the tenth and eleventh centuries that a great number of bishops had no actual right to their high posts.

Several centuries later, the situation had become even more scandalous. We find the Holy Office itself conducting a remunerative business in ecclesiastical posts, and read of Pope Alexander VI (1492-1503), manufacturing eighty new positions for the sake of his son, the infamous Cesare Borgia—positions which retailed for 760 ducats each. Likewise, we learn that Julius II gained 74,000 ducats for the creation of a college of one hundred and one brief writers; and that Leo X profited by more than 200,000 ducats from his appointment of 60 chamberlains and 140 squires.

Worse still, one finds on occasion that even the Holy See is offered for sale precisely like any other valuable property. Thus, following the death of Sixtus IV in 1484, the Tiara "had really been put up at auction, so shameless had been the bargaining"—and the purchaser was Innocent VIII, a man of limited intelligence whose "chief concern was the aggrandizement of his numerous relatives." [7] Similarly, in the eleventh century Benedict IX "sold out to Georgory VI for a goodly sum of money";[8] while Roderigo Borgia (Alexander VI) took office by virtual purchase of the vote of the College of Cardinals. A

commentator on the spotted events of those times has succinctly summarized the situation. Cesare Borgia, as Charles Yriarte points out,
"was confronted with some redoubtable candidates, of whom two were
nephews of Sixtus IV, and another was named Ascanio Sforza. He
triumphed in the end by buying off some of them and making private
treaties with others—treaties which he hastened to forget after his
election." [9]

Another momentous case dates from 1514, when Albert of Brandenburg became established as Archbishop of Mayence, a see which he
held along with those of Magdeburg and Halberstadt. For his con-
firmation in these offices of spiritual leadership, he paid a far from inconsiderable price: 24,000 ducats, which he had obtained in a business
deal with the great banking house of Fugger. But how was Albert to
repay this vast sum? Apparently the bankers took no chances; nor
did Albert. He was to proclaim St. Peter's Indulgence in the provinces
of Mayence and Magdeburg and the diocese of Halberstadt, as well
as throughout the territory controlled by the House of Brandenburg;
and half the proceeds would go to repay the expenses of St. Peter's
while the other half would go to Albert. All in all, a notable deal in
high finance! Ludwig Pastor writes with admirable understatement,
"Though the term of simony has been applied to this case, it is not
quite borne out by the facts. Still the whole thing, looked at from
every point of view, was a disgraceful affair for all concerned." [10] We
may or may not feel with Dr. Pastor that it was "like a judgment from
heaven" that this was one of the direct sources of the Reformation;
but certainly it was not unfitting that this case, and others like it,
should lead toward a renovation in the Church.

This brings us to the matter of indulgences, long a fountain of corruption. The doctrine of indulgences, of course, is a curious thing, less
allied to the original Christian creed than to those old Egyptian
cults which enabled charlatans to sell guarantees of favorable judgments in the beyond. Somewhat like the Egyptian scribes, the popes
and their henchmen professed to have special dispensations from the
Author of all Righteousness, which they were privileged to sell to the
highest bidder. This was possible, of course, only because of a convenient theology, which advertised a hereafter of everlasting torment,
and supposed that human agents could affect the duration or the
very infliction of the penalties. By a partial indulgence, according to
the accepted dogmas, the representatives of Heaven would cancel a
part of the temporal punishment reserved for sin; and by a plenary

indulgence, the Pope in his role as Vicar of Christ could rescind all temporal punishment for wrong-doing.

Here was a powerful rod. And it was one which the prelates used with about as much restraint as one would expect of a bank robber at a providentially opened vault. Neither secular nor religious clergy, as Dr. Pastor declares, "shrank from the direct sale of spiritual gifts," but both alike "gave absolution for money to those who did not profess to have contrition." [11] In other words, the dealing in spiritual exemptions became as much of a financial transaction as the sale of shoes or hardware. Not the least mercenary of the devices was established by Pope John XXII (1316-1334), who, perhaps taking inspiration from the Teutonic *wertgilt* or prescribed money-payment for various crimes, instituted a vertable "price-list for sin"—a specified sum had to be paid to exempt the culprit from the consequences of wrongdoing, the amount being graduated according to the offense. The extent of the credulity of the times may be gauged from the fact that such a prescription could be effective. As Voltaire has put it, "The men who were wicked enough to commit those sins were fools enough to pay for them."

Then there was Boniface IX (1389-1404), who granted large numbers of indulgences with the admitted aim of money-making. In 1390 Boniface proclaimed the Roman Jubilee over a vast territory, and made it possible for any aspiring soul to obtain a plenary indulgence after duly arranging with a collector to pay the amount he would have spent on a pilgrimage to Rome. Thus a commercial air was given to the transaction, and the coffers of the Holy See benefited by 50% of the proceeds.

And if Boniface seems to have gone far, his successors were to outdo him. The sixteenth century thologian Johann Eck would complain that "one indulgence drove out another" and that, as Dr. Pastor puts it, " 'permissory letters' were given as the actual reward of crime." Protestations now were heard from churchmen throughout Europe; a typical complaint was that of Cardinal Egidio Canisto of Viterbo, that the granting of almost unlimited absolution was an inducement to sin. And this, among other things, paved the way for the great revolt of Luther.

Thanks to the expanding market for indulgences, a new type of businessman had become common: the pardoner. Imagine yourself as one of the many pious and hell-fearing souls at the close of the Middle Ages. Suppose that, having committed some crime, you are naturally solicitous as to the welfare of your soul in the Next World,

since the horrors and darkness of Purgatory have been painted for
you in colors more dreadful than any nightmare. New let us assume
that a seductively smiling wayfarer enteres your town or village, announcing himself to be a vendor of holy favors. In proof of this claim,
he displays a carefully guarded relic, which he describes as the elbow
bone of a saint, or as a lock of the Virgin herself, or as a letter received
directly from the earthly legate of St. Peter. Therefore you, a true
son of your age, kneel down and cross yourself, trembling in reverent
awe; and being told to kiss the relic or abase yourself before the letters
of the Holy One, you do not dare to disobey. Truly, a miraculous
opportunity has come to you! For the possessor of the relic assures
you that your sins will be condoned by special intervention of the
saints. There is only one small condition. As a sign of your redemption, you must part with five or ten pieces of gold.

True, if the pardoner's demands are more than you can afford or if
you are of a saving disposition, you may haggle for better terms. But
in view of the black devils with fiery pitchforks which your visitor
discreetly calls to mind, you will end by reaching an agreement, and
may go home rubbing your hands in self-congratulation. Now all
your evil deeds have been erased from the judgment-book of the All-
High. You may sin again with a clean conscience.

Chaucer, in the Prologue to the *Canterbury Tales*, has given us a
good picture of a pardoner. I quote from a modernized version:

> "His wallet lay before him in his lap.
> "Stuffed full of pardons brought from Rome all hot. . . .
> "But in his craft, from Berwick unto Ware,
> "Was no such pardoner in any place.
> "For in his bag he had a pillowcase
> "The which, he said, was Our True Lady's veil:
> "He said he had a piece of the very sail
> "That good Saint Peter had, what time we went
> "Upon the sea, till Jesus changed his bent.
> "He had a litten cross set full of stones,
> "And in a bottle he had some pig's bones,
> "But with these relics, when he came upon
> "Some simple parson, then this paragon
> "In that one day more money stood to gain
> "Than the poor dupe in two months could attain." [12]

III

Even so early as the time of the Crusades, the popes were treating the judgments of the hereafter as merchandise. And it was partly because of this fact that the whole series of disastrous expeditions became possible. Pope Urban II, inaugurating the Crusades in his celebrated speech in 1095, made a promise: death in the Crusades, under the proper conditions, would buy a man exemption from punishment for his sins. *"Deus volt!"* ("God wills it!") shouted back the crowd, in a tumult of enthusiasm, echoing the battle cry provided by the Pope; and there was a scramble for crosses.

To a great extent, of course, the motive is not polluted by earthly greed. But the connection, in various ways, is evident. Among the miscreants whom the papal mandate encouraged to all manner of depredations, thieves were granted absolution and brigands were upheld in the practice of their profession, for had the Pope not assured them that all would be forgiven to him who had donned the Crusading cross? "The fact that they were assured of a plenary indulgence on the completion of their enterprise," writes F. J. C. Hearnshaw, who, after all, but reports the obvious, "no doubt incited them to enlarge indefinitely the list of their transgressions, which, according to contract, were to be washed away." [13] Not only that, but, as H. C. Lea further points out, this extension of mercy was perhaps all the more attractive "because of the demoralizing character of the service, for it was a commonplace . . . that the crusader, if he escaped the perils of sea and land, was tolerably sure to return home a lawless bandit." [14]

Subsequently, still greater remission of sin was permitted, as when in 1291 Nicholas IV offered full pardon to anyone who sent another Crusader or went at the expense of another—which meant that the robber could rob to his heart's content so long as he paid his dues to the Crusades. At the same time, a man going at his own expense was to have an increase of salvation. But all this pales into unimportance beside another profitable new method, whereby a Crusader who could not or would not perform his vows was exempted from responsibility by putting up a sum proportionate to his ability to pay.

Even when the Church did not profit directly—and this applied from the time of the First Crusade—the promise of lucre was held out to many who might otherwise have felt an unholy reluctance to leave home. If a man was in debt, he might avoid liability for principal and interest alike during all the time of his Crusading service. If he were weighed down by taxation, he might ward off the collector by a zeal for recapturing the sepulcher of Christ. And if he seemed likely to lose in a suit involving property interests, he might foil and discomfit his opponent while he departed piously from Jerusalem. At the same time, a devout hope might be kindled in his breast: the hope of loot in the Holy Land.

None of this, however, must be taken to imply that the incentives to the Crusades were primarily economic. No one who has looked even skin-deep into the nature of the times will deny that a leading drive was religious faith. But the power of religion, as we have seen, was not all, nor nearly all; there was also a predatory quality, a rapacity. And this rapacity cannot be called economic in the sense that it fulfilled the needs of existence; it did not serve any economic necessity, in the way of a wheat field or a cotton mill; it was economic merely in the manner of the Huns and Vandals, who gratified their possessive lust by devastating villages and cities.

There is a sense, a very important sense, in which the Crusades can be regarded as little more than a series of great raids for booty. Think of the background of the age in which wars large and small, private and public, had been the regular order of business. On all sides, knights and barons rode forth in armor. Wars in Spain and against the Byzantine Empire, wars in Germany and Italy and elsewhere kept up the military tradition, which was never far from the tradition of grasping the next man's property. Some of the feudal lords, as Dana Carleton Munro has summarized the situation, "fought to aggrandize themselves at the expense of their neighbors; others fought to avenge injuries; in fact, fighting was for many the best loved sport, and any pretext was good. But the zest for combat was keenest when there was likelihood of obtaining booty in some form." [15]

And since this was the background, what shall we expect of the Crusades? Men could not slough off old attitudes as they could put on new garments; it was inevitable that many should regard the Crusades as wars, as in fact they were, in which the hope of loot was never absent. And if some of the Crusaders were actuated by genuine religious sentiment, some quite frankly had gain in mind from the beginning. Thus we see Raymond of Toulouse working steadily to secure an eastern principality; we see Behemond, son of Robert of Guiscord, likewise hoping for a new domain; and we observe Baldwin and Tancred striving for conquests on their own account on reaching Cilicia. These are but several cases out of a great number, and individually they dwindle into insignificance beside the furor of the rabble in pillaging farms and sacking Jewish possessions throughout the journey—a furor shown in all its stark nakedness in the capture of Jerusalem, where, amid a pitiless massacre, the city was plundered and each man marked out whatever he found as his own.

But never were the covetous motives of the Crusaders betrayed in a sultrier light than in the Fourth Crusade. The original idea had been to attack Egypt, the focus of the Near Eastern Moslem power; this would have provided a natural springboard to retake Palestine. The Venetians, however, did not regard the seizure of Egypt as in the line of good business; they were able to make advantageous agreements with the Sultan, promising excellent profits (if the Crusaders could be diverted to some other goal). A much more desirable objective, therefore, was Constantinople, where the Emperor Alexis III had been discriminating against the Venetian colonists.

It has been remarked that nothing was more uncalled-for, nothing more disgraceful than that the Crusaders should turn against Christian Constantinople; this has been denounced as the most scandalous episode in all medieval history. But scandalous or not, Constantinople was overwhelmed in an assault craftily stimulated by the commercial desires of the Venetians; Constantinople was taken in 1204 amid scenes that exposed the Crusaders as little more than booty-bent barbarians. Both by the sack of the city and by the subsequent division of the spoils, the victors revealed their motives. From the common soldier up, all dug their fingers into the loot. A foot soldier took a mere single share of the stolen wealth from the three churches where it was piled high; a sergeant on horseback might carry away twice this amount; a knight might help himself to four times the quantity, and the various nobles enriched themselves with still greater portions. Meanwhile, amid wild scenes of devastation, libraries were ravaged and destroyed, museums robbed and dismantled, and irreplaceable works of art and literature wiped out.

But nothing seemed to matter to the Crusading swarms except the plunder of the moment. Gibbon has vividly described the scene: "After stripping the gems and pearls they converted the chalices into drinking-cups: their tables, on which they gamed and feasted, were covered with pictures of Christ and the saints; and they trampled under foot the most venerable objects of the Christian worship. In the Cathedral of St. Sophia the ample veil of the sanctuary was rent asunder for the sake of the golden fringe; and the altar, a monument of art and riches, was broken in pieces and shared among the captors. Their mules and horses were laden with the wrought silver and gilt carvings which they tore down from the doors and pulpit . . . in the

Church of the Apostles the tombs of the emperors were rifled . . . In the streets the French and Flemings clothed themselves and their horses in painted robes and flowing head-dresses of linen . . ." [16]

While the rank and file thus regaled themselves, the Venetians made sure that they would not lack their rewards. Three eights of Constantinople went to them—the basis for a commercial establishment with far-weaving strands. Undoubtedly the conquerors, blinded by greed, could not foresee that they were preparing their own eventual downfall; that the weakened Eastern Empire would fall to the Turks, with results disastrous to Venetian commerce. But this was still two and a half centuries away: closer at hand were the catastrophic new Crusades sparked by the idea of the attack on Constantinople—campaigns such as those against the Arabs of Spain and against the Albigensian Christians of Southern France, whose flourishing civilization was to be stamped out. The Crusades were now more and more clearly showing their essential nature as mere offensive warfare, much of whose inspiration was in the wealth plundered beneath the sacred symbol of the Cross.

IV

Not only the pillager but the persecutor, as we have noted in passing, came to deadly life in the Crusades. And a cheif target of the persecutor, as throughout many blood-streaked centuries, was the Jew; though in many cases it would seem more correct to say that a chief target was the property of the Jew. This is not to suggest that the acquisitive motive was the only or even the central factor in the persecutions as a whole: there were many other elements, including passionate racial antagonisms, religious bigotry, and artificially stimulated hatred. But even after allowing for all this, one must take account of a large underlying ingredient of plain greed for Jewish possessions—which, if not visible behind all the persecutions, is much too apparent in many.

Thus, in the Second Crusade, when Peter the Venerable, Abbot of Cluny, advised King Louis VII to begin by attacking the French Jews, what did King Louis do? He went halfway; he made capital levies on the rich Jews. Thus, again, when King Philip Augustus in 1180 ordered the imprisonment of all Jews on a charge of having poisoned Christian wells, what was the sequel? He released the prisoners upon receipt of a substantial ransom. Years later, he saw further profit in banishing them; their confiscated real estate fell into his hands, while their synagogues were presented to the churches. The devout St. Louis, in 1254, followed the same system when he also banished the Jews and confiscated their property. Going even beyond this example, Philip the Fair in 1306 threw all the Jews into prison, seized all their possessions except the clothes on their backs and a small quantity of coin, and drove them out of France with no more than a day's provisions—which proved so lucrative that the magnanimous monarch could bestow a synagogue upon his coachman. In Austria in 1420, following a story that a rich Jew had profaned a consecrated wafer, all Jews were imprisoned at the order of the duke; the poor were then banished; but the rich were detained, many were burned at the stake, their property was confiscated, and their houses were given to Christians. In Catalonia the Jews were able to escape massacre by payment of a considerable bribe. In Europe in general, the situation was highlighted by Pope Innocent III, who in 1198 laid down an order that abrogated debts owed by Christians to Jews and later, as if to justify this usurpation, declared that the Jews had earned perpetual servitude by the crucifixion of Jesus.

In England their lot had been comparatively favorable, though they had been regarded as chattels of the king. "The Jew can have nothing that is his own," the commentator Bracton is quoted as saying, 'for whatever he acquires, he acqiures, not for himself, but for the king." [17] But by the end of the thirteenth century, a wave of bigotry, along with a wave of covetousness, began to surge against the Jews. A series of legal restrictions was imposed, and these usually concerned property, as when in 1186 taxes were assessed against them at a fourth the value of the whole country, and when in 1269 they were forbidden to take any land normally coming to them through nonpayment of a mortgage, and in 1271 were prohibited to own land at all, and in 1275 were ordered not to lend on usury, and thus were practically deprived of the means of a livelihood. But worse, much worse, was to come.

In 1290 Edward I issued one of those wholesale expulsion orders in which bigotry accepts avarice as her hand-maiden. The avarice was note quite so extreme as in certain expulsions, for the excluded people might at least take with them whatever they could carry. But it could have been no secret to the king that the victims would be unable to transport their houses; and it would seem more than coincidental that these possessions were forfeited to Edward, although the royal favor did fall upon a few individuals, who were permitted to sell their houses before going forth as homeless wanderers. It is said that the amount which went to the king was not great, but this cannot alter our judgment of his decree—the morality of a robber can hardly be reckoned by the quantity of his loot.

Long before this expulsion, there had been anti-Jewish outbreaks, including massacres in which bloodshed and brigandage maintained their old-time partnership. William, the Austin Canon of Newburgh, an evidently unbiassed chonicler, reports that, at the time of King Richard's coronation, the zeal of the Londoners had risen, "not indeed sincerely (that is, merely for faith's sake), but either in envy of the Jews' prosperity or as gaping after their fortunes". Canon Williams minces no words: "Bold and covetous men thought to do God service if they despoiled or destroyed folk who rebelled against Christ; and they wrought with cheerful fury, hindered by little or no scruples of conscience, the business of their own greed." [18]

Canon Williams goes on to tell how "in a city called Lynn, illustrious for its trade and commerce," an outbreak occurred, and many Jews were slain by sword or fire, and some "foreigners" (men from other parts of England) "laden with booty, took to their ships." Shortly afterwards, there was a great Lenten fair at Stamford, and in consequence some young men bound for the Crusade, "being indignant that the enemies of Christ's Cross who dwelt at Stamford should possess so much," thought "to serve Christ if they assaulted these men whose goods they coveted." Therefore they rushed upon the Jews, slew them, plundered houses, and stole "a great wealth of money"— all of which was tolerated if not approved by the townspeople, for the raiders were unopposed, and "went away with the gain of their work, and none was brought to judgment for public discipline on that account."

In the goriest of all the English massacres, which broke forth at York in 1190, we again see the spiked fist of acquisitiveness. A group of the lesser nobles were deeply in debt to the Jewish money-lenders; and believed it easier to attack the creditors than to discharge their debts. To return to the chronicle of Canon Williams: "The Jews had built in the midst of the city, at most profuse expense, houses of great size, comparable to royal palaces . . . . Therefore very many men of the province had conspired against them, not suffering that these men should be rich while they themselves were in want; and without any scruple of Christian conscience thirsting for the unbelievers' blood in greed for robbery.' [19]

Pursued by the mob, the Jews took refuge in the royal castle, where they were besieged, while several houses were burned and their riches plundered. Many slew themselves, and the survivors were butchered when the castle was taken—in all, about 500 perished. Then, ex-

emplifying the motives behind the carnage, the rabble broke into the
cathedral, and compelled the surrender of the bonds recording their
indebtedness to the Jews. And those bonds were burned in the min-
ster. But "even unto this day," concludes the contemporary reporter,
"no man hath been sentenced for that slaughter of the Jews."

V

The expulsions of the Jews from France and England were but
minor affairs beside the edict by which Ferdinand and Isabella, in
1492, drove the Jews out of Spain. It is a curious fact that Isabella,
who has been commended by historians for piety and tenderness,
should have been behind two of the most monstrously cruel and
needless atrocities of all time: the Inquisition of Spain, and the order
banishing the Jews. Likewise, it is worthy of observation that both,
no less than the Inquisition of the Middle Ages, resulted in the enrichment of the principals and the rewarding of many henchmen. That
gain resulted does not mean that gain was the first objective; but the
pattern repeats itself too often to be overlooked.

We know in any case that Isabella, along with Ferdinand, was
greatly under the sway of the maniacal Torquemada, while the religious superstitions of the times moved mightily in the background.
Nevertheless, while we must allow this much to a devotional zeal
almost indistinguishable from insanity, we have suggestions that Isabella had advisers and collaborators of a more worldly turn of mind,
for the expulsion order was worded so as to drain the last ounce of
profit out of the robbery, the distress, the very death of multitudes.
"Those provisions of the edict which affected a show of kindness to
the Jews," testifies Prescott, "were contrived so artfully as to be nearly nugatory." [20] What, for example, of the provisions that permitted
the unfortunates to carry off personal possessions, but not to take
either gold or silver?

Prescott goes on to describe the inevitable, the foreseeable result:
". . . the only medium for representing their property was bills of
exchange; but commerce was too limited and imperfect to allow of
these being promptly obtained to any very considerable, much less to
the enormous amount required in the present instance. It was impossible, moreover, to negociate a sale of their effects under existing
circumstances, since the market was too glutted with commodities; and
few would be found willing to give anything like an equivalent for
what, if not disposed of within the prescribed term, the proprietors

must relinquish at any rate. So deplorable, indeed, was the sacrifice of property, that a chronicler of the day mentions, that he had seen a house exchanged for an ass, and a vineyard for a suit of clothes!" [21]

If this was not State-commanded robbery, it is difficult to find any word to describe the episode. Why, one is further bound to ask, was the short term of four months prescribed, after which no Jew might remain in Spain under penalty of death? Could it be that the framers of the edict realized that the best way to rob the Jews, and to rob them thoroughly, was to compel their immediate exit?

It may, of course, be argued that the Spanish sovereigns could not really have been ruled by acquisitive motives, since in the long run they lost far more than they gained by the order of expulsion, and in fact hastened the impoverishment and even the ruination of their realm. But the fact that a greedy man is shortsighted does not mean that he is the less covetous. Prescott says but the obvious when he reports, "It would seem, indeed, when the measure had been determined on, that the Aragonese monarch was willing, by the expedient of sequestration, to control its operation in such manner as to secure to his own subjects the full pecuniary benefit of it." [22] And even though "No imputation of this kind attaches to Castile," and though the root of the persecution was evidently bigotry, the expulsion order set loose such a mad acquisitive scramble that one almost loses sight of the original motive amid the grab-and-thrust of bystanders eager to despoil the helpless.

VI

In an even more sinister light, we can see acquisitive fingers weaving their way beneath that organized instrument of persecution, the Inquisition. This engine of mass condemnation, inaugurated when the Papacy already showed signs of declining power, was introduced as a counter-measure against a religious scepticism and revolt which flowed in large part from the avarice of the Church itself; it could never have been attempted nor even conceived had Christianity remained true to her original ideals.

Unquestionably, fanaticism composed its central fabric. But fanaticism, as a glance at the actual workings of the "Holy Office" will show, was aided and abetted by material greed. "History," says H. C. Lea, in his monumental work on the Inquisition of the Middle Ages, "has few displays of man's eagerness to profit by his fellows' misfortune more deplorable than that of the vultures which followed in the wake of the Inquisition to batten on the ruin which it wrought." [23] And elsewhere, in analyzing the Spanish version of the persecution, Lea remarks that "We shall probably do no injustice to the Inquisition in attributing to the profits accruing from the exercise of its temporal jurisdiction the ruthless vigor with which the tribunals sought to vindicate and extend it." [24]

All the evidence supports these conclusions, both with regard to the Inquisition of Spain and to its medieval predecessor. As far back as the mid-thirteenth century, we can see the unholy alliance between piety and profits, when Bishop Bertrand conducted what Lea calls a "thriving business" in selling commutations in sentences of confiscation. In 1264, an advantageous arrangement was made between St. Louis and Bishop Bernard de Combret, and was confirmed by Pope Urban IV: de Combret was to have half the real and personal property confiscated within the diocese and also the king's share of the real estate if this was not sold within a specified period. But these were minor exactions compared with what would come when the prelates had more fully realized the dividend-bearing possibilities of torture, imprisonment, and death.

As we look back, we can almost hear the chuckles of the money-counter rising above the groans of the dungeoned wretch and the screams of the heretic roasting at the stake. Certainly, few businesses were ever conducted more methodically than the Inquisition, nor with a more one-sided concern for its own aggrandizement. It is notorious that its agents frequently did not even await trial before confiscating the victim's property; it is notorious that they had no thought for the wife, children, or other dependents of the arrested man while they stripped him of house and home, and let his family wander forth destitute. It is not less notorious that the Inquisition did not even confine its exactions to the living, and in some instances condemned men dead many years, and snatched their former property from their heirs.

Nothing more clearly illustrates the motives of the so-called representatives of religion than their meticulous attention to details of the seized possessions: "The account of the collections of confiscated property from 1302 to 1313 by the *procureurs des encours* of Carcasonne is extant in ms., and shows how carefully the debts due to the condemned were looked after, even to a few pence for a measure of corn. In the case of one wealthy prisoner, Guillem de Fenasse, the estate was not wound up for eight or ten years, and the whole number of debts collected foots up to eight hundred and fifty-nine, in amounts ranging from five deniers. As the collectors never credit themselves with amounts paid in discharge of debts due by the estates ,it is evident that the rule that the heretic could give no valid obligations was strictly construed, and that creditors were shamelessly cheated." [25]

The mercenary nature of the Inquisitorial transactions is probably nowhere seen more clearly than in the commuting of sentences in return for cash payments. This was, to be sure, only a logical development in a Church that had made a practice of commuting the penalties of the hereafter, likewise in return for cash payments. The condemned man, naturally, would be eager to bargain with his oppressors and to secure remission of his punishment at any price whatever; and the oppressors were not slow to take advantage of this circumstance. An example is that of Guillem du Puy, who in 1264 presented the Inquisition with 150 livres, and in return was granted absolution.

Fines, bribes, and extortions added their unholy aura to the holy operations—it is little wonder that Boccaccio could depict an inquisitor whose vision was as acute for a rich man as for a heretic. When we consider that every person over the age of seven could be placed forever under a shadow by a pointing finger and a cry of heresy, we see that the inquisitors were armed with a tyrant's power over the life, liberty, and fortunes of every man and woman and all except very young children; while not a man, woman, or child would dare to strike back against an instrumentality which would construe even a murmur of protest as an expression of heresy. Thus the inquisitors were being entrusted with authority whose exercise required almost superhuman restraint. And such restraint was the less likely in view of the fact that the agents might be sure of a plenary indulgence, to be obtained by the simple expedient of first sinning and then confessing and repenting.

Certainly, not the least of their sins was that of avarice. And even when this was not aimed at personal profit, it had all the features of the disease. Take the case of the arch-inquisitor, Torquemada. Though he preached disdain for worldly riches, practiced the severest austerities, and slept on a plank, still he was clearly afflicted with the curse of acquisitiveness. This acquisitiveness, it is true, did not take a personal direction; but it was acquisitiveness none the less when he clutched the fortunes of the condemned, and used them to rebuild the church of his native town or to reconstruct the Dominican Convent of Segovia. Though the acquisitions he piled up were convents and churches, they were acquisitions in any event.

One can agree with Lea's conclusions that "greed and thirst for plunder" were not "the impelling motives" of the Inquisition. But Lea is on sure ground when he goes on to observe that "but for the gains to be made out of fines and confiscations its work would have been much less thorough," and "it would have sunk into comparative insignificance as soon as the first frantic zeal of bigotry had exhausted itself." [26] Bigotry, one might say, was the wick; and avarice was the oil that kept the flame burning.

VIII

NEW WORLDS TO PLUNDER

Seen from our distance in time, the expansion of the European world in the fifteenth and sixteenth centuries seems like some great explosive force of nature, some volcanic fury that, long pent up, burst out in all directions with irrepressible violence. Surely, nothing could have been more eloquent of the fact that man had at last broken free of medievalism, which had so long held him in a vise.

Yet it is not hard to detect the various ingredients behind the rush of exploration, conquest, and colonizing. Much as among the ancient Phoenician and Greek sea-wanderers, there was a vast propelling element of adventure. There was also, as never in the rovings of the ancients, a strong blend of religious fanaticism. There was likewise an admixture of what we today would call "patriotism," the spirit of loyalty to king and country, if not the spirit of national vainglory. And last, and certainly not least, there was the great incentive to traders and raiders, the allurement of riches, of gems and silver and gold. And this incentive tended to take on an aura of the miraculous, of the fabled Eldorado and the equally fabled Seven Cities of Cibola.

Had there not been the hope of wealth to lend savor, the expeditions not only would have been conducted with much less zeal, but many of them would not have been undertaken at all. Daring and courage did indeed ride high beneath the bellowing sails of the caravels; but except for the enticement of a gold more tangible than that of the sunset, most of the wanderers would have remained in port.

We can see this in the very term "merchant adventurer," which was applied to many navigators of the great period of modern maritime expansion. These were, in effect, little more than a marine version of the robber barons of the Middle Ages; men like Drake, Hawkins, and other captains of the Elizabethan era were not less seabrigands for being under the protective wing of the State, which encouraged and even knighted them, and shared the profits of their profession. To the Spaniard whose home-bound ship was overtaken and robbed, it mattered not in the least whether the despoilers called themselves Christian warriors, merchants, or corsairs. Like some of the looters mentioned by Homer, the raiders made no neat distinction between piracy and trade; anything that enriched them was part of

99

the lawful order of business, the more so if the victims were the hated subjects of a rival king.

By the mid-fifteenth century there were, to be sure, strong new incentives to legitimate trade. With the capture of Constantinople in 1453 the Turks gained control of the land routes to India; and as they asked a profiteering price for the use of these routes and as the sea roads had long been controlled by the Moslems, Europe was eager for new lanes of access to the silks, spices, and other commodities of the East. Even before the fall of Constantinople, the Portuguese had been adventuring far down the African coast; in 1487 Bartholomew Dias reached the Cape of Good Hope, while in 1499 Vasco de Gama crossed the wide ocean distances to India.

But the Portuguese voyages represented something more than ordinary adventure and exploration; they must be given the dubious credit for initiating the slave trade. "The Portuguese exploration of Africa," as one writer bitingly comments, "lagged until skill was acquired in capturing the natives; and then, the trade becoming profitable, exploration of the 'Land of Wealth' was carried forward speedily." [1] While there are reports of black slaves in Europe even before the time of Henry the Navigator, the regular traffic may be said to have begun with the intrepid prince. It was in 1441 that Antonio Goncalvez, master of the robes to Henry, set out with the alleged aim of capturing some "sea-wolves," but actually captured some two-legged prey in the shape of Azeneghi Moors. In the following year these Moors offered to buy their freedom in return for some Negro slaves; and this exchange was approved by the Prince, who expressed the pious thought that they might thus gain some converts to the faith. Regardless of the religious predilections of Prince Henry, here was an entering wedge for one of the most cruel and rapacious enterprises which history records; the flood gates to the slave trade were to be thrown wide. In 1444, reserving to himself a portion of the gains, Henry granted exploring privileges in Africa to a company formed at Lagos. Whether or not this company was formed for the specific purpose of slave-trading, the sequel is eloquent: the expedition's one achievement was a raid upon the defenseless natives of the islands of Nar and Tider, about two hundred of whom were carried away in chains. One would suppose that if this result had run counter to Henry's principles, he would have rebuked if not severely punished the navigators; on the contrary, he heaped honors upon Lancarote, one of the leaders; and did not disdain to receive his own share of the loot, one fifth of the slaves.

One gets a vivid picture from the chronicle of a contemporary, Azurara—who, though he believes the enslavement to be good and in accordance with the "law of Christ," nevertheless offers us a damning indictment of the acquisitiveness that bade man to treat man as an item of property. Here is an excerpt from Azurara's description: "But what heart was that, how hard soever, which was not pierced with sorrow, seeing that company: for some had sunken cheeks, and their faces bathed in tears; others were groaning very dolorously, looking at the heights of the heavens, fixing their eyes upon them, crying out loudly, as if they were asking succour from the Father of nature; others struck their faces with their hands, throwing themselves on the earth; others made their lamentations in songs. . . . But now, for the increase of their grief, came those who had the charge of the distribution, and they began to put them apart one from the other, in order to equalize the portions; wherefore it was necessary to part children and parents, husbands and wives, and brethren from each other. Neither in the partition of friends and relations was any law kept, only each fell where the lot took them." [2]

As a sort of epilogue, we are told that "The Infante was there upon a powerful horse, accompanied by his people, looking out his share, but as a man who for his part did not care for gain, for, of the forty-six souls which fell to his fifth, he speedily made his choice, as all his principal riches were in his contentment, considering with great delight the salvation of those souls which were lost."

It may be that Prince Henry "did not care for gain" except in the religious sense—but what of the takers of the other four fifths of the slaves? We have the sorry beginning of the modern trafficking in human misery, which was to weave avaricious fingers across the centuries.

II

Behind the voyages of Columbus, though time and fable have suffused them with a golden glow, we can see the same sordid incentives as in many a less renowned expedition. This does not mean that Columbus did not go forth in adventurous excitement to find "the light that never was on sea or land"; but it does mean that he kept a more definable goal before him, and that this more specific goal was in the minds of his sovereigns also. In presenting his case to Ferdinand and Isabella, he may have catered to their desires even more than he unbared his own when he pictured the gold-plated palaces of the Indes, and the long processions of men bearing on their shoulders great boxes of pearls and diamonds. Judging from the outcome, we may suppose that the rulers were impressed by these juvenile forecasts, and did not even ask what value such abundant diamonds and pearls would have. Isabella, in particular, appears to have been moved by the visions of silks and gems; and both she and her spouse shared the illusion that gold and silver and jewels are valuable in themselves rather than because of the worth accredited to them by the peculiar turn of man's thought.

Throughout the subsequent negotiations, the subject of riches is constantly in the foreground. True, pomp and grandeur are not neglected by Columbus, who demands the title of Admiral of the Ocean Sea; nor is the question of power overlooked, since he asks to be made viceroy of all lands he discovers. But not less notable is his claim to 10 per cent of the riches of new-found realms (of course, neither Columbus nor his sponsors seriously considered that the inhabitants of the Indies may have had title to their own wealth).

For some time the sovereigns hesitated. But there were others, such as Santangel, the "Grand Treasurer," who believed that the gold of the Indes would serve most satisfactorily in the royal coffers. And Columbus' own faith in gold was an undoubted factor—gold which, he declared in a subsequent letter to the monarchs, ruled everything and could even free souls from Purgatory or open the gates of Paradise. When finally the agreement was drawn up, it included this crucial term, which Columbus had insisted upon: "He shall have the right to retain for himself, during his Admiralty, the tenth part, after deduction of expenses, of the precious stones, gold, silver, spices, and other articles of trade by whatever means he obtain them: by purchase, barter or conquest." [3]

One must not suppose, however, that while thus providing for the commander, the Crown forgot its own share. The nature of the undertaking is suggested by the fact that, as was customary, the sovereigns were to have a fifth of the gold, silver, and other valuables obtained by the voyagers. Making sure that their Majesties would not be cheated, a representative of the royal treasury, following an invariable rule, was to travel with the wanderers.

In a letter to the rulers, written after his first voyage, Columbus does not neglect the question of riches. The following report was well calculated to awaken the cupidity of contemporary gold-seekers: "So it was found that a sailor for a strap received gold to the weight of two and a half castellanos, and others much more for other things which were worth much less. As for new blancas, for them they would give everything which they had, although it might be two or three castellanos' weight of gold . . ." [4]

"Castellanos," we should note, were gold coins, and "blancas" were coins of silver.

The writer further stresses the importance of gold when, referring to the large island which he had named Espanola, he announces that it is "in the best position for the mines for gold and for all intercourse as well with the main land hereas with that there, belonging to the Grand Khan, where there will be great trade and gain." A little later, Columbus assures his patrons, "Their Highnesses will see that I will give them as much gold as they may need, if Their Highnesses will render me very slight assistance; moreover, spice and cotton . . . and aloe wood . . . and slaves, as many as they shall order to be shipped and who will be from the idolaters." [5]

The latter remark is deeply significant. For these words are at once a dire forecast, and a revelation of a state of mind—an acquisitive psychology that was to shed a blight across Columbus' own generation, and to scatter tragedy far into the future. But this was seemingly not realized by Columbus, any more than it had been understood by the Portuguese navigators earlier in the century. After all he was but the heir to the ideas of his land and age—and few, few indeed are those who break loose from such ideas (even when they favor such customs as cannibalism, headhunting, and heretic-burning). In Columbus' mind, which was better suited to charting the wide thoroughfares of the ocean than the devious byways of social progress, there was evidently nothing wrongful about enslaving the heathen; it was simply good business.

Thus in January, 1494, when the Admiral sends home an account of the state of the colony he is attempting to found, he makes the commercial-sounding, sanctimonious suggestion that it would be for the good of the souls of the cannibal Indians to take as many of them as possible, and that a certain number of caravals laden with the soon-to-be-saved captives should be sent out every year to defray the costs of the livestock and other commodities necessary for maintenance of the colony. It is to the credit of the Spanish sovereigns that they rejected this none-too-veiled suggestion for opening the slave trade.

But small good came of the reprieve. The rulers, in far-off Spain, could not keep a controlling hand on their emissaries may days' sail away. Nor could they thoroughly understand what was happening in the New World, or even weigh the effect of their own edicts, as when Isabella subsequently, and most injudiciously, permitted the enslavement of prisoners taken in "just warfare." Despite beneficent-sounding orders issued by the queen for the physical and spiritual welfare of her new subjects, the branding irons were soon to come out, the whips were to crackle, and men and women once free and happy were to be driven forth to servitude, disease, and destruction by the avid seekers of gold.

After his first conquest, Columbus sent off four ships with slaves to Spain. And already in 1495 he was claiming tribute from all the people of Hispaniola (the future Haiti). Upon every Indian of fourteen or over in the mining provinces, a quarterly tax of a little bell-ful of gold was placed: those in the remainder of the island were to pay an *arroba* of cotton. Brass or copper tags were to be worn about the necks of the natives, to show that they had made payment. But the demands, though considered light by the masters, were often more than the vic tims could bear, and consequently were in some cases modified and tribute was required in labor rather than in goods: in effect, slavery was substituted for robbery.

At our remoteness in time, one has a little difficulty in understanding the bland presumptuousness whereby Columbus (who is considered not to have been avaricious as men went in his day) could thrust himself into the land of harmless and friendly natives, and demand that they pay him for the privilege of existing. Nothing but the traditions of millennia can account either for the harshness of the conquest or for the accompanying acquisitive outlook, extending to the very bodies of the inhabitants.

In any case, the intruders brought down a sorry fate upon the natives of the West Indies. These people, generally described as mild, kindly, and inoffensive, had been leading their simple, carefree lives for an incalculable period; and left to themselves or treated humanely, they would undoubtedly have continued to live on happily. But they could not withstand the brutality of the newcomers. It was almost as when whole animal species, such as the American bison and the passenger pigeon, have faded out beneath the greed of hunters; the West Indians, likewise hunted, were no less surely destroyed; with appalling rapidity, they withered away and disappeared. Already in 1537 the Empress was informed that in twenty *estancias* in Cuba only 130 Indians were to be found, and elsewhere the situation was the same or worse.

Long before this time, demands had arisen for Negro slaves to replace the natives; in 1542 there were said to be 25,000 to 30,000 in Hispaniola alone, serving 1200 masters. Even the kindly Bartholemew de las Casas, the greatest humanitarian of the times, took the step (which he was bitterly to regret) of calling for the importation of Negro slaves to ease the burden of the Indians. Thus, to right one wrong, another great wrong was initiated. And thus the Europeans, having depopulated parts of the New World, began depopulating parts of the Old to fill the gap; and having stolen the lands of the aborigines whom they had slaughtered or enslaved, they imported stolen men, women, and children in order to preserve a profitable balance.

It is to be said for the Spanish administration that eventually, when it was too late to save the Indians of the islands, it did pass a series of beneficent masures for the sake of Indians of the mainland, though these enactments did not also enfold the Negro slaves.

Meanwhile, however, the notorious system of *encomendias* or *re-partiementos* had been established: a system of forced labor on great farms, bringing reminders of the *latifundia* or slave-ranches of the Romans. Here, beneath the lash of brutal overseers, the Indians were often driven to the last inch of their endurance. We have pictures of them herded in droop-necked gangs, lethargic, unsmiling, less like men than like sheep being sent to the slaughter-pen. But not only on the farms; in military expeditions and in the mines the natives were as ruthlessly exploited. Las Casas tells of four thousand Indians forced to accompany a military party as burden-bearers, and of this number how many returned alive? Exactly six! So lightly was the life of an Indian regarded that (so Las Casas tells us) when one of them was too sick and exhausted to proceed, the chain was detached from his shoulders by the simple procedure of cutting off his head. This might have been intended as a means of forcing the remaining Indians on to their last ounce of exertion, but as an indication of an attitude, what could be more eloquent?

In a letter to the King from Don Pedro Sarmiento de Gamboa, a sixteenth century adventurer who for a time was official historian and topographer to the Viceroy of Peru, we find a revealing first-hand account of Indian slavery. Gamboa described a raid led by a brother of the Governor, a raid in which ninety Indians were seized and led away with promises that they would be treated as "hired workers": "But, the slavers ignored their captain's pledge and forthwith divided up the Indians amongst themselves, one taking the husband, the other the wife, and others the children. It is pitiful to see how inhumanely they treat them, and the suffering and distress of the Indians themselves . . . . The slavers seek to justify themselves by saying that the Indians tried to make off and therefore had to be divided up among

themselves. Once this had been done, each went his way with the
Indians he had seized and was free to kill them or do whatever was his
will with them." [6]

The Indians were not only treated like sticks and stones, but were
made into a source of profit. Their masters would raise the price of
bread for their own benefit while depriving the natives of their fair
share of the irrigation water and so running them; they would dispose
of produce at five or six times the normal price and compel the red man
to offer goods at a quarter of their actual worth; they would violate
the law against selling intoxicants to the Indians; and even the Church
would plunder and defraud. So gloomy was the lot of South American
natives that many committed suicide, or slew their children to save
them from oppression; while in their terror of the conqueror they
sometimes flouted the missionaries by refusing to believe in a good
God who had made the white man. After death, they frequently said,
they would prefer Hell if the Spaniards were in Heaven.

Most dismal of all was the fate of those assigned to the mines. We
can picture them climbing in long dark columns on notched log
ladders, bearing loads of as much as two hundred pounds, while trail-
ing like doomed men out of the Tartarean pits, whose unconnected
galleries permitted no ventilation.

Many did, indeed, escape. Some, in order to avoid the virtual sentence of penal servitude, fled to the inhospitable forests to the east;
others were spared owing to bribes which their chiefs tendered to the
Spanish officials. But others, withering away by the wholesale, found
no relief but that of death.

Such was the shrinkage of the population that, by 1630, only a
third as many Indians were reported to be available for the mercury
mines as when the original assessments were made; Don Diego de
Luna, Protector-General of the Indians, pointed out that the system of
slave labor threatened the extinction of the native population. This
warning, unfortunately was little heeded. In the following century,
the people in some districts had reached the borderline of annihilation;
fertile valleys, once thick with a thriving populace, had been emptied
of all but a few scattered descendants of the native race; in the two
hundred leagues between Lima and Paita, according to the Marquis of
Varinas, a bare twenty thousand could be found in place of the previous two million.

Meanwhile, since Negroes were used to replace the natives, the
trade in black slaves continued steadily. A great impetus to the
promising new business had been given by the entry of the English.

In 1530 the notorious corsair William Hawkins transported black slaves from Guinea to Brazil; in 1562 his even more infamous son Sir John proved his enterprise by obtaining 300 Negroes in Guinea and selling them in Santo Domingo in return for goods such as pearls, sugar, ginger, and hides. Three years later he conducted another lucrative undertaking of the same kind, though he encountered business difficulties in the resistance of Spain. He was, however, rewarded for his pains not only by the direct profits but by a coat of arms from Queen Elizabeth.

To be sure, Hawkins was to have rivals. In 1567 Francis Drake commanded one ship of an expedition of five carrying 400 Negroes or more to labor beneath the lash in the Indies. The story is told by the Elizabethan chronicler Richard Hakluyt: "We coasted from place to place, making our traffic with the Spaniards as we might, somewhat hardly, because the king had straitly commanded all his governors in us. Notwithstanding, we had reasonable trade, and courteous treatment, from the isle of Margarita to Cartagena." [7]

Here were only the beginnings. For the better part of three centuries the trade continued, with and without benefit of law; and during the greater part of the time the leading slave traders were the English, though in the early seventeenth century the Dutch had the unenviable distinction of providing most of the vessels. The exact figures are unobtainable, but it has been estimated that by the close of the seventeenth century an average of 20,000 Negroes were being shipped from Africa to the West Indies alone. And so late as the mid-nineteenth century, the captives imported to America are said to have reached an annual 30,000—which represented big business, since their market value was around thirty million dollars.

The way in which Europeans clung to this commerce is indicated by the French ordinance of 1672, which placed a premium on every Negro carried across the sea. But the prevailing state of mind is even more graphically revealed in this extract from a letter of the Chamber of Commerce of Nantes: " . . . and the commerce of Guinea is so much the base of it that if French traders abandoned this branch of commerce, our colonies would necessarily be provided with negroes by foreigners and by infallible consequence with all European goods which they consume . . . the abandonment of the Guinea trade would necessarily mean the loss of (all) colonial commerce. If follows that we have no commerce so precious to the State as the Guinea trade which it cannot do too much to protect." [8]

This, obviously, is an upshoot of the mercantile philosophy. But though such statements are important as showing what psychological currents were blowing, they cannot illustrate the reality—the palpitant, diabolical reality of men, women, and children carried across the ocean naked and bound in the festering, sweltering holds of vessels wherein from 5 to 10 per cent ordinarily died, while in at least one case the fatalities are known to have reached one third. Nor can any words portray the torture of men, women, and children driven to toil in a strange land, often torn from the arms of wives, husbands, sons, daughters, parents, or friends, while goaded on like work animals for gain.

But we may observe the situation a little more plainly in another contemporary description. Here is a picture, provided by the Portuguese chronicler Azurara, of the first arrival of Negro slaves at Lagos, in Nigeria, even before the excruciating ocean passage: "That miserable band of slaves was indeed a foul and melancholy spectacle to those that beheld it: men and women debilitated by hunger and misery, their bodies naked, lacerated, and mutilated. You might behold the wretched mothers, lost in grief and tears, dragging two or three children after them, or carrying them upon their necks or shoulders, and the whole band connected together by ropes or iron chains around their necks or arms or hands." [9]

Not only private individuals but the Emperor himself profited, and this in more ways than one. He claimed a fifth of the human property and made good his demands by means of the letter *C*—designating "Charles"—branded with a red-hot iron upon each of the captives. And he benefited from the import licenses and customs duties for the importation of Negroes—fees which he used to build the fortress-palaces of Toledo and Madrid. "The blood-cemented walls of the Alcazar of Madrid," one commentator concludes, "might boast of being raised upon a complication of human suffering hitherto unparalleled. . . . Each ducat spent upon those palaces was, at a moderate computation, freighted with ten human lives." [10]

Under Philip II, the system of *asientos,* or government contracts for the importation of slaves, became established as basic in the colonial system; the rights were sold to the highest bidder, and the prices constantly increased. Thus a bulwark of the slave-system can be seen in the acquisitiveness of the Crown.

But perhaps an even stouter bulwark was in the lure of private profit. In this word "profit," we can see the incentive that made business go-getters in England and New England, the Netherlands and elsewhere as brutally matter-of-fact as butchers driving steers to market. Without the profit, regardless of the desire of planters for forced labor, there could have been no slave trade. Without the profit motive, with its allurement of gains that might run as high as 200 or 300 per cent, there could have been no slave hunters, no slave ships to bear the victims across the Atlantic in the agonies of the "Middle Passage."

One modern historian has commented caustically on the trade and on some of its paradoxical features: "The African slave trade sustained the rum industry of New England and offered the greatest market for the coarse fabrics of the East India Company. Mercantilists considered its a valuable trade, for no cash was needed for the *carrera de Indias*. The rum made from the sugar cane of the islands was sent to produce drunkenness in Africa and Africa paid for it with kidnaped labor which was to grow more sugar cane to be worked into more rum to buy slaves. The bills on Liverpool for sugar represented the profit. When the great Chatham thundered his eloquent defense of the cause of the 'shugger islands' (for so he pronounced it) right or wrong, this was what he meant: the manufacture of delirium tremens with which to produce cheap labor which could rapidly be used up at hand-worked sugar mills to produce more sugar to be sent through the same round." [11]

It is true that England did eventually abolish the slave trade in her colonies, and even vote the huge sum of 20,000,000 pounds as compensation for the slave owners. It is true, likewise, that the profit motive was challenged in subsequent prohibitions by most of the leading countries of Europe, and by the United States (prohibitions all too frequently and flagrantly violated). But this turn in sentiment, while most heartening and while showing (if proof were necessary) that the acquisitive motive does not always dominate, can no more wipe out the inhuman cupidity of previous centuries than the eventual abolition of the Roman gladiatorial games could erase the memory of the long generations of cruelty in the arena.

III

Among most of the early adventurers and settlers, slaves were not sought (except perhaps incidentally) so much as gold, silver, pearls, emeralds, diamonds, and other valuables. Let us glance first at the Spaniards. The direct connection between gold and the sailings for the New World may be traced not only in the words of the voyagers but in the number of sailings, which were 22 in 1506, 32 in 1507, 45 in 1508, and only 17 in 1510. But sometime later rumors of the gold of Montezuma began to startle the Western World; and in 1520 the departures had reached 71. This is only as one would expect; but one would not so soon surmise that the Emperor Charles V would send men-of-war as escorts for the treasure-bound vessels. These men-of-war, as it happened, would do much more than to protect the caravels against pirates; they would make it impossible for the captains clandestinely to dispose of any of the cargo in profitable deals at ports not under Charles' scrutiny.

Among all the conquistadores, we can see gold operating like a magnet, an enchantment, a hunger and a craze. Galvanized by the thought of gold, men were to endure prodigious hardships, achieve incredible feats, commit monstrous acts of plunder. The savagery inspired by gold may be seen among the lesser adventurers no less than among the world-renowned figures. One of the early Spanish captains, for example, was a rogue named Beccara, who gained much gold and many slaves, and gave the name *el Quemado*, "the burnt one," to one of the caciques or chiefs whose land he had invaded—the implication is that he burnt the poor wretch who could not give him all the gold he expected. And this explanation is borne out by other Spanish activities.

There is, of course, the celebrated case of Pizarro, who after inducing the Inca Atahuallpa to fill a huge room with gold, condemned the unfortunate Emperor to be burned to death, though he remitted the penalty to the infliction of strangling. A less renowed but not less pertinent instance is that of the minor captain Juan de Ayora, who in the course of his Panamanian wanderings, fell in with some hospitable Indians, and was entertained with a feast of roast meat. After the repast, Ayora rudely called for the chief, and demanded, in effect, "Give me gold, or be thrown to the dogs, or else burned alive!" The chief, no doubt terrified, gave all the gold he had, which seemingly was not much—at least, not enough for Ayora, who demanded more, and ordered the chief to be bound until he had produced the required treasure. And when the chief swore that he had no more, the Spaniard made good his threat by having the victim burned alive.

Though not all the Spanish commanders were as cruel as Ayora, nearly all reached the same madness concerning gold—a madness that put the metal above food and shelter, as in the case of Alonso de Ojeda, one of the lesser conquistadors, who permitted the people of San Sebastian to starve while he went off on the trail of an Indian chieftain falsely reputed to have much gold. Quite in the same spirit was

Ponce de Leon, who founded the colony of Caparra with the idea of obtaining gold, of which he could not get enough despite his severities against the natives. Similar, again, was Ferdinand de Soto, who strayed for years over vast reaches of North America, looking for gold to match the wealth of Peru, from which he had gathered a fortune of 180,000 ducats; on all his travels, the Cross accompanied the search, but this was because as Francis Parkman remarks, "These devout marauders could not neglect the spiritual welfare of the Indians whom they had come to plunder."

In the same tradition, once more, was Francisco Coronado, who wandered far through what is now Mexico and the southern United States, looking for the mythical golden cities of Cibola. In this hunt, he was held back by no restraints of common sense: let an Indian point vaguely in any direction as the way to the citadels of gold—and off in that direction Coronado would start. Let him be told of a town where the chief fell to sleep to the golden music of golden bells —and Coronado would give himself to the quest, still with hope that burned strong.

It is a commonplace that we can judge much of men's minds by the stories they tell, and from the myths they cherish. Therefore, just as we may recognize a warlike people from the tales of sworded champions, so we can identify an acquisitive society from its legends of lavish possessions. For men center their myths about that which they admire and desire. From this it follows that the Seven Cities of Cibola, and Eldorado with its naked Man of Gold standing brilliantly in his boat in the sunset rays, were in a sense real: they were real reflections of the minds of the Spaniards, of that which they prized and coveted. Eldorado existed, just as a paradise of material and sensual delights existed for the devout Moslem. It existed as the translation of man's dreams and hopes into a bewitching fable. The fable itself was false, but the impulse that embraced it was genuine.

IV

Among the major conquistadors, we find the same rapacity as among their less renowned confreres. Mainly because their wanderings happened to take them into the heart of gold-producing civilizations, two of the Spanish captains shine above all the others by feats that have dazzled the centuries. Yet a slight turn of fate might have made them of no more importance to history than, let us say, Diego de Niceusa or Pedrarias Davila. Cortes might have roved

futilely through the wide wastes of North America like de Soto or
Coronado; Pizarro might have strayed off into the vast South American desolations, never to be heard of again. True, Cortes and Pizarro
may have had greater hardihood than some of the others; the former
was a more daring and resourceful commander than most; and Pizarro
stood out even from his fellow desperadoes in his ruthlessness and in
the fury of his passion for gold. Nevertheless, both were favored by
facts beyond their control: Cortes by the superstitution of the
coming of the white-faced god Quetzacoatl, which paralyzed the hand
of the religious-minded Montezuma; and Pizarro by the split in the
reigning Incaic dynasty, no less than by the complacent self-confidence
with which the Emperor Atahuallpa permitted the invaders to approach when he might have wiped them out.

But even admitting all this, it is hard to believe that either Mexico
or Peru would have been conquered except for one dominating incentive: gold. Consider first the case of Cortes, unquestionably the less
greedy of the two adventurers. He also, and his followers, were driven
on by gold-hunger. We read repeatedly of the gifts of precious metals
which they exacted from the Aztec king, and of their avarice in the
division of the spoils; and we are told how at times, as after the
massacre of the defenseless Cholulans, they burst into homes and
temples with the fury of Vandals, stripping them of gold and silver,
precious stones and ornaments. The motives of Cortes himself were
frankly confessed early in his career, when he arrived in Hispaniola,
and was assured that he could have a generous allowance of land to
settle upon. " 'But I came to get gold,' replied Cortes, 'not to till the
soil like a peasant.' " [12]

In view of this remark, and considering Cortes' subsequent conduct
and the investment made by merchants in the hope of rich returns
from his expedition, it is not hard to see Mammon marching behind
the adventures in Mexico. We have, besides, many additional lines of
evidence. Take the ordinances proclaimed by Cortes before undertaking his expedition—ordinances which endeavor to justify plunder
by means of piety, and announce that without the devout aim of
converting the heathen "the war would be manifestly unjust, and
every acquisition made by it a robbery." [13] But whether or not the
seizure of booty was just, let any officer or private beware of taking
any gold, silver, gems or other valuables! If he would not face death, he
must bring the loot forthwith to Cortes, or to the official designated
to receive it. In the case of two slaves, the extreme penalty was
applied; and Cortes had a noose put about the neck of one of his own

soldiers, whom, however, he ordered to be cut down before life was extinct.

Some further evidence, showing the emphasis upon gold and the difficulty of enforcing the ordinance, is provided in the chronicle of Bernal Diaz de Castillo, who served under Cortes throughout the Mexican campaign: ". . . on that night of sorrow we were fleeing from Mexico, Cortes declared before a King's notary that whoever should wish to take gold from what was left there, might carry it off, and welcome, for their own, as otherwise it would be lost. As in our town and camp of Segura de la Frontera Cortes got to know that there were many bars of gold . . . he ordered a proclamation to be made, that under heavy penalty they should bring and declare the gold they had taken, and that a third part of it should be returned to them, and that if they did not bring it, all would be seized. Many of the soldiers who possessed gold did not wish to give it up, and some of it Cortes took as a loan, but more by force than by consent, and as nearly all the Captains possessed gold and even the officials of the King, the proclamation was all the more ignored . . . ." [14]

The passion for gold—a passion reflecting the desires of Cortes' followers quite as much as his own—can be noted behind one of the most shameful episodes of his career, the torturing of the Aztec Emperor Guatemozin. After the fall of Mexico, some of the soldiers became disgruntled at the small amount of gold that had come to them; they accused not only Cortes, but the Aztec sovereign, claiming that he could show the location of the buried treasure and should be tortured into unloosening his tongue. Obviously Cortes was under great pressure; but on other occasions he had not yielded easily to pressure, and one therefore suspects that he too had some idea that a little salutary torment might cause the Emperor to reveal the hidden treasure. Ignoring his recent promise of protection, he demanded to know the location of the gold; and receiving no positive answer, ordered Guatemozin and two of his followers to be tied. Then their feet and hands were smeared with oil, and the flames applied. Quatemozin bore the ordeal with a stoical courage; the most he could be made to say was that much of the gold had been thrown into the water—a confession that did his tormentors little good, for Cortes' best divers were able to bring forth nothing of much value.

At about the same time, Cortes further showed his trend of mind who two small detachments were sent by him through the state of Mechoacan as far as the edge of the Southern sea, and returned with samples of gold and pearls. Prescott concludes the story as follows:

"The imagination of Cortes was kindled, and his soul swelled with ex-
ultation at the splendid prospects which their discoveries unfolded.
'Most of all' he writes to the emperor, 'do I exult in the tidings
brought me of the great Ocean. For in it, as cosmographers, and
those learned men who know most about the Indies, inform us,
are scattered the rich isles teeming with gold and spices and precious
stones.' He at once sought a favorable spot for a colony on the shores
of the Pacific, and made arrangements for the construction of four
vessels to explore the mysteries of these unknown seas." [15]

The long-range effects of Cortes' thrust into Mexico were strange
and disproportionate. On the one hand, we find a handful of ruthless
and desperate men, who, whatever the suasions of adventure and religion, could not have been urged forth to the hardships and perils of
the march except for the dazzle of gold. And on the other hand, we
see an empire demolished, its administrative system overturned, its
arts and crafts, its entire way of life obliterated for all time. It is
true that Aztec civilization had appalling faults: it was founded upon
conquest, and it encouraged the rites of human sacrifice, which it
brought to a ghastly extreme. But does this mean that it deserved to
be extirpated?

Take the analogy of a better known and greater empire, that of
Rome. Here too we have a foundation of conquest; here too, in the
wanton slaughter of the area, we have a bloodthirsty custom that demands countless lives—a custom tantamount to human sacrifice, without even the Aztec excuse of superstition. Let us suppose, therefore,
that at about the time of Julius Caesar, some previously unknown
foreign band had burst in, inspired with a lust for the wealth of Rome
and armed with guns against which the defending swords were powerless. Suppose that Rome, with her administrative skills, her law, her
art and literature had been blotted out irreplaceably. Would we say
this was an historical gain? Would we consider it sufficient compensation that the newcomers had enriched themselves while enslaving the
Romans and ending forever their conquering drives and the gory spec-
tacles of the amphiteatre?

Something like this, even if on a less gigantic scale, is what happened
in the case of the Aztecs. There is reason to suppose that, if left to
themselves, they would in time have thrown off their most atrocious
institutions and evolved into something notable and unique. But this
was made impossible by a band of reckless intruders, who placed the
gold of the moment above the civilization of many centuries.

V

With even greater force, these remarks apply also to the conquest of Peru. Pizarro, the guiding spirit of this enterprise, was a man of ruffianly upbringing and experience; until the age of fifty he had been but one of the many illiterate adventurers wandering about with no clear aim or occupation—swineherd, sailor, soldier of fortune, and pearl-seizing and gold-looting colonist of the New World. This man, utterly unfitted by training or character to appreciate the values of the empire he was invading, was drawn on by one great lure. The key to his character, as Roger Bigelow Merriman has phrased it, "was insatiable ambition and lust for gold, and willingness to sacrifice everything thereto." [16] Not the greediest Vandal pillaging the cities of North Africa, nor the most rapacious Crusader snatching the art treasures of Constantinople, was goaded on by a more savage cupidity. True, Pizarro was but one of a type, too common in his day. And his desires had been whetted by the tales afloat in the very air about him, such as the story told to Balboa by an Indian chieftain, who described a land to the south where the people ate out of golden plates. Later, Pizarro's greed was further inflamed by the report of the Panamanian explorer Pascual de Andagoya, concerning a great empire where gold was used instead of stone. At about the same time, also, he was stimulated by accounts of the gold-crowned achievements of Cortes—and if another Spaniard could win so much fame and wealth, why not he?

And now he entered into his celebrated compact with his comrade Diego de Almagro and the priest Ferdinand de Luque—a compact that might be called one of the most preposterous in history, had the fantastic dreams it envisaged not come true. By this arrangement, duly confirmed before a notary, the ambitious three agreed to divide among themselves the gold, the gems, and the other spoils of an empire which they had not yet entered and to which they had no more right than to the mountains of the moon. It is worth noting that the governor Pedrarias, who would have been entitled to a share of the plunder, was bought off for a cash payment of 1000 pesos.

Even before reaching the kingdom of the Incas, the freebooters showed what motives moved them. In the provinces of Coaque, they rushed toward a thickly settled town, whose inhabitants dashed off into the woods, leaving their possessions, which included ornaments of gold and silver, along with many emeralds. " 'We fell on them sword in hand,' says one of the Conquerors, with some *naivety*: 'for, if we had advised the Indians of our approach, we should never have found there such store of gold and precious stones.' " [17]

So little did Pizarro's followers appreciate the value of some of the jewels that they splintered them with hammers. The loot was then heaped all together, one fifth was deducted for the Emperor, and the remainder was divided among Pizarro and his men. But the invariable rule was followed, a rule underscoring the importance placed upon the precious metals and gems: he who concealed his findings, instead of contributing them to the general pile, would die for the crime.

We need not go on through all the tragic story of the conquest. It is only necessary to note how Pizarro's progress was marked with rapine, massacre, the invasion and spoliation of houses and temples, the capture of gold and silver whenever possible, the resort to torch, sword, and gunpowder in arrogant disregard of native rights. The culminating episode, of course, was the one already mentioned, in which the Inca Atahuallpa, at Pizarro's insistence, filled a great room with articles of gold, though this did not suffice to save his life. But having obtained the golden objects, what did Pizarro do with them? The intricate art works of the natives, the birds and beasts wrought out of gold with irreplaceable skill, were melted into ingots for the purposes of trade. "Perhaps never before or since," comments Philip Ainsworth Means, "has there been a more wondrous assemblage of beautiful handicraft productions." [18] No doubt the astonished Indians, as in their rudeness and savagery they witnessed the destruction, felt somewhat as the ancient Athenians might have felt had invading Zulus chopped up the marble statues of the Parthenon to serve as building blocks.

But the loss to art, though irreparable, was not even the greatest of the injuries inflicted by the intruders.

To estimate the extent of the damage, one need only compare Peru of our own century with Peru of the pre-conquest era. In a territory where, according to the estimate of Mr. Means, sixteen million people had dwelt in security and contentment, only eight million survived at the time of his writing, many in indigence and misery. In an area once traversed by excellent roads and bridges, consummately designed and perfectly maintained, only the ruins of ancient enterprise remained. In a region where cultivated terraces had run high along the slopes of the cordirellas the wilderness had wrested back its heritage. Even while admitting the evils of paternalism, we can have no doubt as to the relative wellbeing of the population under the Incaic system and under the slave-system of the newcomers. "The subjects of the Incas," points out Mr. Means in a remark notable for understatement, "were far more free from oppression and misery than were their descendants under the Hapsburgs and Bourbons". For "there was still so much virtue left in the Incaic system of government, and so much felicity and well being among the subjects of it, that all Spaniards who saw Peru in the first years of the Spanish occupation praised it unless some mean-spirited motive caused them to do otherwise. All just men . . . united in saying that the Incaic system, as compared with that which came after it, was the better."

And why was the Incaic system the better? Mr. Means implies the answer when he charges that "the greatest, the fundamental and the universal source of evil brought into Peru by the Spaniards was the money complex whence arose all the endless misery that has weighed down the Andean peoples ever since the money-less empire of the Incas was shattered."

It has been pointed out that the empire of the Incas, at the time of the conquest, was racked by a dynastic quarrel, and might in any case have collapsed. However, we must recall the dynastic disputes and the civil wars that have convulsed other lands without proving fatal. There was, indeed, as Means declares, "much virtue" left in the Incaic system. Of all socialistic regimes ever put into action, this appears to have been the most thoroughly worked out, the most wide-reaching in its ramifications, the most successful in its operations. While doubtless it would have been unsuitable for a more sophisticated people, it seems to have been admirably fitted to the needs, outlook, and traditions of the simple natives of the Andes. Merely as a social experiment, it was unique; and in a world whose social experiments are not to many, too imaginative, or ordinarily too successful, it deserved the opportunity to work itself out on its own merits. The fact that it was uprooted by one blast of the foreign conqueror does not mean that it was inferior, any more than the shooting of a traveler by a highwayman proves him to be less worthy than the brigand.

Although superior might, at any time or place, may win the day, superior might is not necessarily superior civilization. And when the might is fueled by avarice, the repercussions are apt to be especially unfortunate.

Even in the home country, the benefits of the American conquests were mostly illusory. We read, indeed, of the vast quantities of metal shipped to Spain. In the years up to 1560, nearly 225,000 pounds of gold were sent to Spain from the New World; and in the following forty years, more than 15,000,000 pounds of silver were transported, in addition to emeralds, pearls, precious woods, etc. But from all these importations, what was the actual gain? Gold and silver, it was found, raised prices without increasing production, and in effect impoverished or looted a large part of the population for the sake of the metal-possessing drones. A class of parasitic capitalists arose; neither agriculture nor industry was encouraged; and money-lending at high rates became common, rather than socially productive activities. Even the precious metals, obtained by means of such strain, grasping, and oppression, mostly passed through the country. The one positive use that Spain found for gold was, fittingly, destructive: by means of gold the Emperior Charles built up his army; one galleon from America would buy him a regiment. And thus we see the power of Spain spreading, until it becomes a threat to all freer lands, casts its shadow even over England, and, in the challenge of the Great Armada, makes a bid to clamp the inquisitorial fetters about the realm of Marlowe and Shakespeare. Fortunately, Philip II failed in this endeavor; but he could make the attempt at all only because of the stolen gold and silver of the abused and beaten natives of the Americas.

IX

THE CLAWS OF EMPIRE

Though Captain John Smith held that no motive aside from riches would "erect a commonwealth or draw people from their ease," we know that the Pilgrims were inspired by forces other than of worldly gain when they disembarked from the *Mayflower* on a bleak December day of 1620. Yet Captain Smith had grounds for his opinion in the known incentives of other colonists—and not alone the Spaniards. The settlers of Virginia, in their tragic first enterprise, where drawn as into a trap by the example of the Spanish treasure-hunters; and were grieviously disappointed to find neither gold-mines to exploit nor rich cities to loot.

Among the French, likewise—though religion marched with their courageous priests, and high adventure led the way for the explorers—the thought of glittering gold-bars was not absent. Even the great Champlain, a man of a notably higher type than most of the conquistadors, could not put from his mind the dream of easy riches, the riches of the East, which lay beyond a South Sea that could be reached without excessive difficulty. Not disillusioned even after many years of exploring, he related to the King and lord of his Council that the Indians had "given him such and so faithful report of the north and south seas that one cannot doubt that this would be the means of reaching easily to the kingdom of China and the East Indies, whence great riches could be drawn." [1]

It is indicative of a state of mind that the French in early Canada had their own version of the legend of Eldorado. It was not, however, known as Eldorado, but as Saguenay, a sort of fairyland where gold was so abundant that the people wore it in ropes about their necks, while ornamenting themselves with rubies. We may smile at this legend, and Frenchmen themselves were to smile at it (rather ruefully, it is true) after gold in quantities too minute to be useful was brought to France, and "diamonds" that proved to be rock crystal, giving rise to the term "Canadian diamond," which for a time was applied to anything worthless.

But Saguenay may have had a noticeable effect upon history. Such at least is the suggestion of Thomas B. Costain, who has this to say in regard to the free hand given to explorer Jacques Cartier by King

Francis I: "It may be taken for granted that Francis, who was not freehanded to the point of extravagance, and who moreover was burdened with the debts of his interminable war-making, would not have promised the funds for such an ambitious venture if he had not been sure that great wealth would have come of it. He wanted to set up against Spain a rival empire in the western world, it is true, but at the same time his cupidity must have been fired by that magic word, gold. It was the bait of the mythical kingdom of Saguenay which loosened the purse strings of the never too generous Francis." [2]

II

During the sixteenth, seventeenth, and eighteenth centuries, the colonizing nations of Europe indulged in a competition that not only covered much of the New World but reached out to the islands of the Far East and the mainland of India. In this competition, throughout most of the period, they were ruled by the peculiar creed known as mercantilism, whose economic assumptions were accepted almost with the same unreasoning faith as religious dogmas. It was taken for granted that a "favorable balance" of trade was necessary for a nation's wellbeing, and such a balance implied an excess of exports over imports. This excess in turn was considered to be valuable in order that the country might bring in bullion—gold and silver, which were regarded as a positive good in themselves, a source of national strength and prosperity. Correspondingly, it was necessary for a great power to keep gold and silver from its neighbors, and this demanded foreign trade in which it must be as exclusive as possible, debarring all rivals from the trading routes and ports (since the potential amount of trade was thought to be limited).

This produced a triple result. In the first place, the nation would seek all possible colonies as the basis of trade—and these colonies would be treated not on their own account and for their own good, but rather as cows to be milked. In the second place, the nation would pile up restrictive laws regarding imports and exports, raw products, and manufactured products, and their shipment and sale. For example, it would forbid its citizens to trade in foreign vessels; or it would order its colonies to send certain products, such as molasses, coffee, and indigo only to ports of the home country. As in the American colonies, it might permit production of pig iron but prohibit furnaces for smelting steel; or it might allow copper to be mined, but proscribe the manufacture of articles out of copper. From all the above, a third inevitable result would follow: conflict, conflict between the nation and its colonies, and conflict with foreign lands. Time after time actual warfare erupted, as in the American Revolution (whose causes were deeply embedded in the mercantile philosophy), and in the series of trading wars between the Dutch and the English.

Basically, mercantilism was the philosophy of selfishness. It was the expression of the old fang-baring feeling, *Get-What-I-Can*. Its faults were exposed, brilliantly and unsparingly, by the great economist Adam Smith, that apostle of freedom who, by one of the bitter paradoxes of history, spoke out just in time to enable the exploiting classes to use his doctrines as chains. Smith contended that the mercantile system sacrificed the interests of consumers to those of producers—which violated not only good economics but good sense. He attacked the idea of a "favorable balance of trade" and the necessity of storing gold and silver; he struck out at mercantile principles as applied to colonies, and put his finger on a key issue by remarking that the principal advisers of the restrictive regulations were the very merchants who expected to benefit, and who placed their own advantage above that of the colonies.

Although the survivals of the doctrine of mercantalism are abundant even now, in pleas for protective tariffs and other commercial restrictions, in the preoccupation with a "favorable balance of trade," and in the concern of the nations for wealth in solid gold and silver, these remnants of the doctrine give little suggestion of its one-time strength. As if in proof that what men believe is more important than physical actualities, we have the century-long spectacle of the European nations competing like embattled dogs for trade, while descending to piracy, massacre, and warfare, though there would have been enough and to spare for all under a proper system of allocation. And throughout all these dealings, taking strength and thrust from mercantile theories, we can see the acquisitive arm of governments, and of private traders and raiders.

Take the case of the Far East, where Portugal cleared the way for its merchant ships by the voyage of Da Gama. Immediately the trade in spices was made into a royal monopoly; the vessels of the king, commanded by the king's officers, conducted a lucrative business, and all others were excluded. Here, therefore, we have mercantilism with a royal slant. And mercantalism, true to the basic doctrine, endeavored to debar foreign ships by means of its own strong navy, which overcame competition by the simple method of capturing and destroying the competitors. Moreover, lest the navy should be unequal to the task, the Portuguese circulated reports of strange and redoubtable monsters on the sea lanes, boiling waters, broiling suns, and other fantastic obstacles. At the same time, they zealously guarded all the charts and maps of their navigators; they decreed that no Portuguese who had been to the East should serve a foreign master; they tried to make a sealed secret of reaching the East. And they limited their activities to the spice trade, on which they maintained their monopoly throughout the sixteenth century. From this monopoly the king, buying pepper at low rates and selling it at high prices in Lisbon to merchants from many lands, was able to make an estimated annual profit of something like a million and a quarter in American dollars, though his gains assertedly would have been twice as great except for the corruption of his servants.

By about the end of the sixteenth century, the control of Portugal, her wings clipped by her annexation to Spain, gave place to the power of the Netherlands. The attitude of the Spaniards, before the Dutch ascendancy, was as possessive as that of any group: the seas around the Indies were their territorial waters where they had the exclusive privilege of trading; no one even had the right to enter without their permission. This dog-in-the-manger attitude was emphasized by the Spanish President of the Council of the Indies, when he warned the British ambassador that "in coercions and punishments to restrain access to these countries, he had an inclination rather to cruelty than to clemency." [3] However, "cruelty rather than clemency" did not hold the islands for the Spaniards; despite some bitter fighting and much bloodshed in the China Sea and the Malacca Straits, Spanish sovereignty in this area was to be restricted to the Philippines.

The entry of the Dutch was aggressive and firm. The Dutch East India Company was more than an ordinary commercial establishment; much of the original capital was subscribed by the towns and provinces; and it had exclusive rights to trade in the Pacific and Indian oceans, which made it something like a government on its own account. But it was a government for the sake of profit—a government whose shares might be bought at 250 or 500 pounds each and whose dividends soon rose to 25 per cent, and were at an average annual rate of 18 per cent throughout the seventeenth and eighteenth centuries.

Of more basic interest than the rate of return are the methods behind the returns. These usually involved coercion. First there was the coercion of the native populations, which, however, were usually left to themselves when they did not interfere with trade, while they were benefited by the enforced suppression of their wars. But the

Dutch themselves were always ready to fight—that is, ready to fight for the sake of business, though they were quite content if they could prevail by treaty or intimidation.

Thanks to the innumerable restrictions, the natives of the islands were forbidden to sail more than a certain distant from their coasts under penalty of seizure as pirates; they were enjoined from trading with India or other parts of continental Asia; they were forced to uproot their spice-trees when these would interfere with the Dutch product. In the course of time, they were prohibited even from receiving emissaries from continental areas; and a tribute of "full-grown slaves" was levied upon them. In the early yars the Dutch were actually, as they claimed, the deliverers of the islands from Portuguese oppression. But in time they bore down with an oppression of their own. However, this too was for the sake of business.

Meanwhile they were coming into conflict with other business interests—the English. And though they were co-religionists of the English and had been friends in Europe, they gradually assumed the snarling hostility of a dog guarding a bone. In 1613, for example, they forcibly restrained the natives of Machian in the Moluccas from trading with the English; in 1618 they attacked the nutmeg islands of Pularoon and Rosengyn, which had been taken over by the English, and some of the latter were displayed as prisoners in chains; at the same time, they captured two ships, looted a third, and put the crews of all three in irons. But even worse cruelties were to follow, including the quartering of twelve natives for an alleged plot; while the culmination flared forth in the infamous Amboyna massacre, in which eighteen Englishmen were tortured and then sentenced to death.

Doubltless national rivalries, national passions, and sheer sadistic impulses had something to do with all these horrors. But had it not been for the trading antagonisms and the furies they unleashed, the supposedly civilized Europeans would not have been whipped up into a frenzy like that of savage tribesmen in a blood feud.

During the same general period, the antagonism of the two nations was also being fought out a world away. The Dutch, who had aimed to corral the West African slave trade and had established bases in the West Indies, had collided with the English in various ways, largely because of the mercantile philosophy. Both nations were faithful to their religion, "All for me, none for you!" Thus, by virtue of the Navigation Ordinance of October, 1651, the products of America, Asia, and Africa could be transported to England only in English ships, or in colonial ships with English masters, and with crews more than half

English. When the representatives of the United Provinces appealed against the Ordinance, their claim was refused, and the refusal brought the two nations close to war. Then in 1665 the Second Dutch War broke out. The climax approached when Captain Robert Holmes commanded an armed squadron to the African coast to protect English trading; incited by the hostile attitude of the Dutch, he seized various factories (despite the nominal state of peace). In January 1665, the Dutch dispatched Admiral De Ruyter to preserve what was left of their monopoly of the slave trade; his fleet recaptured the island of Goree, took many English-owned slave ships, expelled the English from various slave posts along the African coast, crossed the ocean and unsuccessfully attacked Barbados, and then seized some ships in the harbors of Montserrat and Nevis and destroyed their cargoes. It could hardly have surprised the Admiral that the sequel was war.

And so the rivalries bred by the West African and West Indian slave trade, fanned by the gales of remorseless and uncompromising mercantile beliefs, led directly to a clash between two erstwhile partners.

The Second Dutch War, which brought acute loss to all concerned, including the English, Dutch, and French, and left an enduring hatred between French and English colonies, showed in the beginning one great peculiarity. The English relied largely upon the services of buccaneers: bands of reckless men, desperadoes sprung of many lands, who made their living by plunder when they did not exist by running down the wild cattle of the islands or were not themselves being hunted by the Spaniards. These ruffians, who were mostly without any fixed home other than rude leaf-covered sheds, have been described by a contemporary French observer, the Abbé de Tertre: "They were dressed in a pair of drawers and a shirt at the most, shod with the skin of a hog's leg fastened on the top, and behind the foot with strips of the same skin, girded round the middle of the body with a sack, which served them to sleep in as a defense against the innumerable insects which bit and sucked the blood from all parts of their bodies that were left uncovered. . . . When they returned from the chase . . . you would say that these are the butcher's vilest servants who have been eight days in the slaughter-house without washing themselves." [4]

Such men, trained in a merciless school, could be expected to show neither mercy in warfare nor scruples. It is significant, therefore, of the bitterness of the prevailing passions and the fierceness of the commercial rivalries that the English could call for the help of such offscourings of humanity. True, there was a precedent, as there usually is for anything atrocious; many of the mercenary soldiers of previous centuries had been little better than brigands; and the armed privateers, ranging the sea in search of foreign treasure, had been virtual pirates. Marauding, after all, has never been distinguished by its humane restraints. And a nation can hardly use buccaneers without descending to the buccaneering level.

This was proved by the actions of the hirelings. Even before the outbreak of the Dutch war, they had struck out against the Spaniards; under the typical pirate chief Henry Morgan and other redoubtable captains, they raided the coast of Yucatan, captured the city of Truxillo, invaded Nicaragua, and pillaged the capital city of Granada, from which they emerged with 50,000 pieces of eight and many slaves, whom they sold profitably. Subsequently, wrecked villages and blasted plantations marked the line of march of Captain Edward Mansfield through Costa Rica; Granada was sacked once more, and its seven churches and five monasteries looted. And Morgan, a year or two later, captured Puerto Bello on the Isthmus of Panama; after blowing up some of the Spaniards in violation of a promise of quarter and robbing and torturing the other inhabitants for fifteen days, he and his men retreated to Cuba, where Morgan found that he had a quarter of a million pieces of eight, in addition to captured guns, silks, linens, and other riches—on whose proceeds he and his men lived for a while in high debauchery.

But this was a small-scale raid beside the attack on the old city of Panama, which was never restored from its ruins. For twenty-eight days Morgan and his men searched for treasure, after the Spaniards had done their best to thwart him by burning the city; and meanwhile they followed their usual routine by torturing captives into revealing hidden wealth and so acquired booty estimated to be worth not less than 10,000 pounds. Indicating how a haze of glory can be woven about thievery, brutality, and butchery, we have a modern comment that, "Disgraceful and barbarous as the raid had been, it cannot be denied that as an exploit of amazing audacity it stands high in the Caribbean story that for more than a century and a half had been filled with deeds of daring."[5] Morgan was in due time knighted, and as Sir Henry Morgan he became lieutenant-governor of Jamaica.

In his new office, he gave trouble enough to his fellow Englishmen, the more so as he evidently had a tender spot in his heart for his ex-pals, the buccaneers. For example, when the ports of the Gulf of Hondurus were raided by the English pirate chief Captain Coxon, Morgan enabled the robber to bring his loot into Port Royal; allowed

him to refit there regardless of minor details such as government
orders; and permitted him to sail away with the fruits of his thefts to
Rhode Island, where he would find a ready market. Morgan's dere-
lictions, which included drunkenness and other offenses, became so
serious that he had to be removed from office; but in 1687, the year
before his death, Governor Christopher Monck reseated him in the
post of lieutenant-governor, which led to another period of softness
toward buccaneering, and chaos in the trade of the island. Even to
the end of his life, therefore, Morgan was a power in the land, though
his chief accomplishment had been to sack, torture, destroy, and murder in the cause of national commercial supremacy and personal
aggrandizement.

In many of the plunderings, French buccaneers or "filibusterers"
accompanied the English, as when they joined forces with Coxon
and another pirate chief, Sawkins, and made raids across the Isthmus
of Panama into the Pacific, seized Spanish ships, burned and looted
towns all along the Peruvian and Chilean coasts and disrupted the
trade with the Indies. Meanwhile France, like England, thought of
using the buccaneers as agents of official policy. Dutch corsairs, also,
took part in the merry quest of booty, when the sea-brigands Nicholas
Van Horn and Laurens de Graff transferred their business activities
from Guinea to the Gulf of Mexico, and in 1683 led an expedition
against San Juan de Ulua (Vera Cruz). After taking the town, they
favored it for four days with the usual buccaneering treatment; caught
the governor hiding in a stable, and held him for a ransom of 70,000
pieces of eight; threatened to destroy the city unless they were paid
a very large sum; and finally sailed away with loot estimated to be
worth 3,000,000 reals, including gold, silver, gems, and more than
1,500 slaves to be sold in the markets of Saint-Domingue. It is perhaps worth noting that the pirates were unable to divide the stolen
property amicably among themselves; the leaders had their little
altercations, in the course of which Van Horn was mortally wounded.

Buccaneering had now become such a curse that it had to be
suppressed somehow; its evil, spreading like a disease, had even involved some of the local governors, who found it a convenient source
of private graft, when they issued service commissions to the fili-
busters. The French Government therefore in 1684 sent the Sieur
Tarin de Cussy to Saint-Domingue to subdue the robbers; but the
task proved difficult, and the most effective method was to seduce the
private leaders into the service of the King. Thus the notorious buccaneer, de Grammont, was appointed Lieutenant-Governor of Saint-

Dominque; while de Graff was employed to fight against the English, and subsequently helped to found a new colony in Louisiana.

But as the buccaneers ceased to receive official support, many of them turned to unofficial piracy that made them the pests of the sea. No maritime commerce was safe unless in league with them, or unless heavily protected; the English in particular suffered grievously, as in the colony of Jamaica, where the high insurance rates necessitated by piracy had raised the cost of living.

It is a sad commentary that many supposedly respectable men, in the name of business, were lending support to the pirates, particularly in some of the American colonies—in Carolina, where the pirates were virtually at home, and in parts of New England.

"In the port of Boston," Arthur P. Newton tells us, "the King's proclamations against buccaneering were torn down with derision, and long after the rover captains could hope to get assistance in fitting out their ships or disposing of their plunder in an English port or with any reputable firm, they might rely upon a warm welcome in Massachusetts and plenty of financial help if they would only return a sufficiently high rate of profit upon it. The pious elders of Salem and Rhode Island did not like sea robberies to take place in northern waters, for that raised insurance rates, but in the West Indies they could see no reason why the traditional warfare should not go on as before, and they were not too inquisitive as to whether a captain who came to trade with them had won his cargoes by buccaneering or piracy; the only question was one of price." [6]

It is suggestive of the spirit of the times that when a pirate captain put into one of the New England ports with his booty, hardly a jury could be found to convict him.

III

In the Far East in the following century, European empire building was to take a portentous and unforeseen course. On the face of things, it is hard to see why that vast conglomeration of states and principalities known as India should ever have come under the arm of any nation in far-off Europe—though perhaps this was no more unnatural than that Peru or Mexico should have fallen to the Spaniards. But a basic fact, often remarked by historians, is that England did not intend to take India; she was driven on by circumstances, though largely circumstances which she and the other Western nations had created. And the underlying drive was commercial: the quest for profits, for wealth, in whose pursuit she licensed a private military power that led directly toward governmental control. Few facts in history seem stranger or more unnatural. And few facts illustrate more clearly the unsuspected bypaths of acquisitiveness.

The part played by acquisitiveness is shown not only by the returns of the East India Company, but by the importance placed upon those returns. We may regard it as no accident that the Company at its heyday paid its investors generously, and that Clive in 1765 could estimate the gross revenues from Bengal at an annual four millions sterling, and the net income at 1,650,000 pounds. Nor was it merely coincidental that the stock, after a raise in the dividends, went up to 267, shareholders took returns of 12½ per cent in 1767, and servants of the Company bought countryseats and parliamentary boroughs with the fortunes they brought home from the sub-continent. Again, we cannot overlook the fact that, while the Company was a private one, the whole British nation was a partner in the proceeds: a law was enacted binding the Company to pay 400,000 pounds yearly to the Crown, and an inquiry held in 1773 revealed that the actual payment from all sources, including customs duties, approached two million annually. At the same time, private investors were in a fever; citizens discussed the Company's affairs as they might debate the weightiest matters of state; the latest quotations on its stock were proclaimed in the coffee-houses; the great as well as the rank and file were concerned. Amid all this furor, of course, we hear little as to *how* the Company got its money, and *whose* labor, in far-off India, produced the wealth.

There was much that the investors might have considered. They might have noted that the profits of the East India Company were not purely the fruits of trading but were also the ensanguined products of warfare. "Never before or since in the world's history," Sir Alfred Lyall states the basic fact, "has there been so much bloodshed over commerce as distinguished from colonization." Lyall does give the English credit for "having done their best" to confine themselves to commerce throughout the seventeenth century—in contrast to Portugal and Holland, both of which immediately seized territory. But warfare was implied in the methods and principles of all the contenders: each was obsessed with the mercantilist philosophy which demanded an exclusive control; each was determined to oust the others; and each was empowered to wage war. Yes, strangely, each of the commercial companies was licensed not only to trade but to raise armies and fight. It should therefore surprise no one that fighting ensued.

There were, first of all, the bitter conflicts with the Portuguese, and the naval encounters between the English and the Dutch, which weakened both powers. And later there was the war between the English and French, or, rather, between the English and French companies. True, there was the important modifying fact that war had broken out between the two parent countries in Europe; but even before the start of such war the companies had, at great cost, maintained their armies and maneuvered for positions.

And yet, paradoxically, even if the central motive was commercial and avaricious, the English did much to combat various forms of avarice. There was, for example, the move that they made in the early nineteenth century against the practice of *thagi*—murder and robbery conducted by groups of hereditary assassins known as *thags* or thugs, who, in honor of the goddess Kali, would strangle and loot passing travelers. The suppression of this holy banditry, which was accomplished within ten years, perhaps counter-balances much that was covetous on the part of the Europeans.

Avarice and rapacity also characterized the once-great Mogul empire, which was fast falling to pieces after the death of the Emperor Aurangzeb in 1707, and retained little more than the ghost of power throughout most of the eighteenth century. The depravity of this regime, and the ruinous cupidity that ruled it, have been described by Francois Bernier, Court Physician to Aurangzeb during the early part of his long reign. "The country," says Bernier, "is ruined by the necessity of paying the enormous charges required to maintain the splendor of a numerous court, and a large army maintained for the purpose of keeping the people in subjection."[8] There was, says Bernier, no such thing as security of private property; the tyranny and greed of the ruler and his cohorts were "often so excessive as to deprive the peasant and the artisan of the necessities of life" and to "drive the cultivator of the soil from his wretched home." . . . "It is owing to this miserable system that most towns in Hindustan are made up of earth, mud, and other wretched materials; that there is no city or twon which, if it be not already ruined or deserted, does not bear evident marks of approaching decay."[9]

And if the Moguls in their decadence reached out avaricious claws, their decline aided and encouraged the Marathas, a native military race that preyed upon a great part of the Mogul territory. It has been said of the Maratha government that it "lived by and for plunder,"

and that "It would be difficult to exaggerate the wickedness of the
Maratha hordes and their allies the Pindaris." [10] And this statement
seems justified when we note that the methods they employed, though
much larger in scope, were in some ways similar to those of American
gangsters. Their idea was to levy tribute, *chauth* or blackmail over
a vast area, as well as to conquer territory; they swarmed in with their
mobile horsemen, and took a quarter of the revenue of conquered
states on the promise of protecting them against further brigandage.
There are reasons for supposing that except for the arrival of the
English, though the latter in the beginning were often allied with
them, the Marathas would have swallowed all southern and central
India; in view of the decay of the Mogul empire, it is hard to see what
could have checked them. Therefore the commercial East India
Company appears unwittingly to have done a great service by sup-
pressing the Marathas.

The psychological condition produced by the sudden British opening
of the Indian Eldorado was somewhat similar to that observed in all
gold rushes. Vincent A. Smith has summarized the situation:
"Riches were to be had for the asking, nay, without asking. The
sudden affluence thrust upon the Calcutta community . . . turned the
heads of all, and led to a scramble for riches which brought into pain-
ful prominence the evil features of human nature. Gentlemen who
in the ordinary course of nature would have been content to retire as
successful traders and end their days in respectable obscurity, were
tempted to sell their souls for gain and so condemned to leave for the
scorn of posterity names tarnished by the stain of ignoble greed." [11]

One unfortunate circumstance was that the goldseekers had no more
thought for the wellbeing of the country than Pizarro had for the Incas.
In fact, their psychology was somewhat like Pizarro's; the dazzle of
gold, the lure of sudden wealth had obsessed and enchanted them. One
wonders if it even occurred to them that they perhaps owed a duty
to the land that gave them the golden goose. Take the case of Clive,
whose military victory had made him the first of the takers and getters.
This famous figure has been frequently criticized, and not without
reason. After the Battle of Plassey he received a sum that, one
might suppose, would have satisfied the most avaricious: 234,000
pounds, as against 50,000 to 80,000 pounds for other agents of the
Company. But even these vast returns, whose purchasing power was
much greater than it would be today, did not satisfy the victor of
Plassey. Subsequently he was induced to join a scheme for enriching
members of the Company by a forbidden trade in opium, salt, and

betel-leaf; while he received, upon demanding it, the title of *Omrah* or noble, which took with it a *jagir* or land revenue, in this case amountin gto an annual twenty thousand pounds. This, as Professor Howard Robinson expresses the paradox, "the servant of the Company became its landlord." [12]

In accepting this huge dividend, Clive was doing no more than had been done by Dupleix, the French administrator, and perhaps neither he nor his French counterpart ever paused to consider that land revenues did not grow like cocoanuts on trees, but were the products of man's labor—in this case, presumably, the labor of multitudes of peasants living on the borders of indigence. Even if they had been no less exploited by native masters, did this excuse the grasping hands from overseas?

Clive himself evidently saw nothing wrong about his actions. Five years later, before a Committee of the House of Commons, he demanded, "Am I not rather deserving of praise for the moderation which marked my proceedings? . . . Mr. Chairman, at this moment I stand astonished at my own moderation." Perhaps, in the light of the standards of his times, he really had cause for astonishment; it is extremely difficult for a man to look beyond himself, and see his actions as they would appear to another age. This, indeed, is the view of one of Clive's modern defenders: "It was the practice of the eighteenth century to accept advantages which were consecrated by custom, or which did not threaten the interest of the State provided that they could be reconciled with the private conscience; and the public view of the acceptance of these advantages was principally colored by political feeling. . . . It is hard that Clive should have been accused of misconduct for accepting what few men of his age would have declined." [13]

In exactly these words a pleader of the Roman age might have defended a proconsul for helping himself to unlimited riches in the provinces.

We need not go on to observe the steps by which the English, having thrust their hands into the treasure vault of the East, found that they could not hold it without the twin guarantees of military conquest and political control. In the British management of India there would, indeed, be much that was meritorious, and much that would contrast favorably with the record of other colonizing powers. But this neither explains nor condones the original wrong: that India was dominated by a foreign power for the sake of foreign gain. Even while accomplishing some incidental good, the gods of wealth had planted the seeds of incalculable evil, and these were to be seen in riots and warfare (one hundred and eleven military expeditions were recorded in the nineteenth century alone), in the humiliation and further impoverishment of the people, in famines taking millions of lives owing to the appropriation of native land for growing cotton, jute, and tea, and in problems of racial oppression and antagonism which were softened only with the granting of Indian indepedence in 1947.

X

COLONIZATION, BLOOD, AND PROFITS

During the nineteenth century a very different colonial chapter was being written by the European powers. Now for the first time Africa received leading attention, though important action marked other far-scattered areas. And all this was of major significance for our own times, since it not only presaged many of the disturbances of the mid-twentieth century but was among the factors leading to the First World War, and provided some of the battlefields of World War II.

Basically, what reason was there for France to establish dependencies in far-off Tahiti, the Society Islands, Madagascar, or Indo-China? What reason for the Germans to settle in East Africa, or the Belgians in the Congo, or the British in Burma or the Sudan, or the Italians in Eritrea? Actually, there was exactly as much excuse as for the sovereignty of European nations in the West Indies, Central and South America, and India. That intruders should enter little known lands, put the natives to work beneath the lash, or tax them for the privilege of inhabiting their own homes—this was, unfortunately, not a form of enterprise without historical precedent, but it had often gone by the candid name of brigandage.

Yet this was the form of enterprise wherein European nations specialized in Africa, which they distributed among themselves with the celerity of skilled robbers. The speed of the partition is indicated by the fact that, before 1875, less than half of continental Africa's 11,262,000 square miles was in European possession, while, twenty years later, all but one tenth of this vast area had not been gobbled up, and large sections of the remainder, including the Egyptian Sudan and the Boer Republics, would fall within another five years. This, I submit, represents on the face of it one of the greatest feats of acquisitiveness on record.

It would be possible to linger indefinitely over nineteenth century colonialism in various regions, including Kenya, Indo-China and the Pacific islands. But the story, for the purposes of a general survey, can best be told by concentration upon two or three characteristic cases.

II

First consider the record of the French in Algeria, which has led to recent rebellion and years of terrorism and savage warfare.

It is true, of course, that the conquest of Algeria can be traced to a variety of sources, many of them psychological. It is also true that the French people wre but little interested, and had no general desire for the North African territory; it has even been claimed that Algeria was attacked as a diversion to distract public attention from domestic issues. But whether or not we can detect an original French acquisitiveness, we may read the preliminaries in acquisitiveness on the part of Algeria. For centuries the North African coast had been a stronghold for pirates; the dey of Algiers had been little better than a captain of sea brigands, who captured not only merchandise but human booty, holding thousands of Christian slaves, of whom the women disappeared into the households and harems of the East, while the men might groan out their lives in the galleys. This had produced a long record of warfare with European states, some of which had bombarded Algiers without success, while others had purchased immunity; even England in 1671 descended to buying the safety of her ships.

The actions of France, when at last she made the decisive step against the robbers, were not without comic-opera accompaniments. France was perhaps the logical nation to act, since she had had coral fisheries on the Barbary coast since the sixteenth century, and had had more or less continuous though not untroubled relations with the dey. In 1819 two merchants named Bakri and Busnach became involved in the international situation. They had come to exert an almost princely influence; and they incited the ire of the last of the deys, Hussein, to whom they owed something like a quarter of a million francs. Being unable to collect the debt, he was incensed to learn that the merchants had received four and a half million from the French, whom he blamed for the non-payment of the sums due him. In his anger, he struck the French consul Déval three times with the handle of a fly-swatter. Apparently this did no serious injury; but the insult rankled. Six weeks later, a fleet of French warships demanded an apology of the dey, whose refusal resulted in an attempted blocade of the city. Matters now went from bad to worse; in 1829 some French sailors of the blocading vessels were massacred, and a naval officer, attempting to negotiate a settlement, received his reply in gunfire. Finally in 1830 the weak and slow-moving French king Charles X, in the face of the opposition of the press, launched the expedition that put an end to the power of the dey and resulted in "limited occupation."

This "limited occupation" led to sporadic fighting that lasted for years; not until 1847 could the land be said to have been subdued, though eruptions were to occur throughout the nineteenth century, and, as we all know, deep into the twentieth. It is indeed strange that an occupation begun without popular support, and without any apparent long-range design, should have led to such a tenacious effort to make the country part of France.

We must not, however, consider Algeria as a law unto herself; she was to be an important part of the great French colonial empire, and cannot be viewed without regard to the motives that applied to the other portions of that empire. And what were those motives? Not far from what we might expect on the basis of earlier imperialism. The principles of the mercantilists, who saw in the colonies merely a source of trading advantage and commercial prosperity for the home country, were by no means dead in the nineteenth century. Stephen H. Roberts, in his voluminous study of French colonial policy, has summarized the prevailing attitude: ". . . there was practically a consensus of opinion that colonization should pay, whether or not it actually did so or not. No attention was paid to the question of a development of the colonies as individual entities . . . they were pieces in the wider organism, and their sole function was to strengthen France and to serve her needs." [1]

And what if the interests of the home country and of the colony should not harmonize? One can guess the answer. Even as late as 1914 "it was still clearly understood that, if a conflict arose between those of France and those of the colony, as occurred in the rise of industry in Tonkin and the beet-sugar question in the West Indies, the interests of France, despite the hardship and the apparent injustice of the case in question, were to be paramount. . . . the interests of the natives were in no case given a serious consideration. Always in the background there was the assumption that the goal was to be one in which the colony contributed the maximum to French needs in some form or other. The utilitarian concept was never absent. . . ." [2]

Let us glance at some specific developments.

We may pass over the tariff laws which, by erecting impassable walls against trade with other countries than France, were like throttling hands on the throat of free enterprise, and greatly increased the cost of many commodities. Since Algeria was primarily agricultural, far more damage was inflicted by the laws regarding land.

The Arabs and the Berbers valued their land; the former held it communally; its ownership had religious connotations. But to the French intruders, the original possessors were unprogressive primitives, who could not put the soil to proper use; arrogantly and greedily, the invades took as much as they could of the best areas by whatever means they could devise; the very opposition which they aroused gave them the pretext for further thefts, which they dignified with the forms of legality. The French authority Louis Vignon has summarized this phase of the matter with unusual frankness: "Each revolt, in effect,—and they were numerous, as the repression of one was often the germ of another—served as a pretext for the confiscation of part or even all of the tribal lands. It was thus that the natives were driven back . . . all of their best lands being taken for distribution among the colonists." [3]

This, of course, was consistent with the theory that the natives existed in order to be exploited. But if they were unable to strike back against the loss of their ancestral lands, they could at least harbor perennial resentment.

One great difficulty lay in the total opposition of European and Algerian ideas of land ownership, and in the fact that the French, in their possessive eagerness, attempted to put their own views everywhere into force. Doubtless the French could not understand communal proprietorship; and certainly the Arabs could not adapt themselves to foreign individual doctrines. And so, when the French attempted to ride rough-shod over the native system, the result was chaos.

According to a French law of 1873, any tribesman could apply for his share of communally held land (which destroyed the essence of the communal system, since this was based on the tribesman's inability to claim separate rights). When any man, therefore, asked for a portion of what had been inalienable tribal property, he snapped one strand of an intricate cord; the rest gave way, by legal processes or illegal; and soon the remaining Arabs, unable to compete with the tangle of technicalities or faced with costs beyond their means, saw themselves stripped of their birthright. Since even the poorest or the most unprincipaled member of the tribe could set the process into action, the new law was highly effective in throwing men off their tribal lands. To take a single case, as reported by the Franck-Chauveau Commission of 1893: individualization of the holdings was demanded by one out of 513 natives, who held among them 292 hectares of land (a hectare equals 2.471 of our acres). In return for his rights, the petitioner received 20 francs; but the process of division, having been started, could not be checked; the eventual cost came to 11,000 francs, and in the end the entire strip of land (well over a square mile) was obtained by a French clerk for 80 francs.

True, this case was exceptional. But the natives, thrown off their lands and scattered, could hardly harbor any kindly feelings toward the regime. One does not wonder at the view of Stephen H. Roberts (whose words, published in 1929, might also apply to Algeria of a later date) that "many of the evils of modern Algeria can be traced to the operation of this law of 1873," and that (as he elsewhere puts it), "France is meeting the retribution of a century of a policy based on exploitation." [4]

During the period between 1883 and 1889, the natives lost as much as 40 per cent of their land, including the most fertile. And the worst of the situation, perhaps, is that it has been permanent. An Arabian writer in 1953, after telling us that 70 per cent of the country's economic resources are controlled by 10 per cent of the population (the European 10 per cent), goes on to this summary: "A European feudalism, protected by the State, has sprung up in Algeria. Thousands of European proprietors own more than a hundred hectares each. Their individual holdings average 235 hectares, while many estates are beyond 1000 hectares in extent. This in the presence of a land proletariat living on the verge of starvation in normal years, and decimated during the bad years by famine and epidemics. The European feudality furthermore is almost the only group to benefit from the public works and projects for agricultural development." [5]

One need proceed no further—one need not even consider the excessive weight of taxation, which saddled as much as half the burden of the country's taxation on natives who possessed far less than half the country's wealth. Here, in the acquisitiveness that took much and gave little in return, we can find all the explanation we need of the gory splashes that Algeria has left on the history of the twentieth century.

III

As a second example of colonizing methods and situations, we may turn to the Germans in the West African territory, the Cameroons. Unlike the French in Algeria, the Germans were late-comers, and were early dispossessed; their rule began in 1884, and ended with the First World War. Germany, in fact, seems to have been drawn into colonization more or less in a competitive race with the other great powers, and largely out of nationalistic sentiment. Originally Bismarck had proclaimed himself against colonization; but eventually, with evident inconsistency, he consented to the move under the guise of aiding trade.

The commercial purposes of the Germans—their desire to exploit the natural resources of the colonies—were always freely admitted. But the German traders were in danger of running headon into native interests; constant fighting stemmed from the struggles of the original inhabitants to preserve their trade monopolies. Thus, after 1888, there were few years unmarked by open fighting in some part of the Cameroons; and while most of the outbreaks were of small scope, one of their causes was the interference of the natives with the trade of the white man, in the effort to end the white man's interference with their trade. There were, to be sure, other causes, including raids on the native villages and their women; and one serious eruption arose from the murder of a German official after he had recruited the natives for work on plantations where many of them died.

Meanwhile some of the traders, following the way of their kind, pausd at no measures that profits seemed to demand. In doing business with the natives, they found it helpful to provide the two things that should at all costs have been kept from native hands: firearms, and liquor. The avaricious mood of some of the traders is shown by their argument that certain out-of-date flintlocks could not be sold anywhere except in Africa, and, if not disposed of there, would result in serious losses. And some of the traders held that, without liquor, they could do no business at all. Intoxicants, it seems, were the great allurements enticing many natives into labor contracts; some of the carriers in the southern Cameroons, in fact, accepted their wages in this form of currency.

Meanwhile Adolf Woermann, head of the C. Woermann firm, could make some curious pleas in the Reichstag: that his concern sold the natives only the very best liquor; that the sale of this very best liquor enabled him to run an unsubsidized West African steamship line; that prohibition in the Cameroons should logically be accompanied by prohibition in Germany; and that, in any event, the livelihood of thousands of Germans depended on the trade in alcohol. However, the Government overruled Woermann's objections, and placed an import tariff on liquor, though a year later, in 1889, it did not include this commodity on the list of tariff increases.

But the central issue concerned labor. If the whites could urge, coerce, or force the natives into working for them, they could make the colony pay dividends. But without native labor, in an undeveloped country where even the overland transportation of freight depended upon human muscles, the newcomers would be helpless. At this point, unfortunately, a conflict was involved between the native disposition and the outlook and habits of the white man. With the natural indolence of the dweller in a hot climate, the native was content to lounge beneath a tree, laughing and chatting, and doing no more than the minimum of work necessary to give him the day's food. European ideas of enterprise were foreign to his mind. To work under pressure at continuous hard labor—this was something unknown to him. Yet this the white man demanded. It is not surprising that he did not comply willingly; nor that the white man, when inducements such as guns and whisky did not suffice, should use the obvious alternative. The Cameroons were not the only African colony employing forced labor; this was characteristic rather than exceptional. But the methods used there may be taken as examples of the means widely employed to exact the white man's tribute of labor.

One of the easiest and commonest devices was taxation. If a tax was imposed, and if in the natural course of things the natives were unable to pay, the whites might permit them to work out the bill. The word "permit," however, does not express the situation; the laborers were compelled to work, as surely as if the letters S-L-A-V-E had been branded across their brows. That these people, who for unreckoned time had been living in their own way, should now be forced to live in the white man's way— this was an exaction that could be justified only by superior might. And that they should toil for the gain of the invader, and toil at his command—this partook of the nature of banditry.

The taxes were of various kinds, ranging from tariffs to direct imposts. Thus on July 1, 1903, in Duala, a head tax was imposed on every adult. This applied specifically to all persons capable of working; if any man or woman could not pay the amount, he could work it off at tasks picked by the administrative head of the district. The resulting forced labor was hardly softened by the fact that native chieftains, accepting the bait of a percentage of the returns, were to aid in the exactions. This did not at all help the ordinary native, who could be thrown into jail for tax evasion.

However, not all the natives meekly accepted the imposition. Many left their homes in favor of untaxed regions. And in 1907 the Akwa people, protesting that the tax was required of all persons above sixteen or seventeen and had been raised to five marks in the case of

a grown man, refused to make payment—which led, after some parley-
ing, to seizure of some of the rebellious chieftains and the substitution
of a hut tax for the head tax, though in 1908 the head tax was extended to all the rest of the colony.

In the tax law of 1908, the relation of taxes to forced labor is seen
more nakedly than ever. "It was specifically provided," Harry A.
Rudin points out "that natives unable to pay taxes in cash must not
be handed over to private employers to work for the money, for all
tax-work had to be public work of a governmental character. Thirty
days of work were given as the work-equivalent of a six-mark tax.
Lists of taxpayers were to be made out with greatest care. In the
collection of taxes chieftains were to aid the Government at a commission of 7½ per cent of the amounts collected."⁶

Among the facts which strike one about this summary, not the
least is the suggestion that it had been customary to hand deliquent
tax-payers over to work for private employers (indeed, a subsequent
decree, in 1913, authorized this method). A second conclusion is that
the obligation to work for the Government, rather than for private
interests, did not alter the essential nature of the forced labor.

As an indication of one way in which the tax law worked, consider
the criticisms of the head of the Basler mission, that the education of
students from fourteen to sixteen years of age was cut short when they
could not pay the tax. Or observe the fact that certain native chiefs,
not to be outdone in avarice by the foreigner, compelled some of their
followers to pay double or triple taxes, while themselves keeping the
difference. One simple method was to make the laborer pay where he
worked, and pay again where he lived.

But labor in the Cameroons was not only forced; often it was
forced to its very death, particularly in the early days of the colony.
The black men, taken from the high and relatively healthful plateau
regions to the malarial coastal districts, died in such numbers that
their employment was little better than slow murder. So many were
the deaths that an order of 1900 required each plantation to provide
its own cemetery. Bad treatment, bad food, bad living conditions,
long hours of unaccustomed hard work, an unaccustomed climate,
homesickness, and tropical fevers—all these took their toil. The
exact death rate will probably never be known, but an official named
Mansfield, stationed for years at Ossidinge, "wrote that 50 per cent
of the *Stafarbeiter* taken from his district never returned"; while
"Vietor, a German trader who took an active interest in colonial affairs
and worked for improvements in the treatment of the natives, wrote

in 1902 that the death rate of the plantations amounted to 20 per cent."[7] Even if these cases were exceptional, it is generally acknowledged that the percentage was everywhere high.

One can say, however, that the Government did make an effort to provide hospitals and medical service. One must also acknowledge that, though the Germans made serious inroads into native freedom, they did not destroy it entirely, but left the people with a greater control over their own affairs than they might have exercised under certain other conquerors. One may furthermore take into account these first-hand observations of a traveler in the Cameroons: "Wherever I went, I heard the natives praise the excellence of the German administration. The frequently made comment about the Germans was that they were very strict, at times harsh, but always just."[8] Finally, one should not forget that, whatever may be said of private traders, the colony proved to be of no economic advantage to the German Government. This is not to say that no economic advantage was sought, nor does it justify the exploitation of the natives; but it does throw the picture into fairer relief.

And in any case the situation in the Cameroons, for all its black marks, appears almost of a halcyon blue compared with certain other regions, such as the Belgian Congo.

IV

At least in one important way, the Belgian territory differed from most other colonies. It was not at first, at least in theory, the domain of any European power; it had come beneath the grip of a single man, king Leopold II, who could use it as his personal tool, his private acquisition. This meant that there were not even the meager restraints and safeguards existing in other colonies. What came into being was an autocracy, with absolute rights; and this autocracy did not even pretend to be benevolently disposed; it existed for profits, and the natives were of interest only as pawns to guarantee those profits.

From an undated past, these natives had been living close to nature, without ideas of property in the white man's sense of the term, and without thought of acquiring much if anything beyond the needs of the moment. The land they tilled was theirs, and so were the implements of their rude cultivation; but they had neither money, nor a profit system, nor ideas of the permanent sale of any portion of the country. Therefore they could not understand what the white man meant by his claim to the land.

"It had all begun," Ludwig Bauer tells us, "with the purchased rights of sovereignty. The colonizers behaved as if they had to do with highly devloped and legally instructed Europeans, who could grasp the subtleties of law and politics. It had been as if one should induce a three-year-old child, whom one is leading by the land, to assign one a house in return for a lump of sugar. So magnificent had been the success of their hypocrisy, that the colonizers saw only the signatures to (the 'marks' upon) their charters, and overlooked everything else. Now they could advance further. In civilized countries, the lands which have no specified owner belong to the State. . . . But to apply such notions to a thinly populated country, where there were neither towns nor peasantry, signified the dispossession and enslavement of the inhabitants. That was what was achieved by Leopold's decree of August 17, 1889. . . ." [9]

It may be that the King did not realize the implications of his own decree. But as much cannot be assumed for the mandate of September 21, 1891, whereby Leopold reserved to himself all the riches of the Congo, and particularly the ivory and rubber, which he ordered his officials to gather. And where were they to gather these commodities? Naturally, from those who had them. Foreign merchants were to be expropriated; the natives were to be compelled to give whatever they had of value. And since they had nothing of value except perhaps some stray ivory picked up in the jungle, a further decree perpetrated the same ruse as we have noted in the Cameroons. The natives were to be taxed! Every year each of them must pay from six to twenty-four francs—and Leopold might as well have asked payment in Chaldean shekels. To make up the amount, if they had no francs, th Negroes must turn over food—whose price, incidentally, was fraudulently fixed by the State far below the market quotation. And in the rubber districts, the tax must be met in rubber, for which the natives were to be paid at a rate that varied from about 5 to 12½ per cent of the prevailing world price.

These simple figures, however, conceal more than they reveal. To obtain the required commodities, the natives were compelled to work— were, in effect, enslaved. Each was required, for example, to spend a minimum of forty hours a month gathering rubber, which could be found only after many hours' travel through the storm-ridden, leopard-infested jungle. And even after the rubber had been collected, the victims must often travel long distances through the wilderness to settle accounts with Leopold's agents. But when the agents at last had their rubber, the workers were likely to be cheated by false weights and other tricks, since the officials received a premium on what they took from the Negroes.

Some of the Negroes, it is true, were already slaves who had been sold by the chiefs; these, according to the Belgians, were now "enfranchised." This, however, did not mean that they had much cause to rejoice. "What the enfranchisement amounted to," Ludwig Bauer observes, "was that they were heavily laden, that their skeletons bleached by the roadside, that those who survived were flogged with hippopotamus-hide whips for as long as they could keep afoot. The lash was now beginning to assume a leading role in the Congo. It had become the symbol of the new system opened by Leopold's decrees." [10]

The lash was not even the worst of the afflictions endured by the unwilling workers. The reports would be incredible if not attested by many witnesses, including those before the English Commission of Inquiry of 1904. Torture and maiming, the shooting of recalcitrants, the amputation of hands of grown men and of children, the seizure of wives and children of fugitives as hostages, the intimidation and even the assassination of complainants, the death of multitudes from sheer exhaustion as the cadaverous lines of black porters were driven forward through the jungle—these are but a few of the pictures which come to us from that desolated land.

One fact alone tells the story, the decline of the population under Leopold's rule. The statment has been made that, as against 20,000,000 blacks at the beginning of Leopold's reign, only 10,000,000 remained when his profiteering ended. These figures, of course, cannot be verified, and are probably about as inaccurate as most round numbers. But a steep decline in population is unquestionable. Thus the British missionary Scrivener tells of a district where there had been 3,000 people, and where, after seven years, only 300 remained. And almost no inhabitants were seen in areas which Stanley, on his first voyage of discovery, reported to be well populated. Sleeping-sickness could not have been the main culprit, as has been claimed; this was proved by the fact that Lord Cromer, on his voyage up the Nile to Lado, saw village after village on the British side, but scarcely any on the bank of the Congo Free State. True, most of the vanished natives had not actually been murdered; the greater number had fled from Leopold's slave-catchers, only to starve to death in the jungle or to die beneath the clutches of wild beasts or of tropical disease.

Not that Leopold, in far-away Belgium, was cognizant of all this; he probably did not know and did not want to know of the vast streams of human suffering his mandates had let loose. All that he did observe, all that he cared to observe, was that his undertaking was bringing in returns.

The profits were most gratifying. In fifteen years, the Congo gave Leopold no less than four hundred millions in gold. During those same years the Anglo-Belgian Rubber Company improved greatly upon its original capital of 232,000 francs, and distributed millions a year; in one banner year, its dividends amounted to five millions. Meanwhile the groans of Negroes dying amid the fastnesses of remote jungles made an unheard undertone.

But acquisitiveness in the long run was defeating its own ends. Like the strip-and-leave lumber interests that devastated so much of the American continent, the Belgian rubber-seekers thought only of the momentary gain, while robbing the future. In time, the supply of wild rubber vines was exhausted; and as soon as the agents no longer collected bonuses and the whips ceased to crackle about native ears, the production of rubber came down sharply. This, however, was only after long years in which King Leopold built his palaces and villas and entertained his lady loves on the proceeds of the "red rubber" of the Congo.

V

Another important phase of European activities during the nineteenth century may be seen in China. Here, despite various "spheres of interest," leases, and occupations, as in Hongkong, Port Arthur, and Kiaochow, there was no colonization along African lines. But there was deep economic penetration and an acquisitive thrust that had momentous effects. Particularly in the early years, much of the profit-seeking centered about the exploitation of human beings, though the great destroyer and killer was not forced labor but the opium trade.

To trace the origins of this illicit traffic, we must go back to India at the heyday of the East India Company. There, after the English had superceded the Dutch, opium was a source of gain both for the Company and for its agents. In the beginning, employees of the Company had used the sale of opium to augment inadequate wages; but later the Company itself concentrated on selling the drug to users in India. However, its officers in time made a disconcerting discovery the spread of the drug in India lowered the efficiency of Indian labor. One obvious way of avoiding this difficulty was to sell the commodity abroad—no matter, of course, how it lowered the efficiency of foreign labor! Attention, therefore, turned to the vast and promising market of China, regardless of the minor inconvenience that opium-smoking was against Chinese law—in fact, the trade was later forbidden by a whole series of decrees. Making some preliminary experiments, the Company in 1782 dispatched the *Nonsuch* and other armed vessels in disguise to conduct the illegal traffic; but of the 3,450 cases shipped in that year, much was captured or wasted, and the Company suffered a net loss of 20,000 pounds.

In the following year Warren Hastings issued the double-barrelled statement that opium was "a pernicious article of luxury which ought not to be permitted but for the purpose of foreign commerce only." Some years later, the Directors of the Company made a more humane exception when they announced that "in compassion to mankind" they would gladly stop the shipment of the drug altogether except for medical purposes if it were possible to prevent its use. And Lord Ashley in 1843 declared that the continuance of the opium trade "was utterly inconsistent with the honour and duty of a Christian kingdom."

But despite all expressions of sentiment, the trade continued. Special opium clippers had been built to smuggle the drug into the ports; and "warehouse vessels" were established as floating opium depots, despite the fact that the Chinese Government continued to make anti-opium enactments, which were frustrated by the corruption of port officials. There is something tragic in the tone of the official proclamations, as in the case of one issued in 1799, which let it be known that the use of opium "originally prevailed only among vagrants and disreputable persons, but has since extended itself to others, and even to students and officials. . . . Foreigners obviously derive the most solid profits and advantages, but that our countrymen should blindly pursue this destructive and ensnaring vice is indeed odious and deplorable in the highest degree." [11]

One can agree that it was "odious and deplorable," but the pleas of the Emperor were mere cries in the night. He might decree, and he might declaim, but so long as there was profit in filling the pipes of opium addicts, so long those pipes would be filled—not only that, but new smokers would be sought. The English were not the solitary offenders: in 1818, American sales of opium in China amounted to $303,296, as against $1,648,500 for the British; but fifteen years later, while the American trade had diminished, the British supplied from India a quantity valued at $12,185,100. And this profiteering in human life was not strictly a private affair: despite open prohibitions by the East India Company, the commerce was conducted with the cognizance and even the approval of the Government, which controlled the Company and subjected its activities to continual inspection by committees of Parliament.

The prevailing attitude is set forth unashamedly in the report of a committee, which in 1832 investigated the Indian situation: "The monopoly of opium in Bengal supplies the Government with a revenue amounting in sterling money to 981,293 pounds per annum; and the duty which is thus imposed amounted to 301¾ per cent of the cost of the article. In the present state of the revenues of India, it does not appear advisable to abandon so important a source of revenue, a duty upon opium being a tax which falls principally upon the foreign consumer, and which appears upon the whole less liable to objection than any other which could be substituted." [12]

One reads, and marvels. So the wastage of lives in a forbidden and noxious traffic was "less liable to objection" that the abandonment of "an important source of revenue" or the saddling of the home consumer with taxes.

It is not surprising that the English position led to the Opium Wars, the first of which broke out in 1839. While complicating elements are to be seen in the exacerbated feelings of both factions and the arrogance of race toward race, unquestionably the wars are properly named, and would not have been fought except for opium. Unquestionably, also, the first outbreak would not have occurred had it not been for English opposition to Chinese efforts to end the inhuman trade. A special commissioner, Lin-Tse-hsui, appointed by the Chinese Government, made vigorous attempts at suppression; one of his measures was to destroy 20,291 chests of opium; another step was a proclamation placing a "perpetual embargo" on imports of English goods. Driven from Canton, the English merchants went successively to Macao and Hongkong; and after some rioting, an attack on an English passenger vessel, and an onslaught on a Chinese junk, the Opium War began.

That this war was outrageous and unnecessary was recognized by many observers in England, and not least by Gladstone, who, in the House of Commons, denounced the "infamous and atrocious traffic" in narcotics, and proclaimed, "A war more unjust in its origin, a war more calculated to cover this country with permanent disgrace, I do not know, and I have not read of."

Nevertheless, the war was fought out to its successful conclusion on August 29, 1842—succesful, that is, from the point of view of the British traders, since antiquated fighting methods could not resist European weapons. By the treaty of Nanking, China was forced to pay $6,000,000 for the law-breaking opium she had confiscated; she was also compelled to cede Hongkong, to open three other ports to the English, and to grant various other favors. There was, however, no reference to opium in the treaty, except indirectly, in an expression of pious hope that smuggling would cease—a hope whose transparent hypocrisy needs no comment. The fact was that the importation of opium from India had in effect been authorized. Fifteen years later an English court was to declare that, since opium was not mentioned in the treaty, the compact did not affect the legality of its manufacture and sale by the East India Company.

The feelings of the Chinese Emperor meanwhile may be gleaned from his statement that "I cannot prevent the introduction of the flowing poison, gain-seeking and corrupt men will for profit and sensuality defeat my wishes, but nothing will induce me to derive a revenue from the vice and misery of my own people."

In the course of twenty years, the shipments of opium nearly quadrupled, rising from 20,619 chests in 1840 to 75,822 in 1859. During this same period, opium remained an important factor in the revenues of India—at times it approached a fifth of the total Government income of that vast territory. Without opium, in fact, the Government would have incurred a large deficit. Thus the trade virtually set a trap for the administration and tended to become self perpetuating.

It is true that an increasing sentiment developed against the trade; true that, in 1874, a society for suppression of the traffic was established in England; true, likewise, that the Chinese Government continued its efforts to end the use of the drug, as in 1906, when it formulated a plan to abolish the evil within ten years. It is also true that there have been various international movements toward control, including the Opium Convention held at the Hague in 1912, the previous Opium Congress which met at Shanghai in 1909 and led to the end of the India-China traffic, and attempts at regulation by the League of Nations, and subsequently by the United Nations. Furthermore, it is true that the United States opposed and finally prohibited the introduction of the drug into the Philippines, and that the opium dens of Hongkong were eventually closed by order of the British Government. Nevertheless, opium remains a national and international problem—one that could not have approached its present gravity had the avarice of traders not been permitted to get out of control, and, abetted by great companies and by governments themselves, placed solid returns above the wellbeing and even the lives of men. It may be urged that the very use of opium and its products indicates a sickness in society, and a pathological desire of its victims to escape from life; but this does not make it less a fact that the sickness was fostered and the pathological desire was fed by exploitation of the drug, when the crying need was not a catering to the disease but a way of curing it.

XI

FALLING STARS OF EUROPE

While the beak of acquisitiveness protrudes amid prodigies of pioneering and feats of colonizing that covered several centuries and reached to the far places of the earth, it also sticks out in Europe itself in many aspects, some of which involve the overthrow of thrones and dynasties, and the dismemberment and fall of empires.

We have followed the great god Mammon in the Spanish colonial world and in the expulsion of the Jews under Ferdinand and Isabella. But Mammon, going beyond the work of the persecutors and fanatics, established himself as a leading actor in the drama of the depopulation and delcine of Spain.

Strange as it may seem, a principal element in her decline was the colonial development on which she prided herself. And this was because Spanish psychology placed such value on a yellow metal that it overlooked the country's real wealth: the wealth of her own flesh and blood, the riches of the courage and energy, the strength and activity of her most vigorous offspring. Not gold-mining in the Indies, nor silver-digging among American fastnesses, was the basic need of the Spanish people: what they required was enterprise at home in those humbler pursuits by which men are fed and clothed. Here was the reality; but the reality, as so often, was overlooked. In Spain as in all lands dominated by the acquisitive god, the illusion prevailed; the phantom of the precious metals was pursued, the breath and substance of life were ignored; thousands of men, badly needed at home, went to prosper or perish abroad; in a single convoy in 1681, as many as 6,000 departed; in some years, no less than 50,000 left for foreign shores. And since these were mostly young men of the sort upon which a nation's vitality depends, the country was sapped of irreplaceable riches.

For this reason among others, the mark of degeneration early stamped itself upon the nation. Production waned; industries were neglected; large areas of farmland came to be but half cultivated, or not cultivated at all. Owing to the loss of men from religious oppression, man-power declined constantly; the whole kingdom, at the close of the seventeenth century, had but five million inhabitants, and the population of Madrid had dropped from 400,000 to 150,000.

And while the Spanish heart-blood was being drained away, conditions within the country were aggravated and the decline accentuated by the rapacity of class against class and of government against individuals: by the extortionate duties that throttled trade, and the privileges legally accorded particular groups at the expense of the masses. Meantime the government, acting as a predatory force, accelerated the downfall of the nation it professed to serve. This is indicated by the *alcabala* or indirect tax on sales or purchases, which stimulated smuggling and tended to impoverish merchants and artisans; the imposts on both imports and exports, which stifled the commerce of Cadiz; and the severe taxes that "crushed without pity those who had, at their own risk and peril, grown rich in overseas trade":

"The government policy was really confiscation; they cloaked it by handing over government stock in exchange, though they usually forgot not only to pay back the capital but even to make up arrears of interest. The officials, who had to be bribed, exerted still further pressure on these voluntary taxpayers; if they were Portuguese Jews they got no mercy. Thus the upper middle-class of Spain died almost as soon as it was born, and that at a time when the country stood in dire need of its ability and its wealth." [1]

At the same time as the government thus plundered its subjects, three classes of citizens enjoyed special privileges and immunities, and so tended further to deplete the national strength. These classes were the nobles, the higher clergy, and the sheep raisers.

The first of these groups was distinguished by quantity if not by quality. It is estimated that, before the end of the seventeenth century, the nobility included 625,000 individuals! When we remember that all the members of this horde felt too dignified to work, and that elder sons lived on the revenues of their estates while the impoverished younger sons led a loftily parasitic life, we may begin to realize what a drain these drones constituted on the resources of the kingdom. But this comes far from telling the story. We must also consider the fact that the luxurious habits of this group were destructive of native enterprise: for example, they prohibited the export of fine cloth, so threatening the life of the industry; and under Charles V they even forbade its manufacture, so as to compel import of the Flemish product. Their delicate tastes, it seems, led them to prefer the textiles of the Netherlands, the lace of Paris, the brocades of Florence. Hence the domestic industries continued to shrink.

A somewhat similar but perhaps even more damaging influence was the Church, which owned twice as much land as the secular nobility and was constantly increasing its possessions. In Castile, at the end of the seventeenth century, one sixth of the land belonged to the Church. And since the Church, like the nobility, did little or nothing to improve the productivity of the soil, the result is visible in a further agricultural decline. At the same time, the ecclesiastical hoarding of riches and in particular of deathbed donations—often seized in violation of the rights of creditors—constituted a continual tax upon the nation's vital reserves, and tended to complete the stagnation of industry. And to this accumulation of gold and land we must add another serious source of depletion, the accumulation of men as priests and monks: it is estimated that, by the late seventeenth century, at least a thirtieth of the population, having entered the clergy, was being supported by the non-clerical elements.

As if the self-seeking of the clergy and the self-aggrandizement of the Church did not add sufficiently to the national downfall, the process was accelerated by the league of sheep-herders known as the *Mesta*. Exempt from taxation, and favored continually at the expense of the grower of crops, the herders were permitted to cross the country on a special strip of land known as the *canada*, where the sheep might browse in passing between summer and winter pasturage, and where all enclosures and all cultivation were prohibited. Since its demands grew with its wealth and power, the *Mesta* continued to seek and receive favors at the expense of the dwindling peasant community. And so bit by bit the prohibited regions grew, until "In the end the *Mesta* became almost an autonomous government, a state within the State, with a council and courts of first instance and of appeal, and the interests of agriculture were mercilessly sacrificed to it." [2]

Meanwhile, in the years between 1550 and 1630, a long succession of edicts compelled the return of cleared land to its original condition. In 1580, it was prescribed that all land used for pasture during the previous twenty years must go back to pasture; no land could be sold except for sheep-raising, and sheep-farmers were permitted to use pastures for sums so small as to represent virtual confiscation of the rights of the owners.

Little wonder, therefore, if food production was seriously curtailed—the more so as the food that was raised, such as meat and oil, was taxed almost without limit. Little wonder, also, that the depopulation continued; that many men were driven to emigrate, and that much of the land, whose few trees had been stripped off by the *Mesta* if not by the peasants, began to take on the looks of a desert.

Though many forces were here at work, including an unenlightened national economic policy and the destructiveness of the peasant in furthering deforestation, the central factor in the decline is to be seen in the rapacity of a class—a favored class that put its own acquisitions ahead of the State, and so weakened the fabric of the nation's life.

II

Since Spain in the sixteenth century came into control of much of Italy, we must not be surprised to find many of the same destructive forces in the conquered regions. Take the kingdom of Naples, where, in 1467, the introduction of a system like that of the Castilian *Mesta* brought ruin to the peasantry. Or consider Milan. In view of its prosperity during the Middle Ages, and its vast accumulations of money, this city might have remained one of the financial pivots of Europe, except for the parasitism of the Spanish conquerors, whose exactions were never-ending. Funds to support the royal policy in England; funds to maintain the luxury of the Milanese court; funds for magistrates, ministers, and other satellites of the privileged, were demanded so prolifically as to sap industry and agriculture alike. Private banks were ransacked; taxes were multiplied; the dye-works were driven out of existence by an impost on indigo; the cloth-works diminished in number from 70 to 15 in the short period between 1616 and 1624. At the same time the farmers, seeing no prospect of a profit—in fact, not being sure that returns would equal taxes—were chilled into inertia, the land began to revert to weeds, and famine lifted her grisly head although the region boasted some of Europe's richest soil.

But perhaps an even more noteworthy case is that of Venice, which for centuries had shone among the maritime cities of Europe, not only for the luxuries of its palaces but for the opulence of its Eastern trade. Undoubtedly many factors combined in the decline of this queen of the Adriatic: among others, the downfall of the Byzantine Empire, which, as we have seen, she herself in her greed helped to precipitate; the great explorations and discoveries that had shifted the center of commerce to the Atlantic; the gradual silting up of the canals; and the raids of the corsairs of Barbary and Spain. But another important element, and one that in the long run may have outweighed all others, was the avarice of the rulers, and their accompanying short-sightedness. Unable to adapt their minds to changed conditions, or to hold their desires within the limits of reality, the merchant leaders not only continued to levy high duties on all goods passing through the port, but added new taxes. Consequently, shipping was driven to neighboring cities; and a contraband trade arose, and even was conducted by some of the foremost sons of Venice, with the result that the State was robbed of her revenue. And while the government was growing more corrupt and industry was being crushed by the increasing taxes, the wealthy aristocrats did not put their money into manufactures that might have improved the general prosperity, but invested in their personal villas and estates.

Hence, with private aims opposing the public interest, Venice came to be a state "divided against itself"—and inevitably she met the fate of all states so divided.

III

Traveling north from Italy, we find acquisitiveness prominent in Poland; we see the greed of the classes behind the weakness of the masses, and behind that enfeeblement of the nation which led toward partition. On the one hand the nobles, by their strangling monopolies, reduced the miserable and ill-fed peasants to a halfway state of slavery, in which they could be pursued if they ran away; as a consequence, agricultural progress was paralyzed. And on the other hand, the aristocrats throttled the cities: by the Statute of Piatrkov, which tied the knot about the peasant's throat, they also choked out the life of the townspeople, who thenceforth could not infringe upon the right of the lords to buy land, to make grain alcohol, to navigate the Vistula, to receive benefices from the Church, etc. Consequently the country, hollowed out internally and economically debilitated for the benefit of a parastic group, in time become in easy prey for foreign designs. As if to insure this result, the predatory process was furthered by the power of political veto, whereby one deputy could dissolve the diet: foreign ambassadors might thus maneuver the country to their will, since some deputy could always be bribed to paralyze legislation by ending the parliamentary sessions.

An even more striking case is that of the Netherlands. We of today find it hard to realize that at one time the Netherlands led Europe— their place was very similar to that later occupied by England. Then why did they lose their grip?

The story is not far different than we may see in other lands. For one thing, we find the old spectacle of inequality, a preying of class upon class, lavish luxury and wild speculation while the proletariat languish and suffer. The lot of the city workers, in the latter half of the sixteenth century, became extremely difficult, with rising prices that were not balanced by rising wages. Hence there were many uprisings, some of them of a bloody nature, and all of them tending to weaken the economic foundations of the country. In the early seventeenth century a gambling craze, the furor for shares in the East India Company, further reduced productive enterprise at home. And an additional weakness is shown by something that appears fantastic, inane: the wild possessive rage over tulip bulbs, which suddenly became worth far more than their weight in gold, so that one person offered twelve acres of building ground for the Harlem tulip and another bought the Amsterdam tulip for 4,600 florins, a carriage, two horses, and a set of harness.

Even though this was but a passing phase, it did have a disturbing effect, and raised the prices of all common articles. But a deeper, more enduring source of evil may be traced to the corruption that undermined the very cornerstone of the State, the dishonesty and self-seeking of politicians at the expense of the community, the squandering of the national strength in pursuit of party government for the sake of private profit, "government by a few interested and irresponsible wirepullers and agitators": [3]

"The Dutch merchant politicians sacrificed the national strength to cash profits. Their policy . . . was mammonism of the most selfish kind. The economists in their pay placed property above men, ignoring the fact that . . . the most precious possession of the State is not the dead wealth possessed by a few, but the productive labor of the people. Looking only after their commerce and their capital, largely invested abroad, the Dutch oligarchs callously allowed the Dutch industries, and even those industries which were the foundation of the national strength, to decay, and the Dutch working population to emigrate to foreign countries. . . .

"Ruling for their own benefit, and treating the Netherlands as their farm, the Dutch party politicians exploited the nation, destroyed the power and wealth of the Netherlands, and reduced the foremost power in Europe, and the glorious Dutch world-empire, after untold sufferings, to its present insignificance." [4]

IV

While several empires were crumbling to bits, the seeds of a different sort of transformation were slowly germinating in the great kingdom of France.

It would be absurd to imply that acquisitiveness, powerful as it was, was solely responsible for the vast upheaval of the French Revolution. We have to recognize other factors of high importance, including the misrule of the Bourbons, and the preachments of the philosophers, which gradually prepared the minds of the people to revolt. But without minimizing these influences, one may point out that Mammon, hugging his money-bags, is once more in the background; Mammon laid the foundation by creating the conditions without which revolution would have been unnecessary if not inconceivable. It was Mammon who perverted the authority of the Crown in the direction of callousness and extravagance; it was Mammon whose abuses provided a fertile soil for the ideas of Rousseau, Diderot, Voltaire, and the other Enclycopedists.

Yet nothing in the history of Mammon fully explains why the Revolution broke out when it did, and why it took the particular direction it did. Actually, in many sections of France—and particularly among the peasantry—the lot of the average man was by no means so bad as in previous ages. The dues paid by the peasants had diminished, and in some districts the people went for decades without paying anything at all; in many regions the peasants owned much of the land. Why, therefore, did the Revolution break out?

The Revolution broke out, to put the matter as simply as possible, because the overall situation was not sufficiently improved; because the ancient forces of avarice were still powerful; and because the fertilizing and explosive new ideas of freedom and equal rights, falling on a soil made ready by privilege and by luxury, produced a psychological drive that infuriated men against their oppressors. The Revolution, after all, was but the culmination of a long series of *jacqueries* and revolts reaching back to the Middle Ages. But the will to rebel had been growing in modern times, as in the uprising of 400 workers at Orleans in 1709 in protest against a stamp duty upon stockings, and in the more celebrated episode at Lyons in 1744, when the master-craftsmen and journeymen gained control of the city, forced the officials to yield, and were not subdued for several months. All these scattered revolts, despite their eventual failure, were like barometric readings of the approaching storm. That storm, however, would not have been possible had the ground not been prepared by actual evils, many of which had sprung of a crass and selfish possessiveness.

Consider, for example, the contrast between the condition of the masses and the state of royalty and the higher nobility. To the traveler in modern France, who has visited the palaces of Versailles, the

French Revolution does not appear wholly mysterious. One remembers the elaborate gardens, with their statue-dotted green spaces, their fountains and orange trees, and the mansion which a king built especially for his mistress. One recalls the halls which, even in their latter-day barrenness, bring to mind the garish court life of long ago—the gold-leafed walls, the frescoed ceilings, the variegated marbles, the furnishings tending to excess of ornateness. And one tries to imagine at what expenditure of wealth and energy, what cost in the labor of unremembered myraids, these magnificient pleasure-palaces were erected. In contrast, one thinks of the homes of the humble, the cramped dwellings of the city laborers, the dinginess of twisting lightless streets. One thinks also of hovels in outlying regions such as the French Alps: low-roofed, built of clay, a manure heap in place of front garden, windowless to avoid taxation, in winter the abode of man and beast alike. If such dwellings could continue into this century, one may be sure that there were many such in the eighteenth century. And though the more fortunate peasants were housed in less primitive and even fairly commodious quarters, the contrast was still sharp enough to sow the seeds of resentment and revolt.

Among the social classes of pre-Revolution days, considered in the broadest sense, there were two main groups only: the privileged and the underprivileged. In the first category, we may include royalty, nobility, and the higher clergy; in the second category, we may rank the masses. Between these groups the gulf was hardly less enormous than the abysses of an Oriental caste system; this fact glares at us in a state that, rich in resources, is on the verge of bankruptcy; a state that squanders millions on its titled subjects while the public debt grows more onerous.

The privileged group is estimated by Taine to have numbered about 270,000, of whom 130,000 were clergy, and 140,000 nobility (this enumeration evidently leaves out of account the numerous impoverished or relatively impoverished sons of the aristocracy). Half the public lands, and the richest half, including palaces, castles, convents, and cathedrals, were in the hands of a group of little more than a quarter of a million, who drew an enormous income from this property. The Duc d'Orleans received rentals of 11,500,000 livres; the princes of the blood had incomes totally more than double this amount; the bishop of Strasbourg claimed an annual revenue of a million, while other clerics were close runners-up. "A courtier with no more than 100,000 livres was a poor man."[5] Garments, woven with gold and silver, were displayed by some of the grandees, who gambled profusely, bought elaborate carriages, indulged in lavish entertainments and hunting expeditions, and yet for all their wealth, were deeply sunken in debt. At the same time, there was a monopolistic and bought judiciary, whose offices were passed on from father to son like titles of nobility; the posts were purchased for a high price, and even so, seem to have been paying investments; their possessors in Paris sometimes rivalled great lords in wealth, and in Bordeaux they owned the choicest vineyards.

If any measure of justice had governed, the men of enormous means might have defrayed the greater part of the nation's expenses, relieving the burden of the public debt and taking the crushing weight from the shoulders of the working man. This, however, is just the opposite of what did happen: the classes who received all from the State seemed to regard it as their right to receive all, and to make no return; as a reward for having much, they were privileged to pay little. With a respectful tread, the tax collector passed the rich man's door, making increasing exemptions; he was so thoughtful of the Bourbon princes that he accepted 188,000 livres, instead of the 2,400,000 due on an ordinary basis; and he could make himself so agreeable to the great nobles that the Duc d'Orleans could say, "I settle matters, and pay about what I please."

We need therefore not be surprised that many taxes were levied upon the poor man exclusively, or else were levied so disproportionately that he bore almost the entire weight. Such was the *taille* or land tax, which had indeed undergone some lightening, though the peasant who could not afford it was in danger of losing the ox without which he could not till his land. Such was the salt tax, demanded of the commoner even if he had no need for salt. Such, in its own way, was the corveé, a tax upon the poor man's labor—a regular institution after 1738, which might entail from eight to forty days of forced service. And such, in considerable measure, was the poll tax; this the lords were expected to pay, but they secured large reductions. It was in line with such favoritism that in one province, which expended more than a million and a half livres for public services, the nobles paid not one *sou;* while in other provinces the underprivileged contributed five times the income taxes paid by the titled group.

Correspondingly the Church, being prodigiously wealthy, enjoyed vast immunities. In 1710 it purchased exemption from the *taille* and was likewise discharged from other taxation. And though it made occasional gifts to the State, it sometimes received huge grants from the depleted public treasury, as in 1787, when its receipts from the

Crown amounted to a million and a half more than its public expenditures. Moreover, it was closely in league with the nobility, for whom it provided a lucrative side-line, since titled persons were almost the exclusive recipients of its benefices. Following an example dating back to the Middle Ages, the sons of nobles were sometimes ordained at the age of twelve; while the upper circles of the Church constituted such a closed corporation that not one of the 143 French bishops in 1789 did not claim noble blood. Many of these, naturally enough, continued to lead the life of lords; there were bishops of noble birth who magnificently lived at court, and hardly knew anything about the dioceses whose income they drained.

We must not forget, besides, that the higher ecclesiastics, though comparatively few in number, monopolized five sixths of the religious incomes. Nor must we forget that the country curates lived a hard and penurious existence, so much so that Voltaire refers to them as having to contend for a sheaf of wheat with their miserable parishioners. And finally, we must not overlook the fact that the Revolution found the lower clergy casting their not inconsiderable influence on the side of the other exploited groups—an appreciable factor in the success of the uprising.

Next we should consider the army, whose failure to respond at the hour of peril was largely responsible for the triumph of the insurgents. Here also we find a monopoly of privilege. To the minority, the officers, go all things desirable: the authority of command, the honor of position, good living conditions, social prestige, a sufficiency of money, leisure, and amusement. And, to the majority, a life somewhat below that of the average dog: enlistment through force or betrayal, kicks and blows for several years, labor and weariness, bad living quarters, bad food, and wages at six *sous* a day, with no prospect of promotion.

Whereas a total of 46,000,000 fill the pockets of the officers, a mere 44,000,000 livres are distributed among the far more numerous privates. But the officers, being of noble rank, are protected from base competition by a law made some years before the Revolution, which provides that no one who cannot trace his titled blood back through four generations may rise so high as a captaincy. In 1702, moreover, 7,000 commissions were created for the nobility, whose aristocratic blood elevated the favored ones above all commoners, no matter how capable. Added to this, we must note the direct influence of Mammon on the commissions: officerships might be bought by the nobles for their most stupid and untalented sons, even though but fourteen or sixteen years of age. (On the other hand, a man of sufficient means, even without patrician blood, might at times be permitted to purchase a commission).

In view of such facts, need it surprise us that the army seethed with disaffection? That it was thoroughly unreliable? That, at the moment of crisis, it forsook the monarchy? And that thousands of deserters swarmed through the streets of Paris and led in the revolts?

We might go on indefinitely, glancing at the abuses and blindness of the privileged—observing, for example, the hunting rights of the nobility, which established game preserves for 45 miles around Paris, wherein no cultivator was free to build enclosures. Take the *métayers* (farmers who received payment in kind rather than money). Owing to various factors including the increase in taxation, the requisitions of the army, the forced labor, the movements of troops, and the grasping of nobles, rent-collectors, and other privileged persons, the condition even of well-to-do farmers declined in the latter half of the region of Louis XIV. Not the least afflicted were the *métayers*, who were reduced to eating nothing but buckwheat, and who, "doubled up like animals," would labor at their rough, wheelless ploughs, sometimes with the aid of donkeys, sometimes with their half naked women yoked beside them. Meanwhile the land, in the name of absentee owners, was often let out to sub-contractors, who sometimes instituted what has been described as a reign of terror, and exhausted the land as well as the peasant. Meanwhile other landlords, trying to increase revenues to meet wartime costs, put the collection in the hands of business agents, who guaranteed an exact payment of the sums due—with results that could hardly bear lightly on the impecunious farmer.

It may be hard for us to realize the fact, but serfdom, while widely abolished throughout Western Europe, remained in parts of France until the late eighteenth century; remained in Bourbonnais, Auvergne, Nivernais, Champagne, Burgundy, and the crown provinces such as Franche-Comté, as well as on the estates of the Church. The serfs, despite some improvements in their lot, were still in so abject a state at the time of Louis XVI that they could not make a will without the lord's permission, nor marry out of their estate or rank; upon their death, unless they had direct heirs who had lived with them continuously, their property was taken by the seignieur. Such repressions could not fail to have reactions. Nor could it be purely coincidental that, in the various uprisings, the feudal restraints were the chief objects of the hatred of the peasants, and that the first chateaux were burned in the surviving strongholds of serfdom.

In serfdom or not, the ordinary agricultural worker lived in misery, his staple food a heavy black bread. And there were many times when no bread was to be had; often the *disette* or famine raged through the land, as in the winter of 1663-1664, when one missionary, in the town of Châtearoux, counted nearly 200 children orphaned by hunger. Doubtless such an affliction can be blamed, in part at least, on the wiles of the weather; but the continuance of the famines, though they were fewer and less terrible in the eighteenth century, can be largely ascribed to the exactions on the peasant, the dues and taxes, the forced labor, and the encroachments excluding him from the common land.

These encroachments deserve a special word. The forests, the heaths, the marshes, in which the poor man had been wont to supplement his scanty existence, were being taken from him by the well-to-do —often, indeed, in the name of intensive cultivation. As far back as the time of Henry IV, who ascended the throne in 1589, enclosures of the common land had been known, as in England; even at that early period, we hear the complaints of fishermen being deprived of access to the banks of the stream that gave them their livelihood.

But in the decades just before the Revolution, the outcries became much louder. One can understand the peasant's feelings when the acres which were rightly his, but which he had not the means to work or whose title-deeds he could not show, were seized by powerful companies. Though in many places it had been agreed that the land was to be divided equally among all, usually the lion took the lion's share; in districts such as Champagne, Lorraine, Bourbonnais, Franche-Compté, and others, the effect was to transfer the waste-lands from the possession of all to the ownership of one great lord.

While the country laborers thus found cause to grumble, the lot of their confreres in the city was sometimes hardly better. They were obsessed by taxes, like the one imposed in 1744, for the sake of the wealthy producers, which required 800 livres for the right to manufacture cloth-of-gold, and so lifted a stone barricade against the hope of the master-craftsmen to rise. Then there were the penalties against leagues and small associations of workers, as in a law forbidding more than four laborers to meet, even to form a social orgnization. There was the edict requiring the workman to carry a card showing all changes of employment; there was the decree of 1749, which pinned the workman down like a serf, compelling him to remain at his job when a definite term had been stipulated; and there

were the rises in prices, which, during the last quarter century of the
monarchy, were not equalled by increases in wages. True, the
city workers were small in number compared with their brothers in the
country, but the city men could be organized more easily and effective-
ly, hence would constitute an important element in the Revolution.

It was, indeed, the urban rabbles, which, rising beneath the goad of
long-continued abuses, led the way to the great outbreak. And when
the city had shown the direction, the rural populace followed in rapid
revolt. It was not something marvelous and abnormal; it was quite
in the natural order of things that, even before the fall of the Bastille,
there should be upheavals in the provinces, as when the unemployed
of Lyons set fire to toll-gates and tollhouses. And it is less surprising
than it seemed that an unprecedented storm should sweep the countryside, and that its fury should overturn royalty in its gilded couch,
hurl nobles down from their chairs of purple and gold, and sound the
death-knell of the old regime.

It is true that, amid the subsequent orgies of riot and warfare, the
macabre tragedy of the Terror, the marching of armies, the rise of
Napoleonism, the conflagration that spread to all Europe, we tend to
lose sight of the original causes of the Revolution. The religion of
nationalism sparked by the Girondists, the rallying call of "Liberty,
Equality, Fraternity," the songs and the patriotic hymns and the
preachments, the adoption of universal military service, the marshal-
ling of young Frenchmen for a holy crusade, all tended to obscure the
sources of the Revolution amid a psychological haze. In none of this
do we see any evidence that the acquisitiveness of the masters had
been a leading cause of the gory outbreak—a cause without which an
orderly evolution might have led to a better, freer would.

Had the demons of greed not produced the psychological excita-
tions that spread the Revolution like fire on an oiled floor, how
different the future might have been! Though the uprising brought
many gains, it is doubtful if there were any that could not have been
achieved by more peaceful and less destructive methods. It is doubtful whether, without the Revolution, we would have had the gigantic
series of wars that culminated with Waterloo; the national antagonisms which, marking all the nineteenth century and the twentieth,
have brought military conscription as part of the accepted order,
have encouraged and enlarged arms races, and have led straight to
the cataclysmic outbreaks of the twentieth century. Likewise, it is
doubtful whether, without the example of the French Revolution, we
would have witnessed disturbances such as those in Russia and in

China, which have metamorphosed our era and darkened all the horizons of the earth.

V

In some ways the background of the Russian Revolution is similar to that of the French upheaval, though the tyranny of the Roumanoffs was much severer than that of the Bourbons had ever been. Again we see diverse strands converging through the centuries, but again the Revolution was given its form and character by an infusion of comparatively recent ideas—the doctrines of Karl Marx, with his radical views of the class struggle and the dictatorship of the proletariat. But those views could have had little effect on modern Russia except for the old heritage of resentment, of hatred, of terror, which had descended in a long and unbroken line from a dark and despotic past. This resentment and hatred, in turn, was largely sprung of actual abuses—the acquisitiveness by which one group reaped comfort, convenience, profit and luxury from the calloused hands, the broken bodies and souls of a much larger group.

The germs of the disease can be traced back even to the ancient barbarian society, in which there had been two contrasting elements: the freemen and the slaves, with a middle class, who did forced labor to liquidate their debts. Some of the slaves, as in many lands, were prisoners of war; some were men who had sold themselves into bondage as the alternative to starving. Here, then, we already see one of the acquisitive bases for the woes of later centuries, and an attitude of mind that regarded the man-owner and the man-exploiter as part of the natural order.

This attitude of mind was conspicuous behind the rise of serfdom, which, before its abolition by Czar Alexander II in 1861, was a prominent feature of imperial Russia. Serfdom, however, had been a relatively late outgrowth; in the latter part of the fifteenth century, it could be found only in scattered sections of Russia; but by the mid-sixteenth century it had taken wide hold, and during the nominal reign of Theodore, son of Ivan the Terrible, a legal edict attached the serfs to the land— that is, when their owners did not see fit to sell them into servitude elsewhere.

It is a curious fact that the decree had been encouraged by the eagerness of the peasants themselves to escape their miseries and the burden of taxation. But once established, serfdom grew like a cancer. Under Peter the Great, though he had attacked serfdom as an institution, thousands of forced laborers were worked to death in constructing the Ladoga Canal and building the cities of Petersburg and Kronstadt. Under the Empress Anne (1730-1740) the market in human beings in effect gained the stamp of imperial recognition, since its proceeds were taxed by the Government. Under Catherine II the trade expanded, despite the relatively progressive ideas of the Empress; in 1765, three years after her accession, the landowners obtained the right to send rebellious serfs to Siberia without either a trial or a right of appeal.

Here was outright slavery. Beneath the Russian system, the most valued property rights were those in human bodies; a proprietor's wealth was reckoned by the number of "souls" bound beneath his jurisdiction, and those "souls" were counted somewhat as a chicken rancher counts his hens. The importance assumed by serfdom may be gauged from the fact that in 1825, when the total Russian population was 49,000,000, 36,000,000 were peasant serfs. And the value placed upon serfs may be seen in the statement that, while a pedigreed dog might bring 2,000 rubles, a peasant man was priced at about 400 rubles and a peasant woman at no more than 100 to 150; at the turn of the century, the bargain hunter might have obtained a serf girl in the country districts for a little as 5 rubles. That serfs were regarded as chattels is evident, also, in current newspaper advertisements—for example:

"Barber for sale, as well as four beds, quilts, and other articles. . . . For sale: girl of sixteen, exemplary conduct; and also slightly used carriage. . . . For sale: cook, coachman, and parrot. . . . For sale: young boy trained to groom horses. Also a milk cow. . . . For sale at Panyaleimon's opposite the meat market: a girl of thirty and a young horse." [6]

These human objects of sale, bought and paid for like "young horses" and "slightly used carriages," were subject to any treatment decreed by any eccentric, deranged, or Sultanic master. Like the wealthy Romans, the Russian lords were in the habit of being attended by retinues of slaves, each assigned to some specialized task; a very rich man might have from 300 to 800, while an aristocrat of average standing might claim a mere 100 or 150 who would serve as bakers, tailors, maids, valets, coffee servers, carpenters, coachmen, etc. Here is a description of some of the uses made of this property:

"The functions of each servant were laid down in most precise language, and in a well-kept house minutely written instructions by the master himself were issued at regular intervals. Even the best educated people of their day spent much time and energy in drawing up endless documents as to who should light the candles and who blow them out, while someone else was to trim the wicks, and yet another flunkey collected the melted wax, not to mention such serious points as who should answer what bell, open what door, or attend to what requirements of the masters or their guests. . . . In the antechamber of one gentlemen, seventeen footmen had to sit night and day, of whom one was to fetch the master's pipe, another a glass of water, the third a book, and so forth. The established ritual in the house of another, who kept 300 servants, included a daily dinner of forty courses. . . ." [7]

In the Russia of such lavish idiosyncrasies, the Empress Catherine could dine from massive jewel-studded gold plates; could give her lover Orlov a gold-embroidered coat said to be worth a million rubles; could build palaces for him and later for another favorite, Potemkin; could give away estates with hundreds of thousands of "souls" attached. And members of the nobility, following her example, could employ thousands of serfs to erect pavilions or towers for the amusement of guests, could turn fields into lakes, or alter a riverbed so that they might hear the song of a nightingale. Meanwhile the workers were regarded by the noble "very much like cattle, perhaps not quite so valuable, and as something only fit to be whipped and made to work for him till they dropped dead . . . the significant thing is that even the enlightened or decent kind of representatives of the upper class, even those who lived on terms of comparative affection with their peasants and servants, still considered these as mere cattle." [8]

While serfs swarmed on the farms and in the domestic retinues of the lords, others engaged in forced labor in industry, in the mines or the forests—the property of the State, or of private owners. Even the freemen were lowered to a condition that was slavery in all but name, as will be plain from the edict of 1736, which prescribed that the toiler and his family must remain attached for life to his factory or mine. This meant that, no matter how miserable his situation, the employee had no hope of improvement.

Hence it is not surprising that revolts were frequent. During the reign of Catherine, outbreaks were recorded in no less than fifty districts; and one of these, led in 1773 by the Cossack Emilian Pugachev, was so wide-reaching that it may almost be called a revolution, a general uprising of the peasants, a revolt which, as the prominent war-leader Marshal Bibikov stated, was really a rebellion of the poor against the rich. Pugachev, it is true, was eventually captured, after

reducing the city of Kazan to ashes and aiming a threat directly at
Moscow. But the officials and landowners, drawing exactly the wrong
lesson from the insurrection, pulled the reins tighter than ever about
the serfs and further darkened their already dark lot. Had they been
gifted with the foresight so seldom given to men, they might have
looked forward to a greater outburst nearly a century and a half later.

The nineteenth century, though it did bring the end of serfdom,
did not solve the problems of the workers, and particularly of the city
workers, who were exploited by the new industrialism very much as
in other lands. In the factories employing the new machine methods,
they were regarded as mere necessary adjuncts of the machinery, who,
as one writer puts it, "might have less consideration than sturdy working animals. Their health and safety were of themselves of secondary
import. It was not even pretended that the welfare of the workers was
the uppermost or even a prime consideration. Wages could be low,
even a pittance; hours could be long, unbearably so; conditions of
work . . . could at times be described as not less than horrible or
shocking. Child labor could be employed, even the labor of children
in their tender years, unfitting them for their future years. . . . And
all this was for the financial gain of the factory owners . . ." [9]

As in the West, *laissez faire* was supreme. But also as in the West,
the factory system threw the workers together in groups, so that they
began to ask each other why they had to wear out their lives, and who
benefited, and whether there was no way of improvement. From such
questioning, with their reachings toward a more beneficent and a more
just system, it was only a short leap to socialistic principles. Few
turns of fate could have been more unfortunate than that the particular form of socialism which rose into favor was that of the aggressive-
minded Karl Marx, who, as an author of the *Communist Manifesto*
(1848), put forth his celebrated appeal to the workers of the world
to unite, since they had "nothing to lose but their chains." Marx and
his confreres, of course, would have pleaded in vain had there been no
background of deep-seated and smoldering grievances, by which the
labor and the very lives of non-possessors had been at the disposal of
the possessors. It was this that gave an effective ring to the call for
the class war. It was this that made possible the eventual Bokshevik
triumph.

It may be that, except for the weakening effects of the First World
War, the ineptness of the Czarist regime and of Kerensky's Provisional
Government, and the craft and unscrupulousness of the rebels, the
Russian Revolution would have brought a milder group than the

Communists to the foreground. Yet the essential fact is that the
Revolution was aimed not only against the political but against the
economic leadership. It was pointed both at the capitalistic state
and at the capitalistic system, and it could not conceivably have succeeded had great numbers of people not been convinced of the iniquities of capitalism. And so we find that all the Revolutionary
leaders give their pronouncements an economic stress. It does not
follow that the sources were in economic realities as much as in economic ideas; the outburst occurred not simply because men were exploited, but because they reacted to exploitation with revolutionary
views, which in turn swept all things before them and cleared the way
for the Bolshevik experiment. Nevertheless, those particular views
could not have developed as they did except for a long brutalizing experience, which fired the victims of the old system with hatred—a
hatred which, calling for the smashing of the supplanted order, was
passionate, often irrational, and pathological to the point of sadism.
Consider this from the call of the First International Communist Congress, as heard over the Petrograd wireless on January 23, 1919:

"The present is the period of *destruction* and crushing of the capitalist system of the whole world." [10]

Or take this, from an early proclamation of the Communist International:

"Conquests of the political power mean not merely a change in per-
sonnel, but *annihilation of the enemies' apparatus of Government.*
The revolutionary era compels the proletariat to make use of the
means of battle which will concentrate its entire energies, namely
*mass action, with its logical resultant, direct conflict with the govern-
ment in open combat.*" [11]

In more moderate terms, Lenin expressed his motivations: "The
essence of the Soviet authority consists in this, that the permanent
and sole basis of all State authority, of the entire apparatus of government, is the mass organization precisely of those classes which were
opposed to capitalism, that is of the workmen and of the half-pro-
letarians, peasants who did not exploit the labor of another and constantly had to sell at least a portion of their labor strength." [12]

In this, as in almost all statements of the leaders of the Revolution,
we can see the resentment against the ancient injustice, the ancient
oppression. This does not mean that the reaction inevitably led to a
new oppression, of an equal and possibly even more onerous nature.
It does not mean that the Revolution need have taken the tyrannical
forms it assumed under Lenin and Stalin. But it does mean that fury

in the face of long-continued avarice and inhumanity was so deep-rooted, and had spread to so many minds, that a cataclysmic outbreak was the natural sequel. And perhaps it was no more than an historical accident, even though a tragic one, that gave the controlling power to the particular clique of rebels who unseated the moderate Kerensky in 1917 and established a "dictatorship of the proletariat."

XII

MAMMON AND INDUSTRIAL MISRULE

In the latter part of the eighteenth century, the world was visited by an Aladdin's genie, who held a treasure unequalled in value since the discovery of fire thousands of years before.

The new boon was, in a sense, a second gift of fire, for it made use of the heat of the furnace and the boiler to increase the productivity of man's work and to extend his conquest over nature. Now, at one magical stroke, the power-driven machine made it possible for a single laborer to accomplish the task of scores, and for a single factory to produce more than could once have been turned out by thousands of workshops. Not only a new era in industry but a new age in history had been inaugurated—an age that might reasonably have been expected to provide all with an abundance and a security never known before.

Today, after two centuries of the revolutionary changes, we see the Utopian possibilities indeed fulfilled in some directions, but only in some directions, and in part. Conveniences and luxuries have truly been scattered broadcast. But what a multitude of problems have arisen! What gigantic inequalities, what antagonisms of class against class, what disease-breeding and death-breeding exploitation! Between the glamorous *might-have-been* of modern industrialism and the mean reality of its beginnings and of many of its subsequent years, what an unbridgeable abyss!

But why have the glowing original expectations not been fulfilled? Why has the lady Bountiful revealed, beneath her silken garment, the claws of the wildcat? Just wherein did we go wrong? Was it that the machine was inherently treacherous? Or does the fault lie elsewhere, within the hidden webs of man's mind and spirit?

One thing we must admit. Since civilization is a continuing process, not even the most radical innovation can develop without foundations, like an island supported on air; the Industrial Revolution had to root itself in pre-existing soil.

But what was the pre-existing soil? We have already glanced at much of it. We have seen how the image of riches, in ancient, medieval, and early modern times, was frequently before the minds of men. We have observed how the thought of gold wove a glamour;

168

and how acquisitive hands reached out, and scheming minds contrived meshes, and brigands thundered on land and sea, and kings and barons and prelates, landless adventurers and ambitious business-getters paused at few extremes of destruction, torture, or murder in their craze for the glittering seductress. With all this in the background, and with avaricious desires quickened by new ideas and incentives, it was hardly to be expected that the opportunities offered by the machine would be translated into a code of *Save-the-world* or *Relieve-the-underdog*.

Actually, conditions in the late eighteenth century had come to a prime state of ripeness for the disciple of *Help-myself-and-the-world be-damned*. On the land, this tendency had long been seen in the process of enclourse. And in trade the ancient stigma, evident when the Church condemns all interest-taking and when "gentlemen" look down upon businessmen, was in the process of disappearing. Then, again, an impetus to greed had been given by the very agency which might have been expected to suppress it, the Puritan Revolution, which had accepted money-making as a goal in itself, and had condemned the poor as if poverty were a crime. Transportation of some of the non-possessors—"rogues," "vagabonds," and such, who might be any of the unemployed—was prescribed under Cromwell, considerably to the profit of rich proprietors in Barbados and Jamacia. Here, indeed, would appear to be a by-product of the atmosphere of the age, as can be seen when a philosopher such as Bishop Berkeley can propose seizing and enslaving "sturdy beggars" for a period of years. What we observe, therefore, is first of all a reversal not in economic currents, but in trends of thought, which in turn did change the economic trends. And it is peculiarly unfortunate that the changes in thought preceded a transformation of the greatest social and economic potentials, and directed that transformation not toward the public betterment but toward private enrichment.

The ideas of various social philosophers—Adam Smith, Ricardo, Malthus, and others—all contributed mightily to the same end, and developed the idea that it was not only wrong but unnatural to interfere with the private entrepreneur as he maneuvered for his own advancement. What serves the welfare of the individual, argued Adam Smith, in a bit of seeming logic that may have done more harm than any other dictum of modern times, is certain to serve the welfare of the community—so long, that is, as we leave the individual unobstructed in the quest of his own interests. Unfortunately, Smith was not thinking of the industrial era, which was just about to dawn. If he

had been thinking of this era, he might have paused to consider two
salient facts: first, that men trained in acquisitive traditions would
put acquisitive ideas ahead, so that it would be merely coincidental
if the public good was advanced; and second, that the unusual prospects for self-aggrandizement provided by the new industrialism
would whip the acquisitive desire into a frenzy, a mania as of men who,
launched on a gold-rush, rudely sweep all obstacles and all other men
aside.

One of the ironies was that the industrial gold-rush, like panics and
stampedes of all kinds, created a drive that could not be stopped automatically and made victims of its very participants. The factory
owner, caught up in the swirl of the costly new processes, was thrown
into competition with other factory owners, and felt bound to produce
at the lowest price if he was to be sure of surviving. This meant that
he must squeeze the last ounce out of his workers; even if not by
nature inhumane, he would shut certain windows in his mind and not
permit himself to see the agony just beneath his nose. Nevertheless,
the example of Robert Owen, who ran his mills on humane lines and
yet made a profit, indicates that the average capitalist may have been
ruled quite as much by his fears, ambition, and avarice as by the
realities. In any case the blind creed of competition, "Yourself first,
last, and always!", had closed his eyes to the realities.

And if the capitalist was thus entrapped, what of the laborer?
Spokesmen of liberalism favored the new order because of the opportunities it supposedly gave to the enterprising poor man; yet in the
great majority of cases, the worker was no more free than an ant hur-
ried along by a torrent. One of multitudes, he had been driven to the
city by the enclosure of the common land for the benefit of the
wealthy. Or he had been victimized by the inability of cottage industries to complete with the great new monster, factory production, and
had had no choice but to become a servant of the new order.

The early features of the machine age have often been described.
We know how, receiving its original impetus in England, it rapidly
transformed the countryside; blackened wide regions with smoke;
created huge slums in the cities; introduced a gruelling peonage in the
coal mines; fed upon the bodies and the lives of women and children
both in the textile industries and in the mines; and produced a warped
and stunted race from the waifs sacrificed in one of the most brutal
enslavements ever known. So late as 1834, for example, the Supplementary Report of the Factory Commission estimated that the employees in the cotton mills included 60,000 men, 65,000 women, and

84,000 children, 41,000 of whom were girls, and half of whom were under fourteen. But such statistics give little idea of the actualities. We come a bit nearer to reality in the report made to a Parliamentary Committee on Children in Manufactures by John Moss, the governor of the workhouse at Preston. The regular working hours, he stated, were from 5 a.m., to 8 p.m., Saturday included. The actual hours, however, sometimes extended to 9 or 10 p.m., with two half-hour breaks for breakfast and dinner (though there were no places where the children could sit down). Sunday, on the other hand, was an easier day; the little workers had nothing to do except to clean the machines from 6 a.m. til noon. But such leniency could not always be expected; we hear of cases in which the mill owners, during rushed periods, kept their small charges busy from 3:30 a.m. til 9:30 p.m., holding them to their tasks in the stifling atmosphere by the terror of constant whipping.

But even worse than the lung-destroying, wizening textile mills— if anything could be worse—were the coal mines, where women, boys and girls were harnessed like beasts. An indication of the attitude of the times may be seen in the report of a medical witness from Shropshire, who spoke reassuringly to a parliamentary commission in 1842. There were, he announced, "very few under six or seven years employed to draw weights with a girdle under the body and these only where the roof of the pit is so low for short distances as to prevent a horse of the smallest size or asses from being employed." [1]

A report of the Commission itself, however, is a little less complacent in its references to the girls of the mine: "Chained, belted, harnessed like dogs in a go-cart, saturated with wet and more than half naked, crawling upon their hands and feet and dragging their heavy loads behind them, they present an appearance indescribably disgusting and unnatural." [2]

Or consider this statement to the Commission of an eight-year-old girl "trapper"—one of the children who, from the age of five, had to go down into the pit for periods of twelve hours and more in order to open and shut the ventilating doors:

"I'm a trapper in the Gamber Pit. I have to trap without a light and I'm scared. I go out four and sometimes half-past three in the morning and come out five and halfpast five [in the evening]. I never go to sleep. Sometimes I sing when I've light but never in the dark. I dare not sing then." [3]

A quarter of a century later, children were still being put to work in the mines. And meanwhile, despite some signs of an aroused social conscience, all efforts to ameliorate the lot of the working children were bitterly resisted. For example, in 1802, when Sir Robert Peel managed to put through Parliament a bill limiting the hours of pauper children to twelve a day and prohibiting night labor for the younger tots, protests against such unheard-of humanitarianism came from mill owners in Leeds, Glasgow, Manchester, Keighley, Preston, and elsewhere. Such a restriction would, they maintained, be "prejudicial to the Cotton Trade." There was also an outraged complaint against a provision requiring that the child receive some daily instruction in reading, writing, and arithmetic. This, objected the mill owners, "would amount to a surrender of all the profits of the establishment."

Parenthetically, we may note that the Lancashire textile mills, in which not only children but adults were forced to the lowest debasement, were precisely those in which the most rapid fortunes were made.

No wonder then that Lord Belgrave, one of those wild radicals who wanted to extend the protection of the law to all indentured children, could remark that "Wealth is pursued in this country with an eagerness to which every other consideration is sacrificed."

And yet not all the guilt attached to the employers. Many parents likewise regarded the children as a source of profit. A measure of the degradation of some elements of the population is to be seen in the "Burial Clubs," which might make it profitable to permit children to die; some parents insured in no less than three such organizations, receiving triple payment on the death of an infant—which, if we are to believe one commentator, sometimes left the fathers and mothers with "a desire for the burial payment stronger than the normal anxiety for the child's life. Rent collectors testified that they had been told to postpone expectation of the rent, until some member of the family, usually a child, should die and so bring in enough to pay what was owing." [4]

One must remember that child labor did not originate with the Industrial Revolution, which merely contributed its most extreme and ugly forms. Child labor had been encouraged even before the day of the power-driven machine—had been encouraged by the penny-pinching parishes that had charge of poor relief, and by the possessive ideas of the age. One cannot forget the sentiment expressed in 1723 by Bernard de Mandeville, the Dutch physician who was an influential exponent of *laissez faire*: ". . . every Hour of those poor People spent at their Books is so much time lost to Society. Going to school by comparison with working is idleness." [5] In keeping with this ideal, we hear one charity school being commended because the girls had worked twelve hours a day; and we see that charity to children is concerned only with practical training in earning a living, no matter in what difficult ways. We must therefore not be surprised if the early industrialists built upon the pre-existing ideas and institutions, while overlooking the fact that no previous laboring conditions had been so wearing, monotonous, or murderous as those of the mills and mines.

The same explo. ting psychology applied, unfortunately, not only to the children but to their working mothers, who were sucked to the limits of their energies, and whose babes were almost of necessity neglected, and in some cases stupefied, enfeebled, or even killed by the opiates used in the effort to keep them quite. In all directions, the story is similiar: everywhere, in that early, gold-bemused industrial world, we can see the ravages of the same disease, which spread like a blight to all mine and factory areas, and attacked the health of the people, their cities, their homes, their enjoyments, their morality, their culture, and their longevity.

Take the matter of living conditions. The very growth of the industrial districts implied overcrowding—Lancashire, for example, rose in population from 672,000 to 1,052,000 between 1801 and 1821, and increased even more in the next twenty years. Had there been as much thought of the general welfare as of the pound sterling, there would therefore have been planning, regulation, provision for health and for recreation. Actually, however, nothing so extravagant was supplied. The two hundred thousand people of the new Manchester did not enjoy the benefit of a single public park or garden; near Preston, according to a report made by the Health of Towns Commission in 1844, there were houses that stood back to back in open country without green growing things of any kind, and separated by small back yards featured by open sewers. In some districts of Wales the poor had to go a mile for water, and wait in line much of the night. In the chief town of this rich district, neither public lighting nor drainage had been arranged. In the industrial town of Merthyr Tydfil, where the forge and furnace were amply fed, the people had to drink whatever the river offered. And yet the machine methods had made it easier than ever to provide the necessities of the people.

But neither the necessities of others, nor their convenience or health nor such an immaterial essence as beauty meant anything at all as the determined individualists of the new age gave themselves to the service of their own profits. J. L. and Barbara Hammond have made a pertinent comparison: "Mankind did not admire wealth for the first time; but the rich merchant of Bruges, Genoa or Norwich, like the rich pope or the rich noble of the Middle Ages, had regarded the beauty and culture of his town as a sign of his own importance and success." [6]

In the great cities, the congestion of population was fantastic, almost unbelievable. It will convey only the vaguest idea to mention that an investigating commission in 1844 found nearly 243,000 people inhabiting one square mile in London, while in Liverpool in a certain district the ratio was 657,963 to the square mile. But a clearer impression may be gleaned from the statement that a family might be lodged in a single all-purpose room, where one bed might have as many as five occupants—in the cellars of Manchester, in 1845, no less than 27 cases were found in which a bed accommodated seven.

Consider this report: "A doctor once visited a patient and found her at home in one corner of the room. The landlady herself occupied the central part, near the fireplace, and had rented three of the corners to tenants. In one corner was a widow with three or four children; in another was the doctor's patient, who was unable to earn money to pay her rent and had followed the landlady's suggestion to sublet her bed to another person." [7]

Not only were the rooms overcrowded; all available ground was overcrowded with houses, which were cheaply built to bring a high income (costing no more than 65 or 70 pounds each, they might rent at first for as much as 12 pounds a year). The ghastliness of these dwellings almost passes description: frequently set back to back, and facing their neighbors across spaces seldom more than 15 feet wide, they might receive no light or air except through the narrow courts, might have no means of refuse disposal except by open sewers, and might look down upon great cesspools or "middens" which filled the courts, or upon hills which contained the accumulations of the slaughterhouses.

And yet the residents of the courts were less unfortunate than the multitudes whose homes were in cellars—dismal caverns 10 or 12 feet square, and reaching from 3 to 6 feet below ground level. In seven towns, 14,847 such cellar dwellings were found, containing 67,726 men, women, and children—dim holes, without drainage, with no opening in most cases except the one front door and sometimes with no paving except the earth.

Under these conditions, life expectancy could not be high. As far back as 1757, long before the worst of the industrial evils, the death-rate in Liverpool was found by a Dr. Percival to be one in 27, and in Manchester 1 in 25, whereas in Monton, only a few miles from Manchester, the death-rate was 1 in 68. From this we may conclude that a man in the city had only forty per cent the chance for survival of his brother in the country. But this ghastly state of affairs—though, of course, one cannot vouch for the universality of the same ratio— only aroused the well-to-do when they perceived that cholera, typhus, and other diseases respected no boundary of caste, and might spread to the favored areas from infection centers in the slums. It is true that little was then known about the protection of health; yet it is noteworthy that the Industrial Revolution was about three quarters of a year old before, in 1846, serious sanitary measures began with a number of Nuisance Removal Acts, followed two years later by a General Public Health Act.

In what may seem an over-simplification, though it is a telling summary, the Hammonds have uttered the thoughts of many observers of the early industrialism:

"Thus England asked for profits and received profits. Everything turned to profit. The towns had their profitable dirt, their profitable smoke, their profitable slums, their profitable disorder, their profitable ignorance, their profitable despair. The curse of Midas was on this society, on its corporate life, on its common mind. . . For the new town was not a home where men could find beauty, happiness, leisure, religion, the influences that civilize outlook and habit, but a bare and desolate place, without color, air, or laughter where man, woman, and child worked, ate and slept. . . . The new factories and the new furnaces were like the Pyramids, telling of man's enslavement, rather than of his power, casting their long shadows over the society that took such pride in them." [8]

II

And yet things need not have taken shape so monstrously. The machine method of production was, after all, only a method of production; it was not a malevolent thing, a dragon, but was subject to man's will. More than that! it was a method whose one innate advantage, its reason for being was that it could produce more easily and bountifully than the older system. But if it could produce more easily and bountifully, why did it not lead to an easier, more bountiful life for all persons whom it touched? Logically, this should have been the result; nothing in all man's strange and contradictory history is stranger or more contradictory than the early course taken by the Industrial Revolution. For what more ironic than that the machines, able to produce much more prolifically than the unaided hand, should compel workers to drudge as never in the day of the handicrafts? What more paradoxical than that the tool of liberation should bring chains? What more tragic than that the instrument of widened opportunities should incur a contraction of horizons, and that the means of prosperity should scatter improverishment?

For these absurd and costly results, there can be but one explanation. And this may be found not in the machine process itself but in the use made of that process. Beneath a wise public regulation, which recognized that the benefits of the miraculous scientific discoveries should be shared by all, the new industrial age might actually have brought the bright new world envisaged by dreamers. But the new industrialism burst upon mankind at a time of narrow individualism that channeled all advantages down private streets The simple fact is that the profit-seekers, supported by the ruling philosophy of the day, sought to usurp every benefit of the Industrial Revolution. Caring nothing for the next man, and desiring only to grow rich, they denied their servants all opportunities for decent living, cleanliness, and education because they saw such things as superfluities that earned no dividends. And since they considered the good of the public no more than that of their own employees, they worried not at all how they injured the community.

One evidence of this attitude crops up in the position toward labor organizations. Here we find a queer inconsistency in the interpretation of *laissez faire*: this malleable doctrine was not construed to justify any interference with associations of employers, but was held to make associations of employees wrongful and even iniquitous. And this applied to associations for political as well as for economic purposes.

By the terms of the Combination Bill first brought before the House of Commons in 1799, no workman could lawfully join others in the attempt to obtain increases in wages, reduction in hours, or other benefits; no workman could even attend a meeting to discuss betterment of conditions. The offender could be brought before a one-man court, perhaps consisting of the very employer he was rebelling against; and if found guilty, might serve three months in prison, or two months at hard labor in the House of Correction. There was no remedy except by an appeal to the Quarter Sessions; but this recourse existed in theory rather than in reality, since the required surety of twenty pounds stood like a fortress wall in the way. So strictly was the law a class weapon that an employer, wishing to hold his men down to a prescribed wage, might intimidate them with threats of imprisonment or of incarceration in the navy. Nor would such threats lack power in a day when men in Manchester could be sentenced to long terms for conspiracy for the crime of forming a Friendly and Burial Society, and when eleven women at Middlewich could be punished with prison sentences for the offense of quitting their jobs when their pay was reduced.

It is true that, in 1800, the law was relaxed somewhat in its workings, but its central provisions remained until 1824. It is also true that it supposedly applied to employers no less than to workers; but no action against employers was ever taken. Furthermore, it is true that the law failed in its main purpose, since the workers were merely driven to clandestine action. After a quarter of a century, the repeal of the Combination Laws, even though accomplished stealthily and almost unnoticed, was tacit admission of the failure of forcible suppression.

The repeal, however, was far from bringing a panacea. The effect was a little like that of the abrupt removal of a lid from a boiler. There was an epidemic of strikes, violence against the machines to which the workers ascribed their sufferings, counter-violence in the action of troops, and the dislocation of business, which in some cases was serious, as in the disorganization of shipbuilding on the Thames. All this, naturally, disconcerted those who had urged repeal of the Combination Laws. But after all, what could they have expected? The possessors had shown no regard for the general welfare, and had made use of the new conditions in every way they could to further their own interests. And what more human than that the oppressed, when their long-awaited opportunity came, should likewise attempt to further their own interests, again without regard for the general welfare?

III

Meanwhile the industrial age had brought misery also to the farm laborers who were unable to scrape out an existence on their wages. It was evident that they needed help; but the effort to succor them was so ill-judged that it virtually made their wretchedness official, and opened the doors to the exploiters and profiteers. It was in 1795 that a group of Justices, meeting at Speenhamland in Berkshire with the idea of aiding the farm worker, made the decision that would aggravate and prolong the very problem they were trying to alleviate. Reaching the unfortunate conclusion that "it is not expedient for the Magistrates to grant the assistance by regulating the wages of Day Labourers" according to the directions of pre-existing statues of Elizabeth and James I, they proposed to supplement the low payment of the workers by means of parish relief, and actually published a scale of such relief for "the poor and industrious person."

In other words, they recommended that the community rather than the farmer bear the burden of paying the farmhands. They converted even the full-time toiler into the receiver of a dole; now, if a man were to support himself by his own labor he had to be, in effect, a beggar, an acknowledged pauper. This debasing innovation, which was actually a contribution to the large employers of farm labor rather than to the employees, inspired rapid imitation throughout the country as farmers perceived the benefits of shifting wage burdens to the shoulders of the parish. Thereceforth the farmer paid as little as he chose, even if that little was almost nothing; there was no way of forcing him to offer more, and if the hired help could not live on what they received—then that was the concern of the parish, which might even hire out paupers to the farmers for less-than-subsistence wages while the parish itself made up the difference.

Not surprisingly, the system was ruinous in its working. Everywhere demoralization was encouraged. "The most patent evils," as W. Cunningham well points out, "arose from the fact that this scheme tended to render the inefficient pauper comfortable at the expense of the good workman who really tried to earn his own living." And this was almost inevitable because of a vicious circle: only the destitute could get help from the parish, and only those who got help from the parish could obtain employment, while it was impossible for the worker to seek a job in other districts, since movement from village to village was still forbidden by the settlement laws.

Little wonder that, while the nobles regaled themselves in the palatial halls built at this very period, discontent seethed among the farmhands as they eked out an existence on bread and potatoes while remembering the meat, cheese, vegetables, and home-brewed beer enjoyed by their fathers. Little wonder that their feelings were manifested in spasmodic revolts, in which buildings and farm equipment were attacked. Little wonder that violence, as almost always, provoked counter-violence, and that military force was used against the demonstrators, many of whom—though their only offense had been to ask for higher wages—were thrown into jail. Thus, in the winter of 1830, starving laborers marched with unruly demonstrations, demanding wages of half a crown a day. Many were arrested; three were hanged for crimes not involving death or even serious injury; 420

were let off with transportation to Australia (which, in most cases, meant separation for life from home and family).

"The scenes of distress in and about the jail are most terrible," reported the *Times* correspondent. "The number of men who are to be torn from their homes and connexions is so great that there is scarcely a hamlet in the country into which anguish has not entered. Wives, sisters, mothers, children, beset the gates daily, and the governor of the jail informs me that the scenes he is obliged to witness at the time of locking up the prison are truly heartbreaking. . . ." [10]

As an indication of the sort of crimes for which the ferocious penalties were exacted, take the case of the carter's boy, William Sutton. During a drunken fit, he had stolen four pence. And for this he was condemned to die. Or consider what happened to William Farmer, a laborer alleged to have cried out during an unlawful assemblage, "Money wa want and money wa will haw." For the expression of such dire intention, the death penalty was recommended; but the judge had perhaps taken to heart Shakespeare's lines about "the quality of mercy." All that Farmer had to suffer was transportation for life, in order, as the magistrate proclaimed in his lecture to the condemned, "to show the people of the class to which the prisoner belongs that they cannot with impunity lend their aid to such outrages. . . ."

It is a curious fact that the extreme impoverishment and degradation of the farm laborer came at the very time when prices were high, often exorbitantly high, owing to rising population and warfare. For example, wheat, which had brought 43 shillings a quarter in 1792, sold at 130 shillings in 1800. But the great profits that flowed to the farmer were not shared with the worker, who was often hard put to pay for his bread, and for whom almost no provision was made. Thus, since the producer sought larger markets, it became impossible for a laborer to get milk unless he owned a cow. And sometimes the villages were starving while the produce went to the new industrial cities.

Meanwhile the process of enclosure, which reached back as far as the sixteenth century, had come to its fateful climax. Farm-houses had fallen into ruin; whole village had disappeared; in the course of converting grain-lands into grass-lands for the sheep, "It seemed that sheep were eating up men." [11] After 1750, the consent of the owners of four fifths of the land was all that was required to make the enclosures legal—a purpose furthered by a powerful commission, which happened to be under the influence of the rich landed proprietors, and compelled a redistribution that was confiscation in all but name. By means of various pressures, by fraud, coercion, or sheer overweening might, the peasant was driven from his land, sometimes in return for a new patch of inferior ground which might actually be of little use to him. At the same time, the agricultural capitalists, investing in the land of whole districts, were able to make as much as 14 or 18 percent and to live in high style, clad in luxurious coats and drinking the choicest imported wines. It was of this situation that Goldsmith wrote:

"Ill fares the land, to hastening ills a prey,
"Where wealth accumulates and men decay."

IV

But we have been glancing only at one side of the picture. There was a less conspicuous side, concerned with the struggle of the forces of anti-rapacity against the dominant avarice. Slowly, uncertainly, with many setbacks, many delays, these beneficent forces gained in power, bringing less intolerable working conditions and a less unfair distribution of the proceeds of labor. But the battle they waged was to continue through all the nineteenth and much of the twentieth century, since they were warring with giants. Not all those giants represented greed undiluted; there were also the obstacles of old, implanted, and erroneous beliefs, such as that the improvement of working conditions in England would give an advantage to other countries, and that the distress of the workers could not be relieved by shorter hours, and that the agitators were mere sentimentalists, since the result would be lower wages (later it was proved that men would work much more efficiently on a shorter schedule, as when in 1859 the hours of Yorkshire miners were cut from twelve to eight and they produced more coal than before).

But despite all theories, working conditions were improved step by gradual step, beginning with the law of 1802, by which Sir Robert Peel sought to regulate the labor of child apprentices. In 1819, Peel made it illegal to engage children under nine in the cotton mills, or to employ boys or girls more than twelve hours a day before their sixteenth birthday (this proved of small value, since the Justices of the Peace who supposedly enforced the law were mill owners or sympathizers with the mill owners). Not until fourteen years later was a relatively effective factory law put into force, and even this did not provide nearly inspectors enough. Some idea of the currents and counter-currents of the times may be gleaned from the fact that when the Government in 1844 passed a provision for a ten-hour day for women, the

Tory Home Secretary, Sir James Graham, threatened to resign, and the House revoked the measure. The act of 1844, however, prescribed a twelve-hour day. Furthermore, the law required dangerous machinery to be fenced—a step that surprises one only because it was not enacted until after about three quarters of a century of limb-wrecking machines. Three years later, in 1847, the ten-hour limitation for women and children was written into law.

In its operation, however, the enactment was disappointing. It was not extended to adult males; while the factory owners sought to evade the law by means of a provision enabling them to employ women at any time between 5:30 A. M. and 8:30 P. M.; through a relay system, they kept the women in the mills for twelve hours or more, and so in practice denied them the benefits they had received in theory. It required two subsequent laws, in 1850 and 1853, to remedy the situation. But the mood of the employers was once more shown by their formation of a National Association of Factory Owners, which Dickens not unjustifiably satirized as "the Association for the Mangling of Operatives"; its aim was the repeal of the Factory Laws, and its retrogressive trend is to be seen in an amendment to the law which it obtained, making it unnecessary for mill owners to fence machines where only men were employed.

Nevertheless, the reactionaries were fighting a losing battle. Important measures of control were applied to the mines, when in 1842 it was forbidden to employ women or children underground; and further laws were to follow at intervals, though often only after bitter struggles, until the establishment of the eight-hour day and other provisions now taken for granted. Sometimes, indeed, the advances were made only after strikes, riots, and wild industrial turmoil. The great wonder, however, is not that the avarice of England's private owners was eventually controlled. The great wonder is that it remained dominant over so many decades, and was curbed so slowly and so falteringly.

V

Among the other countries that followed England into the industrial age, the English course of development was repeated with variations. In France, paradoxically, the exploiters were favored by the progressive ideas of the Revolution, which had been intended to set men free; the doctrine of individual liberty, conceived to liberate the masses from the tyranny of nobles and kings, was used to prevent humane legislation and the checking of abuses by greedy factory owners.

Some progress, to be sure, was made; for example in 1813, nearly thirty years before England took the same necessary step, the hiring of children in mines was prohibited. But the French waited until 1841 to pass their first factory law, making it illegal to engage children under eight, and fixing a twelve-hour day for youths under sixteen. Unhappily the law was not implemented by any satisfactory means of enforcement.

Subsequently, as in England, there was a slow movement upward, as in the law of 1900 establishing a ten-hour day in all industries employing women and children. But in France, as in all industrial countries, the fight against grasping employers was almost continuous. Thus, when in 1892 the law limited women to eleven hours' work a day and children to ten while still permitting men to serve for twelve, the proprietors invented a relay system similar to the one devised in England several decades before, and so kept women and children on the job for the full twelve hours. This abuse had to be corrected by legislation, which did not come for eight years.

In Germany, wherein Prussia took the lead, abuses as to child labor began to be reported about 1818; but not until 1824 did the Minister of Education try to pass restrictions. Immediately, however, he was balked; the Minister of the Interior argued that the limitation of child labor would handicap German manufacturers in their foreign trade. Then, in 1828, a more persuasive objection to child labor was heard from a general in charge of the Rhine provinces. The employment of children was indeed an evil; it caused a physical deterioration in the industrial population, and stood in the way of a proper supply of recruits for the army. So now at last the Prussian Government ordered curtailment of child labor. However, bureaucratic frictions intervened and nothing was done until 1839, when the agitations of a humane employer, Schukhardt, led to the passage of a factory law, by which children under nine were kept out of the labor force. Fourteen years later, employment of children under twelve was prohibited; for those between twelve and fourteen, the hours were limited to six. But Prussian employers did not take lightly to this interference with freedom and profits. They coerced the young workers into lying as to their age; they stationed sentinels to warn of the approach of the inspectors; while local officials, siding with the factory owners, produced so difficult a situation that no more inspectors were appointed.

However, the battle would go on and on. Many years later, the extension of factory inspection was opposed by no less a figure than Bismarck; but the Reichstag insisted on universal, compulsory inspection —a provision which the Iron Chancellor had to accept, though he did succeed in undermining the legislation and preventing its effective operation.

But in Germany, as in all countries, the movement away from unleashed rapacity gained momentum with time. And in Germany, as in all countries of the western world, a triumph of the common man over the exploiter was achieved in subsequent international labor agreements, and especially in the convention adopted by the Washington Conference in 1919, which provided for an eight-hour day or forty-eight-hour week in all the signatory nations. The significance of this step is to be seen in the fact that the signers, within ten years, numbered fifteen, and included all the leading industrial powers aside from Japan.

VI

What part meanwhile had the United States been playing? The situation was unique, for much of the energy of her hardiest sons was absorbed in pioneering in the mountains, forests, and grass-lands. of the West. This meant that the factory, during the early days, was less important than in England and Western Europe. Acute industrial problems did, however, develop in the second half of the nineteenth century.

As in England, not the least of these problems was in the rise of noisome slums, some of them hardly more savory than those of Manchester or Liverpool. Speculators drew profits by erecting firetraps in solid blocks, with rear houses crowded behind the front ones, packed together at any odd angles, often five or six stories high, unheated, mostly unconnected with sewers, and almost airless and lightless. Thus in Gotham Court, in Cherry Street in New York, each home of two rooms housed an average of from two to seven people. "In some districts," says Allan Nevins, "there was a congestion that had probably never been equalled in any other great city of Christendom." [12] It was estimated that, of 100,000 slum dwellers, nearly 20,000 lived in cellars. An investigator, in a block off Hester Street, found a room no more than twelve feet by eight and only five and a half feet high, which served as home for nine. And another room, in a basement, provided living, working and sleeping quarters for two men and their wives, five teen-aged boys, a girl of fourteen, and two single men.

Such conditions did not develop in a day. As far back as 1867 the New York Board of State Charities could report that "the innocent are mingled with the vicious; young and simple-hearted children with their callous and corrupt elders; the sexes mingled indiscriminately by day and often by night."[13] Meanwhile garbage collected in many streets, some of which were ridged high with the accumulation; and vice, crime, and disease found a fertile breeding-place. It is not at all astonishing that in a single year, from a single building in East Seventeenth Street, New York, 35 typhus patients were sent to the city hospital.

Improvement did, to be sure, come in time, as the humanitarian and anti-acquisitive forces gathered strength. In the sixties the first large coordinated drive against the slums began; but the process was a slow one, reaching across generations. So late as 1901, it could be found necessary in New York to pass a law requiring all rooms and hallways to be lighted and ventilated (previously, in 90,000 tenement houses, only 4 rooms out of every 14 had had direct access to light or air). During the twentieth century, there has been much anti-slum agitation and much slum clearance, though admittedly far from enough; New York, Chicago, and many other cities have still seen crowded, malodorous districts, where human beings have swarmed in rickety old buildings like beetles under a log, and where squalor and wretchedness and the lack of any green open space have testified to the continued reign of *Profits First*.

In the field of labor, the history of the United States has been spotted. In one glaring respect, the record has been the worst in the Western world—in the existence of Negro slavery in the Southern states until it was uprooted amid the trial and terror of civil war. The subject of American slavery is, however, far too involved to be considered here at any length; many elements were intertangled, including local tradition and pride, the prestige of slave-owning, and sectional bias and antagonism. But there was also a pronounced acquisitiveness, as we may see in the markets where men, women, and children were brought and sold, in the advertisements for runaway slaves, in the civil suits over slaves, in the breakup of slave-families for the sake of profit, and in a thousand other ills. It was in the cotton fields of the far South that avarice cracked the harshest whip; yet it has been suggested that slavery in the South might have ended of itself, like slavery in the North, and therefore the Civil War and succeeding evils might have been avoided except for the invention of the cotton gin, which made it possible to use slave labor profitably in the cotton fields, and encouraged importation of Negroes from the middle tier of states. It is known that these slaves, even as the factory and mine workers of the same period, were brutally ill-used (Simon Legree, apparently, was not wholly a character of fiction). Hence there is some justification for Bertrand Russell's gibe that "The less Southern slave States thus became breeding grounds for the profitable Southern graveyards." [14]

Turning to free American labor in the nineteenth century, we witness some stormy strife, involving a clash of two opposing principles: that a worker had a right to a fair return from his toil, and that capital had the right to any return it could grasp. The conflict of these points of view was seen, for example, in the celebrated Pullman strike of 1894, which was prompted by a 25 per cent cut in wages, along with exorbitant rents in company-owned houses. After the magnate George Pullman had doggedly refused to confer with the employees, and had discharged three who came to him with pleas for relief, the strike was called—and did not at all follow the peaceful course of many later labor disputes. Under the direction of Attorney-General Richard Olney, formerly attorney for the Chicago, Burlington and Quincy Railroad, the Chicago marshal engaged 3600 deputies, which the Chicago superintendent of police described as "thugs, thieves, and ex-convicts"; and these hirelings incited a disorder that gave an excuse for calling in federal troops, which in turn produced rioting and several deaths. Order was restored only by the State militia. One result was the arrest of Eugene Debs and three other union officials on a charge of violating the Sherman Anti-Trust Law—a charge which could not hold, and was changed to that of contempt of court, for which Debs received six months in jail, and the other defendants three months each.

Speaking of the strike and its accompaniments, Governor John Peter Altgeld of Illinois had some pungent remarks: "At present the status seems to be this: Combinations of Capital against the public and against labor have succeeded, no matter by what means, and the men who have accomplished it are now patriots; while combinations among laborers for self-protection have failed, and the men who advocate it are enemies of society" [i. e., "anarchists"].[15]

The actual danger, however, was not from the alleged anarchists but "from that corruption, usurpation, insolence, and oppression that go hand in hand with vast accumulation of wealth, wielded by unscrupulous men." [16]

True, the Pullman strike represented but one violent uprising out of many. But violence was not always possible, since great numbers of the exploited workers were women and children. The case of the sweatshops, particularly those of New York, was notorious. There, beneath the twin orthodox doctrines of *laissez faire* and non-interference with profits, as many as 15,000 women at the close of the Civil War, in a time of steeply rising prices, earned no more than from $2.50 to $4 per week. The labor of these sweatshops, whose abuses continued well into our own century, was supplemented by that of the piece work which the employees took home, and at which children as well as women might drudge, the former perhaps for a penny an hour while the latter's wages might go as high as ten cents for work that, during the rush season, might hold them down to five hours' sleep a day. It is said that, of these workers in sweatshops and tenement homes, three out of five eventually were taken from their misery by tuberculosis.

Meanwhile child labor was becoming scarcely less of a scandal than in England generations before. From the earliest times, there had been child labor in America; but no previous child labor could match the extent, the callousness, or the cruelty of the institution in the closing decades of the nineteenth century. The census of 1900 placed the employed children in the United States at about 2,000,000. But numbers mean less than specific working conditions.

We say that slavery in the United States had been abolished, but surely no supposedly free labor is nearer to slavery than that of children, who do not ask for the work, who are unable to refuse it, who drudge at it for long hours under conditions prescribed by adults, and whose earnings are in large part used by adults. The conditions prevailing at the turn of the century have, fortunately, ceased to be; but they are hardly less revealing than the oppression that once made a stench in British industry.

To begin with, we find the cotton mills in which children from the ages of six and seven worked on twelve-hour day or night shifts, with an extra half day on Saturday and ocasional night-work that sometimes led to continuous stretches of seventeen hours. And while the backs of small girls were hunched into unnatural shapes and their eyesight was ruined, they might earn as high as four cents an hour. Here is a picture of one such child, from a Government report on *The Cotton Textile Industry*: "One of the children is an emaciated little elf, fifty inches high, and weighing, perhaps, forty-eight pounds, who works from six at night until six in the morning, and is so tiny that she has to climb up on the spinning frame to reach the top row of spindles." [17]

In the coal mines, conditions were hardly better. We see small boy "breakers" who pick out the pieces of slate and stone from the anthracite rushing along the chute; in return for nine hours spent crouching over the chute without standing room, while their hands were cut and bruised by the hard black mineral, they could average something like sixty-three cents. It was during this very period that a powerful lobby, operating in the Pennsylvania Legislature, for years prevented the increase of the minimum age to sixteen.

But let us turn elsewhere. In the canneries, six-year-olds earned three cents a bushel for husking corn; eight-year-olds passed nine hours a day capping cans at the rate of forty a minute. In the oyster sheds, where shucking sometimes began at three in the morning, a child who paid strict attention all day might open shells enough to make him twenty cents richer. And in the glass works, whose molten fragments might burn or blind the worker, the activity of smal boys was almost constant. The folowing is from a report of the United States Bureau of Labor:

"Into the work of the snapping-up boy there enters the hardship of looking into the bright, glaring light of the glory-hole. . . . Not only is constant walking necessary, but also constant arm movement, some bending, and, in general, an incessant activity of the entire body. . . . In a Pennsylvania establishment, where the temperature on the outside was 88 degrees, the temperature at the point where the snap-up rubs off the excess glass was 100 degrees; in front of the glory-hole it was 140 degrees. . . . The speed rate of the snapping-up boy is fixed by the output of the shop, and in the case of such small ware as one ounce and under he must work with great rapidity." [18]

The condition of these glass workers is further indicated in another report:

"A child of fourteen, a little old worker with seven years at the glass-works to his credit, was found by a school-teacher in Pittsburgh, with his head buried in his arms, fast asleep on a doorstep. His hands and clothes were covered with factory burns. His home was far from the works, and the exhausted little fellow had been sleeping for hours out in the chill night. Another boy of twelve, in Pennsylvania, who can neither read nor write, has been a worker for years, and often does not go home at all after his night's work, but sleeps in any corner, and hangs around till time to work again. Such a boy is ripening, of course, for a common loafer or criminal." [19]

Such a boy, however, had only a limited life expectancy. Reporting on all the Southern mills, the Washington *Post* declared that the average life of the children after they entered the mills was four years —which, even if an understatement, does point a finger toward the truth, since the deaths were innumerable from accidents no less than from disease. But the wheels of industry must roll on. The precious right of free citizens to a profit must not be curtailed.

Of course, we know that this precious right *was* curtailed. Child labor laws eventually were passed in all the States, though sometimes, and particularly in the South, with inadequate provisions. The beginnings, ironically, represented not a direct reaction to the exploitation of children, but a throw-back from the movement for the humane treatment of animals. And the advance, having begun, was combatted at every step by entrenched acquisitiveness. This was the power that blocked an attempt to impose a 10 per cent federal tax on the net profits of factories employing children. This likewise, until 1919, was the power that defeated all efforts to bar from interstate commerce the output of establishments employing children under fourteen. And this was the power that, after the measure at long last was passed, prompted its invalidation by the Supreme Court.

VII

In connection with all the abuses cited above, the basic truth seems simple enough: that money has obscured all other standards. When a man draws profit from women moiling their lives away in sweatshops, or from the pitiable exertions of little children bent unnaturally over rumbling machines, he may not consciously pause to consider what he is doing; but, in any case, he is not sufficiently concerned with what he is doing. He does not notice the fact of human wretchedness, for the reason that all he does notice is the sign of the $. And this is true not because he is a monster of covetousness, but because the ends he has been trained to value center about the sign of the $; because this is the symbol of aspiration in the society that surrounds him, the object of competition, the doorway to praise and honor, the fulcrum of power, the magnet of pride and display, and the guarantee and proof of success. The sign of the $, to the men about him, is the testing rod not only of bread and cattle and steel, but of all objects; of majestic natural landscapes, of forests, lakes, and bays; of the intangible products of the mind, such as symphonies, poems, and philosophic concepts; and of men and women themselves, who in common parlance are "worth" so many dollars, and are interesting to the public not so much for what they *are* as for what they *have*. And so we worship not only wealth but the possessor of wealth, who has more or less taken the place occupied by the nobles in other lands and ages. Because of our reverence for the rich man, any incompetent who inherits a fortune

or any pirate who embezzles it will automatically rise to a recognition
not easily matched by the inspired sage or the saintly public benefactor. And because we worship the possessor of wealth, we do not ordinarily inquire too closely how he obtained his resources; and, as a result, he himself is less particular about the means than about the fact
of accumulation.

In all this, it is true, our age is not unique. But in our age the tendencies have been accelerated by the machine process, which has
increased the pace of all activity, multiplied the possibilities for material wealth, and extended the potential range and power of the grasping
hand beyond all previous imagining. The machine process exalts quantity at the expense of quality; it gives us many products but products
tending to a universal sameness, and so concentrates our attention
upon the acquisition of *much* rather than of the *best*. Thus it turns us
from craftsmanship and art to mere multiplicity. And thus, at the
same time, it diverts us from abstract possessions to concrete, and
from invisible matters such as human feelings to visible concerns such
as refrigerators and television sets. It has little interest except in tangible results. Moreover, it has placed its tangible results within reach
of the majority, at least in the more favored lands. And so, for a larger
proportion of the people than ever before, the symbols of opulence
have become the goals of existence; the dog in the manger has made
himself the god of the temple.

The over-concentration upon wealth and its over-valuation, rather
than any inherent baseness, account for the dire human afflictions that
have fallen upon the world since the birth of industrialism—the slave-
labor of pauper children in England, the almost equally cruel slave-
labor of children in America, the draining and harrowing of the
mothers of the race in workshops and mills, the exhaustion of men
through overlong hours and needlessly dangerous conditions in mines
and factories, the growth and overcrowding of slum districts, the
abuses in the colonies of European nations, and notably the inhumanities in the Belgian Congo. In most of these cases, if not all, one feels
safe in asserting, the authors of the outrages did not look them in the
face; their minds retained "watertight compartments," which made it
possible to seal up annoying or conflicting ideas. Hence they could
blithely cash their dividend checks while never pausing to think every
penny had been earned with sighs and groans, and spotted with blood.
In their concentration upon the shining goal of riches, they were like

men bewitched, who see but one object in a landscape; and that object was all they wished to see. This has been the general story of the wealthy possessor in the modern world. And this has been the explanation of much of the tragedy of the modern world.

A wide further elaboration of the story may be noted in the growth of the great fortunes of the nineteenth and twentieth century, particularly in the United States. This story has so many facets and ramifications of its own as to be worth separate treatment.

XIII

THE NEW NOBILITY OF MILLIONS (I)

The words *millionaire* and *multi-millionaire,* as used in the modern world, are things new in history. Not that no immensely rich men have ever lived before; some of the wealthy of ancient Greece and Rome might have been known as millionaires had the term been invented, and so might some of the Medici, and some of the early modern merchant class in Amsterdam, Bruges, Hamburg, and other centers of northern and western Europe, and also the banking lords of Genoa and Venice, and certain more recent European financiers such as the Rothschilds, the von Habers, the Frenchman Gabriel-Julien Ouvrard, etc. Nevertheless, the designation *millionaire,* as applied to a modern moneyed man, and especially an American moneyed man, has a somewhat different connotation than it would have had with reference to any of his distant predecessors.

The reasons are to be seen in three interconnected sets of facts. First, there was in the United States no acknowledged aristocracy, no lordship of birth; and this meant that there was a hiatus which had to be filled somehow, and which a less material civilization might have reserved for men of distinction in literature, philosophy, scholarship, or the arts. But since such fields of attainment were not generally appreciated, while every man could understand and admire the glitter of gold, a self-seeker need only succeed in his quest of riches in order to be elevated to acclaim. This meant that, without realizing it, we had one of the great qualifications for a nobility of wealth.

The second qualification, which was equally important, was connected with the individualistic ideas that had flowered in the latter half of the eighteenth century: the ideas of "natural rights" and of freedom—ideas which, by the process of illogic which is one of the great dictators of human affairs, became transplanted from the political sphere where they were born to the economic, so that a man who had escaped the autocracy of the State never questioned that he should be undisturbed in the private autocracy of his own business. Thus persons of unlimited avarice might follow their impulses without regard to their neighbors. In any land, and under any system, such a situation would be evil. But in the United States the circumstances were especially ripe for the despoiler, and the need for firm control was therefore even stronger than in most countries and eras. And this brings us to the third of the interconnected series of facts which have given the terms *millionaire* and *multi-millionaire* a particular connotation in modern America.

The private *entrepreneur*, in the early days of the country, did not find a settled and established region, with a developed countryside and cities of great antiquity, as would have been the case with a contemporary merchant of Padua, Lyons, Brussels, or Cologne. He found himself in a new land, not completely known or explored, but understood to be teeming with resources—unlimited birds and beasts to be slaughtered, inexhaustible forests to be cut down, mines of fabulous riches, and virgin farmlands so vast as to dazzle the imagination. Here, as in the Peru of Pizarro, was wealth for the looting. And since the newcomer was ruled by an individualism that brooked no checks, why should he not loot to his heart's content? Far from being reprehended if he succeeded, he could look forward to a virtual title of nobility. Admittedly, in the resultant quest, many a constructive deed was accomplished, many a trail was opened, many a discovery was made, many a rich and promising strip of land was thrown open to the cultivator. But all this might have been accomplished, and accomplished much more beneficently, beneath a system that did not exalt the law of the wolf-pack. One has only to look closely at our country's so-called development—first, in the opening of the West, and, secondly, in the rise of the industrial giants—in order to realize that the rule of pillage predominated.

II

Consider, first of all, the vast expanse of the West—all the millions of square miles beyond the Appalachians. Who had created the great wealth in timber and wild life, in minerals and water-power and soil? No man had so much as flicked a finger to produce these riches—therefore what man had more right to them than any other? Were they not, in so far as they did not belong to the Indians, the common possession of all? This does not imply that, under an individualistic system, settlers might not legitimately be granted some of the land —as much as they and their sons required for self-support. But it does mean that there was no excuse for monopolistic control; it does mean that wholesale appropriation of the land by any man or group would represent the robbery of the many for the sake of the private profit-seeker. Even when sanctioned by current precepts and authorized by law, such robbery represented a raiding of the common birthright. But the most cursory examination will show us that the legal rights were often as tenuous as was regard for the public interest, while the spirit of the bandit was as much in evidence as when Henry Morgan and his gay buccaneers sailed the Caribbean.

The mood, in some respects, was that of the participants in the California gold rush, though with the important exception that it was not the rank and file who piled up the fruits. At the sight of vast resources with no owner but the public, the large-scale gamblers and financiers seemed to be whipped into a mania; as good orthodox disciples of the creed of private property, they held that these resources should be in private hands—and what private hands but their own? Therefore the seizing and plundering began.

To be sure, this was nothing unprecedented in history—had it not been an old custom of the predatory barons of Europe? What of the *Mesta,* or league of sheep-herders, which had monopolized so much of the farm-land of Spain? What of the aggressive interests that had enclosed great strips of the common land in England and on the Continent? These all, along with many nobles of the Dark Ages, who left a lineage of aristocratic blood by virtue of having taken what they could and excluded whomever they could, were similar in spirit to the raiders of the American continent. The latter, however, enjoyed an inestimable advantage owing to the fact that there was so much more territory to be looted, and that it was so much richer on the whole than anything in Europe.

Wherever we look, amid the enormous spaces of the new continent, we note the same processes at work. In scores of directions, we see fraud against the Indians, who are the victims of every sort of bad faith, misrepresentation, violent eviction, and bare-faced robbery. Yet the dispossession of the original inhabitants forms but one passage in the tragedy. From the banks of the Hudson to the timberlands of the West, the leading principles are *to get* and *to hold.* Sometimes the getting and holding are done under the forms of law, and sometimes without even the pretense of legality. Take the occupation of the land. The official policy, from the earliest days of our nation, put an unfair burden on the poor settler, as it did not allow him land enough for living under the conditions prevailing in most of the West. But no such handicap impeded rich companies or individuals, whose desire was not to settle but to exploit. These were able to grasp huge territories for small sums, sometimes selling them to settlers at immense profits; we see the process in effect as early as 1792, when an

Act of Congress presented 100,000 acres to the Ohio Land Company, which bought another 872,000 acres for something under 75 cents an acre, and then sold the land to settlers at much higher prices. This was, of course, all strictly legal, and in conformity with the ethics of business, though one would like to know what inducements had prevailed upon the members of Congress.

This question is the more pertinent in view of what happened elsewhere—for example, in Georgia, where, in 1795, the Legislature sold various parts of the State to four land companies. The belief was widespread that the law-makers had been bribed; and in the following year, when a new Legislature had been elected, the act of 1795 was rescinded on the ground of "improper influence." In other cases, according to Gustavus Myers, "the purchasers cheated the Government almost entirely out of what they owed. . . . The land frauds were great and incessant." A committee of the United States Senate on Public Lands, reporting on June 20, 1824, "detailed how these companies and individuals had fraudulently bought large tracts of land at $1.25 an acre and sold the land later at exorbitant prices. It showed how, in order to accomplish these frauds, they had bought up United States Land Office Registers and Receivers. . . . The Committee told how an attempt had been made to assassinate one of its members." [1]

Lands newly taken from the Indians were often seized for small sums by private speculators, with large consequent private gain. Lands designated as "swamps," and so procured from the Government for a pittance or nothing at all, were in many cases valuable mineral, agricultural, or grazing territory, which had been deliberately misrepresented as worthless. And lands donated for a specific project, such as the construction of a canal, were frequently made the pretext for obtaining further donations, when the recipients would appeal to legislators that they had encountered unforeseen obstacles and required new appropriations and grants. The territory presented to the canal companies was staggering in extent: for example, in the decade between 1824 and 1834, the Wabash and Erie Canal Company obtained from the Government 828,300 acres, while the total grants to all the canal companies in the same general period were well over 4,000,000 acres. Surely, it was not merely coincidental that some of these lands contained highly valuable deposits of copper.

But the excavators of canals were, after all, petty operators compared with certain other interests, such as the lumbermen and the builders of railroads. The method of the former, who not only robbed the Government financially but robbed their descendants and all the people of natural resources matched in no other land, were true to the established ways of practical-minded, grasping men—that is to say, men shrewd enough to sense the profit of the moment, but not clever or public-spirited enough to perceive or care about the long-range gain. One of their schemes, which illustrates their characteristic low cunning, was to send in trainloads of pseudo-settlers, who would take advantage of the law permitting any homesteader to purchase 160 acres of timberlands for $2.50 an acre. These pretended settlers would come equipped with the requisite $400 each, and doubtless some additional funds provided by the lumber kings; and having secured the property, they would turn over to their benefactors land worth $100 or more an acre at fantastic bargain prices. Gustavus Myers, writing in the first decade of this century, reports that over 10,300,000 acres, or substantially more than 15,000 square miles (almost enough to comprise the whole of New Jersey plus Massachusetts) had been taken by the lumber interests in sales consummated by this deceiful method and others no more scrupulous. And Charles and Mary Beard, referring to the lumber interests and their kindred, make some sweeping assertions that, unfortunately, are upheld by the records:

". . . . the extractive and lumber interests owed a large part of their prosperity to the benevolent paternalism of a government that sold its natural resources for a song, gave them away, or permitted them to be stolen without a wink or nod. Indeed until the second administration of Cleveland, the public land office of the United States was little more than a center for the distribution of plunder; according to President [Theodore] Roosevelt's land commission, hardly a single great western estate had a title untainted by fraud." [2]

Note that the Government, acording to this analysis, bears its own heavy share of responsibility. But what, in large part, was the Government? It was permeated with the influence, the lobbyists, the personal representatives of the plunderers. Not all, indeed, went so far as the "Big Four" of the railroads, who not only had the State Legislature of California in their pockets for years, but sent one of their members, Leland Stanford, to the United States Senate. Yet agents of the great companies did frequently sit in Congress or in other high office; the occasional national scandals were but indicative of the reeking subsurface, as in the notorious case of Albert Fall in the Harding administration, or when, years earlier, Senator Joseph Foraker of Ohio received as much as $40,000 within a six-month period from Standard Oil—a fact not to be considered apart from his strategic committee positions and his work in preparing the Republican anti-trust planks.

But let us return to the land-grabs. Here, undoubtedly, the worst of the many offenders were the railroads. But here, as in other cases, there was at least a pretext of plausibility about many if not most of the grants. In a new and sparsely settled continent, a land of vast distances which could be welded together only by quick and dependable transportation, there was obvious need to encourage the railroad-builders. How, without encouragement, could they be expected to lay and maintain thousands of miles of track through country still populated mainly by bison and prairie-dogs? Obviously, they needed public assistance. This was the theory; and though patently inconsistent with the philosophy of strict private initiative and control, it had considerable justification.

The trouble, however, was not so much with the theory as with its application. The line between legitimate aid and illegitimate may be narrow and hard to define; but there is no doubt at all that the railroad magnates not only crossed the line, but passed far beyond it, and manipulated legislators and legislation so as to help themselves to milions of acres of the public domain (and, incidentally, millions of dollars of the people's money). We read, with a sense of astronomical magnitudes, that between 1850 and 1872 the railroads obtained more than 155,000,000 acres of public land (nearly, though not quite as much land as goes to make up the two states of California and Oregon). On the face of things, it is hard to see how any private companies could either need or merit such imperial dominions, or what excuse they could have except that of greedy acquisitiveness. One should therefore not be surprised to find this acquisitiveness tainted with corruption and fraud.

One of the great recourses of the railroads was tax exemption—why contribute to the support of the Government when it was possible to make the Government contribute to their support? The tax evasion was often accomplished by legal subterfuges, as when the railroads had a harmless-looking law passed, to the effect they should not obtain the patents to the land before paying a prescribed small fee—this fee was never paid, and consequently taxes on the land were avoided until purchasers were at hand to give a good price. At the same time, the railroads were often permitted to enter the public domain free of charge, and strip it of valuable resources such as stone and timber, as in the case of the Union Pacific, which was granted such privileges by acts of Congress in 1862 and 1864. On other occasions, when the public domain or its products could not be seized entirely without payment, the railroads arranged for exchanges of bad land for good—deserts and glaciers and denuded woodlands in compensation for valuable virgin areas laden with minerals and timber. This was brought to light on May 21, 1900, in a speech made in the United States Senate by Senator Pettigrew, of South Dakota. But by then the theft was a *fait accompli.* The subsequent repeal of the law was like the closing of the proverbial stable door after the horse has escaped.

But to understand the attitude of the railroad chiefs, one need not turn to the rare fulminations of men like Pettigrew. Sometimes the position of the magnates is frankly expressed in their own words. Consider, for example, these remarks of Colis Huntington, one of the "Big Four" of the western railroads, in a letter to his partner Crocker:

"If you could get the right man on *that line* in Arizona to work . . . there, to agitate a question in the territory . . . offer the S. P. a charter that would free the road from taxation, and one that would not allow interference with the rates until ten per cent was declared on the common stock, I believe the legislature could be called together *by the people* for $5,000 and such a charter granted." [3]

Or take this, written by Huntington to David D. Colton on October 29, 1877, regarding Governor Axtell of New Mexico:

"I saw Axtell and he said he thought that if we would send him such a bill as we wanted to have passed into a law, he could get it passed with very little money; *when, if we sent a man there, they would stick him for large amounts.*" [4]

Not less to the point, and not less revealing, was Huntington's candid self-justification, as expressed in a letter of 1877:

"If you have to pay money to have the right thing done, it is only just and fair to do it. . . . If a man has the power to do great evil and won't do right until he is bribed to do it, I think the time spent will be gained when it is a man's duty to go up and bribe the judge. A man that will cry out against them himself will also do these things himself." [5]

It would be easy to paraphrase these assertions: for example, "If a man has the power to do great evil and won't do right unless you murder him or kidnap his mother, I think the time spent will be gained when it is a man's duty to go up and shoot him or kidnap his mother." There is, in other words, no act, of fraud or of violence, which could not be justified by Huntington's philosophy. And the man so cynical as to regard everyone else as corruptible, certainly casts doubt on his own incorruptibility. In the ugly starkness of his self-revealed thoughts, Huntington has shown the state of mind that has made possible the rise of the wholesale modern brigands, the land pirates, the exploiters in all fields. His principles, and those of his partners in the Pacific quartet, were the simple ones beloved of marauders ever since the earliest raids on roperty: all things possible are permitted, and all things are possible to the strongest arm. Thus their activities were never complicated by abstract considerations of the rights of others or duty to the community.

There was, for example, the matter of rates. Were these based on what was just to the customers, or what would bring the railroad a fair return? In those days when *laissez faire* still reigned unchallenged and public regulation of transportation was among the socialistic measures that belonged to the future, probably no theories as to fair-dealing entered the heads of the managerial group. Take what you can! Charge what the traffic will bear! These were the laws to which they were loyal. Consequently, if a shipper was making money, you raised your rates, even though your profits were already excellent—this enabled you to transfer the customer's gains to your own account.

Consider the case of the lemon growers, who were driven to uprooting their orchards when an increase in transcontinental freight rates would have given all their profits to the Southern Pacific. Observing the sorry results, the railroad officials reconsidered, and found that they could, after all, haul the fruit at the old prices. At about this time, a wider market for California lemons was indicated by a tariff newly placed on the Italian product; whereupon the Southern Pacific announced a 15 per cent increase in shipping charges on lemons—which would make the Company the sole beneficiary of the tariff changes. But now, for the first time, the strong voice of Government control was heard; the newly formed Interstate Commerce Commission ordered the old rates restored; and the railroad was compelled to cancel the increase in rates.

Even more flagrant overcharging was to be seen in a twenty-one-mile branch of the Southern Pacific, operating between San Pedro and Los Angeles. For this forty-five-minute haul, the rates were around $2 a ton—in strange contrast to the $4 charged for carrying the same freight the thousands of miles from the Orient or Europe. But the lack of competition or control, along with the creed of loot-and-grab, provides all the explanation we need.

One might go on to describe the discrimination that for years bore down against inland points (which, having no alternative route, could safely be charged much higher prices than the seaports). But even more indicative of the principles and methods of the railroad lords was the violence which they sometimes employed, as when their ferryboats habitually pursued a zigzag course in the Oakland Estuary to black the passage of a speedier rival boat; or when, on one occasion, they discharged half a ton of coal dust upon the patrons of the rival line; or when they attempted to put a "wall" around the Oakland waterfront, monopolizing the property, until challenged by a certain John L. Davie, who tried to build a warehouse in defiance of the railroad monopoly—with results that read like undiluted melodrama.

Though Davie had properly leased the land, his warehouse was demolished by a railroad gang. And in the ensuing melée, in which Davie was bruised and lacerated by the railroad's wrecking crew, the defiant warehouseman was assisted by the crowd, whose anti-railroad sympathies were pronounced. For a time, therefore, he prevailed, though only by remaining on the property day and night along with a militia of young roughs and an ample supply of rifles. The railroad, shunning legal measures, met the challenge by means of a grain barge and some armed men, which it tried to land on the disputed territory. Thereupon some of Davie's young desperadoes put out in a skiff toward the barge, whose chains they began cutting with hacksaws. On the barge, men with guns glared down at them; on the shore, other men with guns crowded to their support. And yet no one used the firearms except to threaten. The chains of the skiff were cut; a few clubs swung, a few fists launched out—and victory was with Davie. Unfortunately the rabble, with something of the spirit of Comanche raiders, crowned the victory by ripping up railroad tracks and generally destroying railroad property, with one resultant though accidental death. As for control of the waterfront—the case was taken to law and the attempted usurpation was finally halted by the Supreme Court.

A still more striking case—one that provided Frank Norris with the material for his novel, *The Octopus*—occurred in the San Joaquin Valley. In the Fresno and Tulare region, settlers were lured by railroad prospectuses into land at first so unproductive that they named it Starvation Valley, though after years of devoted toil they irrigated it and converted it into a garden-land. Naturally, they expected to remain in possession, the more so in view of representations by the railroad that their title would be respected and that they would have the land for an average of from $2.50 to $5 an acre as soon as title was confirmed by the federal government; the documents specifically stated that the value of improvements would not be considered in fixing the price of land. But after a time the farmers were to receive a rude education in business methods. They rubbed their eyes, and thought that there had been a mistake when the announced price

of the land was finally placed not at $2.50 an acre nor at $5 but at
$25 to $40, including charges for the orchards laboriously planted
by the settlers, the irrigation ditches dug by them, and the houses and
sheds they had built. When at last they had made sure that there
really was no mistake about the prices, the farmers formed a Settlers'
League, which took its case without avail to their representatives in
Congress and subsequently, levying assessments upon its members,
carried the matter to the courts. In 1879 the decision was made—in
favor of the railroad.

Then, while an appeal to the Supreme Court was pending, the Company secured writs to eject several settlers, and hired two thugs
named Hartt and Crow, who came armed with orders directing the
local marshals to install them in place of the evicted farmers. The
result was the so-called Battle of Mussel Slough, in which the two
railroad strong-arm men and five farmers were killed. This "battle"
was misrepresented by the railroad, which claimed, for example, that
the telegraph office at Hanford had been closed and its operator driven
away by the bellicose farmers; whereas the operator on reaching San
Francisco several days later, testified that the railroad and not the
farmers, had closed the office. But in any event the Company ruthlessly proceeded with the evictions, the arrest of many settlers and
the jailing of five. For lack of funds, the farmers were forced to abandon the fight; and the "Octopus" triumphed. But when, a few years
later, the same question came up in another part of the state, the
Supreme Court upheld the settlers' original agreement with the railroad.

III

Side by side with the deeds of violence we may note various less
dramatic activities: the watering of stocks and the manipulation of the
stock market for the sake of private gain, as when the onetime drover
Daniel Drew moved the quotations of the Erie up and down almost
at will; the cutthroat competition, whereby one line deliberately forced
another to the wall; the hand-in-glove attitude toward political corruption, as when Jay Gould seated the notorious "Boss" Tweed and one
of his henchmen on the Erie's Board of Directors; the cavalier position
toward legality, as when the Southern Pacific drove an unauthorized
line through an Indian reservation in Arizona; and the tendency to

regard railroads as assets to be maneuvered for financial advantage, rather than as living links affecting the life-courses of millions.

One may argue that the railroads, in the face of gigantic engineering difficulties, did magnificent jobs in throwing bridges of communication across the country; in opening the land to homesteading; and in speeding the consolidation of the sparsely settled territories into a nation. All this may be conceded; yet had acquisitiveness not dominated the onrush of the "iron horse", all the results could have been attained, and attained at much less cost in money and vital resources.

Take, for example, the matter of the construction of too many lines. Here, while on occasion there was great gain for the individual, there was great economic loss for the nation. Some roads, such as the Hudson River's West Shore, were built not for their own sake but for their nuisance value, in order to embarrass competitors and to make possible a sale at an inflated price. Other and more important lines, such as the Northern Pacific and the Great Northern, ran competitively through enormous stretches of mostly uninhabited country where one railroad would have served the needs more amply (though James J. Hill of the Great Northern did have the excuse of trying to bring in settlers and encourage the growth of communities). By the mid-eighties there were five trunk lines between New York and Chicago and two more were being built, where three would have sufficed. Meanwhile most of the roads tottered on the edge of bankruptcy. In 1879 alone, no less than 63 railways were foreclosed. A decade and a half later, in 1894, according to the estimate of Alexander Dana Noyes, no dividends were paid on 61 per cent of the shares outstanding on American railroads; a quarter of the roads, including the Santa Fe, Union Pacific and Northern Pacific, had gone bankrupt. Here we find capitalism outreaching itself. Under any law except the bandit's code of *get-there-first*, it might have been possible to coordinate railroad construction to serve the public interest and avoid wasteful duplication, a burden of debt, and bankrupcy.

It was competition that explained, at least in part, the unscrupulous methods of the railroads in their efforts to remain out of the receiver's hands—the gangs of thugs, the rebates to favored customers, the discriminatory rate structures, the fraud and the bribery. If the iron of public control was eventually to hang heavy about the necks of the railroads, this was because they themselves had invited such restraint. It is one of the ironies of our industrial history that public regulation became tightest and most cramping at the very time when new economic forces, in the shape of the motor truck, the private automobile, and the airplane, were exercising a regulation of their own and tending to make many of the previous legal controls unnecessary. But traditions die hard; and the tradition of the railroad as a devouring monster remains at a time when this means of transportation is fighting for existence and when there is a widespread trend toward the cutting of services and the abandonment of lines. This is perhaps a just even if a bitter nemesis. For the railroads themselves, in this later day, have become the victims of the one-time railroad magnates.

THE NEW NOBILITY OF MILLIONS (II)

The dukes and barons of the railroads, though they included some of the most picturesque rascals our country has produced, were representative rather than exceptional. They were representative of a class who sought to draw opportunity and fortune on the highways and byways of a largely unexploited continent; and they turned to the railroads mainly because these were the greatest, the most promising, and in many ways the most alluring industries of the day. In methods, in ethics, and in outlook they are hard to distinguish from their brothers in other fields, ranging from investment speculation to steel, and from real estate to copper, meat-packing, and oil.

Over the whole group, the same acquisitive philosophy hung like a cloud. All were disciples of *laissez faire*, the creed of *look-out-for-yourself* and *devil-take-the-underdog*. All were willing to cut, tear, and slash. All were participants in a game whose foremost aim was *to get;* among them all, pity and compunction were rare visitors, while thought of the larger aim and the wider interests might occasionally be expressed in devout platitudes, though it rarely found voice in action. These men were the products of an era, and of a social tradition and code of belief, and they were but acting as they had been trained to act, and as they saw men all about them behaving. In a war of the ruthless, it was not accidental that the most ruthless so frequently prevailed.

Let us glance at several prominent examples. One of the earliest and most notorious was John Jacob Astor, a butcher's son born in Germany in 1763. Twenty-three years later, when he started a small fur business in New York, one would have seen no reason to predict that he would pile up one of the greatest fortunes of the day. How, then, did he gain riches given to few? The answer may be that he used methods employed by few.

To begin with, he left the stamp of death upon the wild life of the country. The hunters and trappers, upon whose kills he originally fattened, were of the rapacious band who all but wiped out the fur-bearing animals of the East. However, there were many more creatures to be slain in the mid-West and in the Rocky Mountains; in this slaughter great profit might be had. No matter if Astor and his agents were depleting or destroying priceless natural assets. After all, he was not unique in his standards—he merely had a stronger thrust to his arm than many others. By 1808, he was rich enough to supply half a million dollars as the capital of the American Fur Company, which operated in the vast region of the mid-West and Southwest—an area whose wild life had as yet been little impaired.

In all the wide territory stretching from the Missouri to the Rockies and east and north to the Great Lakes, Astor's company was, as Gustavus Myers puts it, "a law unto itself. That it employed both force and fraud and entirely disregarded all laws enacted by Congress, is as clear as daylight from the Government reports of that period. . . . The exploitation that ensued was one of the most cruel, deliberate and appalling that has ever taken place in any country."[1] The Company's morality was that of the pirate captain. No competitor, no rival trader might operate within the empire of the American Trading Company—not unless he was willing to face violent counter-action, even to the extent of murder.

Meanwhile, following a good old custom instituted more than a century before by the Hudson Bay Company and practiced by various French and English traders, Astor's agents set about to make the Indians malleable by means of the reliable ally, "fire water." When a man was intoxicated, it was easy to cheat him out of his furs, or to procure them for a song. Truly, a lucrative method, despite some small side-effects in dissipation, broken lives, and wrecked tribes! The profit, moreover, was all the greater since the Company made money directly from the sale of the liquor as well as indirectly from its effects. The prices paid by the natives were reported to be as high as $25 to $50 a gallon.

Incidentally, while cynically flouting the rights guaranteed to the Indians in federal treaties, the fur-dealers reaped further profit by selling the Indians large quantities of inferior merchandise at superior prices. At the same time, they resorted to the shabby old trick of short-weighting on the furs. One must not suppose that the aborigines were always so naive as not to suspect what was being done to them; but when they took their cases to court, the majesty of the law upheld the exploiters. And if the Indians became too vehement in their protests, they could be silenced by the argument of the smoking rifle. Any demonstration on their part, besides, might give an excuse for an appeal to Washington for troops to put down an uprising. And this in turn might lead to a virtual blood feud; for the Indians, seeing their braves cut down, would retaliate in kind at any available white man.

But in the long run, the odds were stacked too heavily against them.

All, however, was to be condoned in the good name of profits. Not profits to the ruffians who did the company's bloody task—these agents might receive as much as $130 for ten or eleven months' work (only to be cheated out of much of their earnings). But for the company the returns were magnificent—just how magnificent was revealed by William B. Astor, who in a letter to the Secretary of War, dated November 25, 1831, stated that, on a capitalization of $1,000,000, the company's profit might be estimated at $500,000 a year.

One might suppose that dividends on this scale would have relieved the Astors of the need of supplementary income. But accumulation is like a cancer; it only leads to further accumulation, under the impulse of an insatiable desire. And so the fur trade did not suffice for the wily John Jacob; he must also seek profits in real estate. And some of his transactions were notable.

Take the case of the Morris estate, which covered nearly a third of Putnam County, in New York. During the Revolution, this stretch of more than 51,000 acres had been confiscated by the Government, and had been sold to farmers; in 1809 it supported 700 families, who had long been peacefully settled there, and had not the dimmest suspicion that their claim would ever be challenged. Astor, however, was to give them the shock of their lives. From the lips of a lawyer, he heard that the State's claim to the land might be upset; and consequently he began, by devious methods, to seek out the Morris heirs, from whom he was able to buy their supposed rights for $100,000. Then, taking advantage of the legal technicality that the Morrises had had a life lease not subject to confiscation by the State, he declared that all the 51,000 acres were his. Not only that, but it was his right to evict the 700 families.

This announcement, naturally, creater a furor—and not only among the men and women whose homes and livelihood were threatened. The public, as well, was outraged, the more so as Astor not only claimed the right to take the land without paying the possessors, but held that the improvements—buildings, fences, etc.—also were his free of charge. Doubtless that was all quite in tune with the time-honored traditions of brigandage. But rarely had the freebooter so blatantly unbared his intentions. The State of New York, responsive to the general indignation, decided to contest Astor's claim, which he then offered to sell for $667,000. This offer the State rejected; and the matter dragged through the courts, which in the end, apparently preferring technicalities to justice, issued a verdict in the claimant's favor.

In 1827 the Legislature voted to pay Astor $500,000 in special 5 per cent State stock. Thus did the marauder establish one of the bases of his great real estate holdings.

II

Another of the fabulous early American fortunes was that of Cornelius Vanderbilt, who had been brought up amid the rough-and-tumble of the New York waterfront, in a world where books and learning meant nothing, but the strong arm was a favored means of progress.

Though later known as a railroad magnate, Vanderbilt achieved his beginnings in maritime pursuits. In 1829, at the age of thirty-five, he graduated from running his own schooners into building his own steamboats, while advancing rapidly through the tried old methods of push-and-shove. He was an expert in the art of shouldering rivals out of existence; for example, if they lowered their pay scales and freight rates, he would reduce his own pay scales and freight rates even more, until his competitors quit or were driven to bankruptcy. And when all rivals were safely out of the way, he would charge exorbitantly for his services. Ah, halcyon days of one hundred per cent private initiative, when there were no public regulations to choke free enterprise! By virtue of his unimpeded liberty of action, Vanderbilt had piled up half a million dollars by the time he was forty, while his competitors went to their financial graveyards and the public paid heavily for his monopolies.

All this, to be sure, might seem strictly in the line of business, were it not for certain methods. The all-important dock privileges were controlled by the New York Common Council, whose members had a taste for the sugary sweetness of a bribe; and one of the most effective ways of getting rid of business enemies, accordingly, was by out-bribing them. In this craft Vanderbilt was able to hold his own, as in the corresponding science of corrupting federal officials, and particularly those who controlled the millions in subsidies granted to steamship companies. Not that Vanderbilt was alone among shipowners in this form of plunder, which, thanks to sums known as "postages," paid not only for the transportation of the mails but for the construction of new ships. Thus, according to Myers, "Practically none of Vanderbilt's ships cost him a cent. . . . In fact, a careful tracing of the history of all the subsidized steamship companies proves that this plunder from the Government was very considerably more than enough to build and equip their entire lines." [2]

Another tool of the new prince of commerce was blackmail. At one time, for example, his steamship company charged as little as $35 steerage for the long passage between California and New York. But he sold his steamship *North Star* for $400,000, and blackmailed the purchasers into paying further sums as his price for not competing with the new owners; the latter, in consequence, were able to raise steerage rates to $125. According to a charge made in Congress on June 12, 1858, by Representative Davis of Mississippi, the rival companies gave Vanderbilt $30,000 a month in order that they might be free to charge double fares to passengers; while he received an additional $10,000 a month for carrying mail between New York and Aspinwall.

Thus $480,000 a year went into his coffers so that he might stand by idly while the public was being fleeced on freight and passenger rates.

It was the heaven-sent opportunity of the Civil War that gave Vanderbilt some of his lushest harvests. Acting through an agent named Southard, he would charter dilapidated lake or river vessels for use as federal troop transports on ocean voyages. He appears to have given no heed at all to non-commercial considerations such as whether the men would survive the voyage; sometimes he violated the supposedly invariable maritime rule that at least two persons capable of navigating a vessel must be aboard, and in other cases he did not provide charts enough. A flagrant affair was that of the S.S. *Niagara*. which was described by a member of an investigating committee, Senator Grimes of Iowa: "In perfectly smooth weather, with a calm sea, the planks were ripped out of her, and exhibited to the gaze of the indignant soldiers on board, showing that her timbers were rotten. The committee have in their committee room a large sample of one of the beams of this vessel to show that it has not the slightest capacity to hold a nail.'" [3]

There has been a tendency to gloss over the gross self-seeking, not to say gross fraud, with which Vanderbilt operated the ships. A Senate resolution, after some salutary wire-pulling, went no further than to censure Vanderbilt for negligence. Far from being punished, he received a medal from Congress at the war's end. "Although Vanderbilt had been tenderly dealt with in the investigation, his criminality," reports Myers, "was conclusively established." [4]

A more recent commentator, Matthew Josephson, calls Myers "severe," as undoubtedly he was, since the facts plainly call for unequivocal statement. One cannot, therefore, accept the half-hearted explanatation Josephson proposes: "It was a time of such notorious hurry and confusion, so much mischief was more or less unwittingly done . . . so many shoddy blankets, so many doctored horses and useless rifles, so many stores of sickening beef, were directed toward the front during the general excitement, that Commodore Vanderbilt's errors or shortcomings were largely overlooked." [5]

Even if Vanderbilt's shortcomings were largely overlooked (and that they were not entirely overlooked is shown by the statements of Senator Grimes) he is hardly to be pardoned because of the existence of a wide company of soundrels. One would be naive, moveover, to suppose that mere hurry and confusion account for the wholesale unloading of worthless, rotten, or dangerous supplies upon the Government. The evident fact is that Vanderbilt, like others of his kind, was so imbued with the philosophy of private gain that he was willing to swell his already swollen fortune at the risk of the lives of his countrymen as they went about their task of defending the Union. It was merely a happy dispensation of nature, and owing to no merits of Vanderbilt, that a ship such as the *Niagara* did not encounter rough weather and founder with all aboard. He was an old and experienced shipping man; he knew the requirements for safety at sea; and the Government and the people trusted him precisely because they were aware that he did *know*. Hence only a heinous breach of trust could have impelled him to palm off unseaworthy old tubs upon the hard-pressed and imperilled North

All this, perhaps, can be better understood when we realize the philosophy of the man. His position was the same *Myself first* and *The public be damned* which we have observed in Huntington and his fellow railroad magnates. Whether or not he ever uttered the phrase accredited to him, "What do I care about the law? Hain't I got the power?" certainly these rhetorical questions are suggestive of his attitude of mind. And the same is true of his brusque query, "Can't I do what I want with my own?" after being chided for his disregard of the public convenience at a time when, as a strategic move in a railroad war, he was halting his trains beyond the Hudson from Albany, compelling passengers to walk across the frozen river in the bitter cold of winter. This absence of a sense of responsibility, this arrogant contempt for the general interest in the name of self-interest was, as we know, to win him money—far more than any man can use. At the same time, it indicates the wild extremes to which acquisitiveness can go—that acquisitiveness which admits no duty to the community on which it battens, has no regard for good faith or fair dealing or morality, and recognizes no standard of measurement but money, and no aim but to get rich, and then richer still, and then richer yet, while piling up a colossus of power and wealth whose sole object in existence is itself.

III

"Nothing is lost save honor," is the statement accredited to Jim Fisk, the partner of Jay Gould, after he had become involved in a financial scandal. And this remark, whether meant facetiously or not, does indicate the ethical code that moved not only Fisk but the whole circle of capitalists and stock manipulators among whom he moved. When nothing but the honor of such men had been lost, little indeed had been relinquished. Nevertheless, there are deeper implications in another assertion, ascribed to Gould by his biographer Robert Irving Warshow: "Once in an enterprise, it is very hard to leave it. We are all slaves, and the man who has one million dollars is the greatest slave of all, except it be he who has two millions." [6]

Here in an admission of unusual frankness, is one of the clues to the fortunes of Fisk and Gould and a whole celebrated company. Once having entered an enterprise, they had great difficulty in leaving it; and once having piled up their riches, they were enslaved, increasingly so as the wealth mounted; their possessions came to possess them, tying them with unseen cords amid a dazzle and seduction that gave them no peace. This in itself does not account for and much less justify the lack of morality; but it does to some extent explain why some of the magnates would go on from acquisition to acquisition and from rascality to rascality, never seeming to pause.

Out of the whole group of nineteenth century financiers, the man usually singled out as the villain of blackest dye is Jay Gould—certainly, one of the slyest and most cold-blooded of all the manipulators. But that he was any more wicked than his associates and competitors is questionable: they were all playing the same game, and by much the same methods and rules, and with the same ethical standards, though Gould did differ from most of the others in being more clever and resourceful, and by his daring in venturing where most would have hesitated to tread.

A single instance will illustrate his horse-trading type of shrewdness. During the rate war which his Erie Railroad was waging with Vanderbilt's New York Central, the charge for transporting a carload of cattle from Buffalo to New York was reduced from $125 to $100, then to $50, then to $25. Finally, in an audacious stroke calculated to annihilate his competitor, Vanderbilt lowered his price to $1. And at first this strategy seemed to have accomplished its objective—Gould withdrew from the race and raised the charge to the old $125, while Vanderbilt (at a great loss) did all the cattle-carrying. Not until too late did he learn that Gould had been secretly buying cattle in Buffalo and shipping them in great numbers over the Central, reaping a fortune from his rival's low rates.

This man, whom Warshow calls "one of the greatest financial freebooters of all time"—an opinion shared by other commentators—began humbly enough, the son of a New York farmer who had fought tooth-and-nail for subsistence on his barren land It may be that his own early hardships, which included work from 6 a.m. till 10 p.m. in a country store, filled him with an inordinate desire to get ahead. In any case, his rise was rapid, as a surveyor, as the manager of a small run-down railroad, as a leather dealer, and as a Wall Street operator. The details need not concern us; by whatever methods, he quickly rose to a dominant position on Wall Street. And having risen, he used his power to upset the financial market for the sake of personal gain. Thus, after manipulating himself into control of the Erie Railroad, he maneuvered to use its stock as the means of great profit, when, having sold large quantities at high quotations, he planned a depression in prices by withdrawing $12,000,000 suddenly from circulation, which would embarrass the banks, force the brokers to sell their stock, and so reduce prices as to enable Gould and his henchmen to buy back at bottom prices the stock which they had sold at top rates. While making millions by such cunning, he incidentally drove his erstwhile partner Daniel Drew to bankruptcy.

This little episode, however, was less audacious than a grandiose later scheme: to corner all the country's gold. Here was an idea that would have intimidated a less bold or a less imaginative brigand; it would have seemed impossible, if only because the Government held something between $75,000,000 and $100,000,000—roughly, four to five times the market supply. The latter, however, might be frozen if the Government could be prevented from dumping part of its resources into the market. But how hold the Government's hand?

Here was, indeed, a problem. But Gould thought that he knew how to solve it. And his method sheds light on his mentality. The particular agent of his schemes was Abel Rathbone Corbin, a lawyer, lobbyist, and speculator, who, at 67, had married a sister of President Grant; Corbin was very close in Grant's confidence, and the President stayed at his home whenever he came to New York. Clearly, a man to cultivate! In May, 1869, in the course of a social visit, Gould made full use of his opportunities; somehow he brought the conversation around to the price of gold. And before the visit was over, Gould had made various arrangements for Corbin, such as to buy $1,500,000 of gold on his account, without any harassing necessity on the latter's part to make payment. Gould, incidentally, maneuvered to have himself invited to Corbin's home during Grant's next visit to New York, so that he might, as a patriotic American, have a chance to put his ideas before the President.

Meanwhile Gould was buying all the gold he could. He also made other preparations, as in helping to entertain Grant at a theatre party given for him by Gould's partner, Fisk. In the course of the dinner, a sly question was put to the President as to the price of gold; but the answer, Gould later declared, was like a "wet blanket" to his schemes. Subsequently, through the compliant Corbin, Gould obtained the appointment of a henchman, General Butterfield, to the Assistant Treasuryship at New York, from which valuable information might be drawn. At the same time, Gould engaged a reputed English expert on financial affairs, Dominick Henry, to prepare newspaper and magazine articles, which appeared throughout the United States, and purported to show the beneficent effects upon the country's economy of a rise in the price of gold. The stage meanwhile was further set with hundreds of persons placed at strategic positions, ready to offer Grant their rehearsed advice. Then, as the hour to strike drew near, Gould presented Corbin with a small token of his esteem, a check for $25,000 (the check was made blank, as Corbin, being a man of delicate sensibilities, did not like his name to appear needlessly). At about the same time, Gould purchased $1,500,000 in gold for the account of General Butterfield without payment on the part of this useful minion. And as an additional help, Gould was planning to back his vast purchases of gold by certified checks on a small bank he controlled, without reference to the amounts on deposit.

So far all was progressing smoothly. But now the master manipulator, becoming just a little less adroit in his eagerness, made one or two errors, such as to have Corbin address a letter to Grant, which chanced to be opened in Grant's presence by General Porter, whose suspicions were aroused, so that he in turn stirred the suspicions of the slow-thinking President. After various frightening signs, including a letter of warning from Mrs. Grant to Mrs. Corbin, Gould perceived that he had lost the great gamble—from which, however, he was to emerge financially unscathed, for he began selling gold in large quantities without the knowledge of his partners (so little were they aware of his doings that they bought the very metal he sold, without knowing the source or suspecting the change in his plans). Thus he saved himself when the Government released its gold and the market broke on "Black Friday"; and subsequently he provided for Fisk and one or two others faithfuls, who would otherwise have lost their all.

But what of the persons outside the charmed circle? They might perish, for all that Gould was concerned. Hundreds of firms had been ruined, thousands of individuals had gone bankrupt. Paralysis and terror, according to the committee report of James Garfield, had spread to the business of the entire country. Years later James Brown, the Scottish banker, could echo the general verdict: "Houses were brought to tumble then that will probably never recover from it. That conspiracy caused more mischief than any other thing in the history of finance that I ever remember to have read." [1]

One may add that Jay Gould did not end in jail. Bribery, unauthorized use of bank funds, the effort to corner a market—these were mere commonplaces in the financial world of that unregulated day. So Gould was to survive to perpetrate still other piratical raids, by which he gained control of various institutions, including some of the Pacific railroads, the Manhattan Elevated Railroad of New York, and the Western Union Telegraph Company. On one bleak occasion he did face what looked like a certain prison sentence, when he was arrested and put under heavy bond for having converted securities of the Erie Railroad into stock, and then sold something like 407,347 shares and transferred the money to his own account. Resourceful as always, however, he brought pressure to bear upon Watson, the newly made President of the Erie, who agreed to drop the charges if Gould made restitution, though without admission of wrongdoing. The restitution, as might have been expected, was in stock that was nearly worthless, or (worse still) stock that was never issued.

The effect upon industry of a man such as Gould is shown by the fact that the Erie, when Gould was ejected from its control, had a debt of $86,000,000—an increase of $64,000,000 during his regime. To offset this huge burden, not a penny had gone into improvements enhancing the actual value of the line. Despite the fact that it did an immense business and was one of the most important railroads in the land, it long remained in a receiver's hands, and for about twenty-two years it paid not a penny in stock dividends.

In the case of Gould, therefore, one has difficulty to accept the frequently made assertion that men of great wealth, even when they draw

vast amounts from society, justify the drain by that which they give
back to society.

IV

Jay Gould, though he delved into various industries and particularly
into railroads, was primarily a financial operator rather than an industrialist—he did not create or expand industries, but merely manipulated them for his financial advantage. But there is another type
of capitalist whose returns come not so much from the movements of
the money market as from the control of factories, mines, or oil wells.
And not the least notable representative of this type was Andrew
Carnegie.

Carnegie was in some ways a more complex character than Gould.
The latter, despite all his intricate weavings, was essentially simple in
his aims: it was his object to get more money, and get all he could, and
get it by any means that the law allowed, and even (safety permitting) by means that the law did not allow. This, however, was not
true in the same degree of Carnegie, who in early manhood and in
old age showed that he realized the futility of limitless accumulation,
even though during most of his days he was unable to keep himself
from the pitch-and-scramble of get-and-gain. A notation which he
confided to his diary at the age of thirty-three makes curious reading
in view of his subsequent career:

"Thirty-three and an income of $50,000 per annum! By this time
two years I can so arrange all my business as to secure at least
$50,000 per annum. Beyond this never earn—make no effort to
increase fortune, but spend the surplus each year for benevolent purposes. Cast aside business forever, except for others.

"Settle in Oxford, and get a thorough education, making the acquaintance of literary men. . . . Settle then in London and purchase a
controlling interest in some newspaper or live review and give the general management of it attention, taking a part in public matters,
especially those connected with education and improvement of the
poorer classes.

"Man must have an idol—the amassing of wealth is one of the worst
species of idolatry—no idol more debasing than the worship of money.
. . . To continue much longer overwhelmed with business cares and
with most of my thoughts wholly upon the way to make money in the
shortest time, must degrade me beyond hope of permanent recovery."

This is worth quoting because it shows that Carnegie, unlike most
of his fellow capitalists, did upon occasion perceive the truth—did

realize the worthlessness, the vapid ignoble quality of a career given wholly to accumulation. Later in life, when he took half-year holidays from his business, and again when he distributed major portions of his holdings in liberal benefactions, he showed that his earlier realization had not wholly left him. Although at one time his fortune rose to $400,000,000, he gave away more than $350,000,000 of this during his lifetime, and when he died he bequeathed his family less than $25,000,000 (more than enough, one assumes, to keep them from public charity, though far less than other tycoons have passed on to their heirs).

Yet somewhere within the mind of this strange man there was a contradiction. The money standard, which in moments of clearer insight he abhorred, had somehow possessed him. This is indicated in an incident recited by Matthew Josephson:

"Carnegie playing golf with the publisher of books, Frank Doubleday, asked him: How much did you make last month, Frank? It was impossible to tell but once a year, the publisher replied. I'd get out of it! said Carnegie firmly. The immortal donor of free libraries who was the most articulate of the industrialists had no further thoughts upon the making of books than the cash profit to be derived from them."[3]

It is evident that the modes of thought of the society about him, the modes of thought in which he had been steeped for years, had taken firm grip upon his mind.

This was certainly true when he plunged into action as a industrialist. As a steel magnate, he was a man of steel, who reaped returns that few men in any age have been able to match. As early as 1880, when he was but 45, he and his partners pulled as much as $2,000,000 in a single year from their steel mill, and subsequently the amount mushroomed into many millions—far more than, on any conceivable theory of service rendered, one man could legitimately claim of society.

But the sums obtained are of less interest than the methods employed. It is curious that, while Carnegie could be a humanitarian in theory just as in theory he opposed excessive accumulation, in practice he was as hard as his most relentless union-busting contemporary. "Thou shalt not take thy neighbor's job," he piously proclaimed in opposing the use of "scabs"; but the depth of his conviction was subsequently shown. What, for example, when he found that steel mills in Chicago were paying less than he did for labor by operating on twelve-hour shifts, in contrast to the eight-hour shifts at his Edgar Thomson works in Pittsburgh? Did he congratulate himself on being a more humane employer than his rivals in Chicago? Far from it! He set out to imitate their inhumanities. Having installed new equipment, he returned to the twelve-hour shift—which he forced upon the men after a long lockout, when they had to come back without benefit of union and with cuts in wages and man-power. Doubtless this was all highly effective—that is, as a means of overtopping competitors and bolstering profits. But the story was a different one for the men who, in order not to starve, must now slave for half of each twenty-four hours amid the withering heat of the mills.

But the dispute had at least been non-violent. As much could not be said of the more celebrated Homestead affair. This episode, one of the most disgraceful in the history of American labor relations, can be traced to an effort on the part of Carnegie and his second-in-command, Henry Clay Frick, to break up labor unions and so clear the way for an unimpeded dictatorship of management. This is plain from many facts, including the notice which Carnegie sent Frick to be posted before the mills at Homestead, under date of April 4, 1892:

NOTICE

To Employees at Homestead Works

"These works having been consolidated with the Edgar Thomson and Duquesne, and other mills, there has been forced upon this Firm the question Whether its Works are to be run 'Union' or 'Non-Union.' As the vast majority of our employees are non-union, the Firm has decided that the minority must give place to the majority. These works, therefore, will be Non-Union after the expiration of the present agreement." [9]

The illogic of this is transparent. Because most of the men had never been unionized (or had been forced to accept non-union engagements), they were never to be permitted to form a union! And because the rule of the majority was to predominate, the Company—which hardly could be said to represent a majority of the workers—was to make the final decision for all the men!

Carnegie was evidently content that the burden of the negotiations should rest upon the shoulders of Frick. And when this hard-minded industrialist issued a declaration of relentless war by announcing that the works would close on July 1st and open five days later with any obtainable help, the men blamed him alone, and thought that his announced reductions in the wage scale would be countermanded by Carnegie, the "Little Boss," upon whose friendliness they relied—for had he not at times passed among them with a personal word of apparent regard for their interests?

Here we note in Carnegie a duplicity that could only have sprung of moral cowardice. While Frick was receiving the brunt of the blame, Carnegie was not "traveling on the Continent" as the men had been led to believe, but was hiding at isolated Loch Rannoch, in Scotland, thirty-five miles from any railroad or telegraph, where he was in no danger of being embarrassed by a demand that he rescind Frink's non-union proclamation. The men who relied upon the "Little Boss" would have been astonished to learn to what extent Carnegie stood behind Frick, as in his message of June 10: "You have taken your stand and have nothing more to say. . . . The chances are you will have to prepare for a struggle, in which case the notice should go up promptly on the morning of the 25th. Of course you will win, and win easier than you suppose, owing to the present condition of markets."

If Carnegie was hardly acting like an honest man, Frick is not to be exculpated. Whatever his personal convictions, he was not unaware that the Company was earning around $4,000,000 a year at the very time when he proclaimed that it would face bankruptcy unless it broke the power of the union— the very time when he allegedly found it necessary to lower wages. But Frick, at least, was not taking shelter behind another man's cloak. And it was he and not Carnegie who was wounded and narrowly escaped assassination beneath the bullets and explosives of the anarchist, Alexander Berkman.

But to return to Homestead. The strike began on July 1st, while the workers burned Frick in effigy. Characterized by a Congressional committee as "stern, brusque, and autocratic" in his negotiations, Frick defended the "inviolability of property" and "life and liberty" by bringing in 300 armed Pinkerton men in a tugboat and two barges. The workers, who had already attempted to organize on a military basis, regarded this as a challenge to be met by any means, though the actual means was that of mob action. By the discharge of a cannon, by the explosion of natural gas, by the ignition of oil to set fire to the barges, by rifle shots and sticks of dynamite and kicks and clubs and every other weapon within reach, they attacked the Pinkerton men, and subsequently looted the barges, while beating and mangling the guards. It is remarkable that only one man on the barges was killed and eleven injured, though two who had been captured were killed, one was driven insane, and thirty others, badly battered, had to be taken to hospitals.

Meanwhile Carnegie, safe in his Scottish lake retreat, was peacefully unaware of all this frenzy and gore.

The workmen, manifestly, had won a battle. But their victory of the moment could not save them from eventual defeat. Unlike their employers, they felt the lash of hunger; despite the blows they dealt at the Company, they could not hold out indefinitely. On November 21, Frick cabled triumphantly to Carnegie: "Strike officially declared off yesterday. Our victory is now complete and most gratifying."

Thus, for a generation, union labor ceased to be a problem for the steel magnates, and the twelve hour day and reduced wages reigned in all their glory.

In a different area, the Carnegie works were not superior to a form of fraud that had become almost orthodox in the case of Vanderbuilt and many others. To cheat on federal supplies, evidently, was not regarded as dishonest; it was merely good business. However, the report of the Chief of the Ordnance Bureau took a different view when he reported on some armor plate supplied by Carnegie's lieutenant Charles M. Schwab:

"Mr. Schwab admits that the ends of the pontoon plates were treated to such a temperature as would draw the temper and afterwards were retempered without reheating and tempering the whole body of the plates, which treatment is not only expressly forbidden by the instructions of the bureau, but also is manifestly improper. . . .

"There is nothing in Mr. Schwab's statement which would modify the bureau's opinion that fraud was practiced at the works of the Carnegie Steel Company, with the knowledge and under the direction of the superintendent and other leading men." [10]

But was this with the knowledge and under the direction of Carnegie himself? It would be no more illogical to ask whether the activities of Frick in the Homestead strike had been a secret to Carnegie. Not all the facts, unfortunately, were subjected to the light of day; but we know that on December 20, 1893, several months before the public learned at all about the frauds, Carnegie paid a visit to President Cleveland, and thereupon made a public appeal to his fellow Republicans to support the President's favorite measure, the Wilson-Gorman tariff bill—an appeal that aroused amazement and indignation among the steel magnte's old associates and allies. Three weeks later, writing to Secretary of the Navy Herbert, the President glossed over the "alleged irregularities" in the quality of the armor plate, and suggested a forfeiture by the Carnegie Company of 10 per cent of the value of the metal (namely, $140,484.94) as a proper penalty. It may be merely coincidental that this light tap on the wrist was the only chastisement administered to the great industrialist at the very time when Carnegie had rallied to the President's political support.

Nevertheless, Carnegie and his associates did not entirely escape rebuke. A congressional committee of investigation held them to be guilty; and various organs of public opinion spoke out, as when an editorial in the *New York Tribune* excoriated Carnegie and Frick as "sordid and ignoble," and went on to say: "In palming off those defective and inadequate armor plates upon the government they were imperilling the lives of thousands of our seamen and jeopardizing the nation's honor and welfare, but they were making money. . . . The expenditure of money in ostentatious charity and beneficence will not excuse the shameful means by which that money was acquired. The relinquishment of a moiety of plunder does not condone the theft."

V

A celebrated contemporary of Carnegie was his fellow industrialist, John D. Rockefeller, Sr., who achieved fame while piling up probably the largest fortune any man had ever accumulated. Even during his lifetime, Rockefeller was a controversial figure; both bouquets and brickbats were thrown at him. In an article published in 1881, "The Story of a Great Monopoly," and thirteen years later in his book *Wealth Against Commonwealth,* Henry Demarest Lloyd assailed Rockefeller with more fury than justice, publishing some charges that later proved to have been based on fiction. In 1904, Ida M. Tarbell came forth with her two-volume *The History of the Standard Oil Company,* in which she attributed the growth of the great corporation mainly to special privilege, intimidation, and fraud. Two years later, a more virulent attack was launched by Thomas W. Lawson's volume, *Frenzied Finance.* And attacks have continued to be printed, both here and abroad. Thus H. G. Wells, in a book issued in 1932, declares of Rockefeller that there is "legal proof . . . that his business methods have included lying, perjury, the bearing of false witness against his neighbors, widespread bribery, the corruption of other men's servants and of public officials, the use of threats, and the obtaining of illegal drawbacks and rebates. His whole career indeed has displayed a very complete disregard for the rights or interests of anyone opposed to himself and his projects."[11]

In this indictment, as in most of the attacks, there are elements of truth; yet any such summary gives a distorted picture. If we fasten our eyes upon the man Rockefeller, we can no more see the devil incarnate than we can identify an angel in white robes: rather, we observe a typical product of modern business, who avails himself more thoroughly and more successfully than most others of the business methods, the business *mores,* and the business philosophy of his day. In some ways, he was a model among rich men. He lived with comparative simplicity; he gave copiously to philanthropic enterprises when others, such as Jay Gould, refused all calls for charity; he was evidently sincere in his religious convictions (as were, strangely, a number of the most remorseless tycoons); and he was energetic in collecting funds for the Church.

This harvester of a fantastic fortune was not born with the proverbial "silver spoon." At sixteen he took a job as a bookkeeper at Cleveland at $15 a month, though eventually he rose to the heights of $50. That he was already money-minded was shown by the parsimony which enabled him to save $800 in three years out of his small pay. One should not place too much emphasis upon the remark he allegedly made to a schoolmate upon seeing the house of a rich man: "When I grow up, I want to be worth $100,000"—how many boys have had similar dreams! A bit more significant, as shedding unconscious light upon his aspirations, was the jubilant exclamation that once burst from him when, as a young man, he heard some favorable news: "I'm bound to be rich! *Bound to be rich!"*

Rockefeller's golden road to wealth, as everyone knows, was smoothed by a black fuel spouting from the earth's interior. His acquisitions had their base, first, in a natural resource that neither he nor any man created; and, secondly, in his exploitation of that resource at the very time when it was about to rise into world importance. Had the resource not existed, or had society not possessed the will or the mechanism to utilize it, Rockefeller either would have found wealth through some other channel, or would have remained poor. But the significant thing is the use he made of petroleum in achieving riches. For all his religious convictions, his ethics did not exclude sharp practice. Consistently his efforts were bent toward creating a monopoly; and on the way to that monopoly he picked up whatever special privileges and exerted whatever pressures he could. One of his favorite methods was to obtain rebates, as when he secured from the Lake Shore Railroad a secret pay-back fifteen times as large as that openly allowed the smaller refiners—which put his adversaries at such a disadvantage that soon they had dwindled in number from thirty to ten; twenty had

either closed their doors or accepted amalgamation with the Rockefeller group.

When in 1870 Rockefeller and his associates formed the Standard
Oil Company of Ohio, one of their cardinal principles was the elimination of competition, first in the Cleveland area and then elsewhere; competitors must join Rockefeller or be annihilated. In this there appears
to have been little more than a wolf-slash-wolf attitude, though it was
possible for Rockefeller to rationalize and hold that competition meant
inefficiency, and that only the efficient deserved to survive However,
some of the inefficiency of Rockefeller's rivals was Rockefeller-induced.
How could they equal him in efficiency when he coerced the railroads
into making more favorable rebate arrangements with him than with
his antagonists? and when Standard claimed monopilies, including the
exclusive right to export oil?

One of Rockefeller's schemes for self-advancement was through the
pleasantly named South Improvement Company, which represented a
device to take control of refineries and their outlets by a system of
rebates in which Standard Oil was greatly favored and was even to
receive a "drawback" taken out of the high rates paid by its rivals.
As an engine for strangling competition, the South Improvement Company has rarely been surpassed. Few commentators can be found to de-
fend it. Stewart H. Holbrook expresses a majority opinion: "The
South Improvement Company was surely the coldest, the most naked
effort at dry-land piracy that had been conceived." [12]   And Allan Nevins, in his restrained and carefully reasoned two-volume work in
which he is often an apologist for Rockefeller, speaks of "the savage
and destructive drawbacks specified in the South Improvement contracts" and goes on to remark:

"To give a large shipper a rebate was standard practice; but to pay
him in addition part of the higher rate imposed upon his rivals—this
was as devastating as it was unusual. It was utterly indefensible; and
Rockefeller committed one of the great errors of his career when he
hurriedly aligned himself with such an arrangement." [13]

Elsewhere Nevins adds this comment:

"The Standard Oil by 1879 held a position new in economic history.
It had attained monopolistic power in a great industrial field by its
own efforts, and not by state grant, patent rights, exclusive control
of raw materials, or special geographical position. The means by which
it had gained this power offered wide scope for criticism. It had been
ruthless at times in exploiting its advantages in transportation rates;
it had frequently been tyrannical in making competitors 'sweat' or

'feel sick'; it had employed deception in a reprehensible manner . . .
As for the end-result, the monopoly itself, the healthy instinct of Eng-
lish-speaking peoples since Tudor days had been to detest monopoly,
and the stronger the monopoly the greater was the detestation." [14]

There are other indictments to be made. Standard Oil resorted to
espionage—not, indeed, the only large business firm that descended to
this method, though it outdid its competitors in this as in most things.
Again, it sometimes accomplished its ends under a mask of deception,
employing dummy companies; and in the case of the competing Tidewater Pipe Line Company, it first tried to force the concern into a re-
ceivership by means of a stockholder whom it supplied with funds,
then obtained control of the Pipe Line's officers at a stockholder's
meeting and secured a contract reserving to itself 88½ per cent of
Tidewater's business.

All the while, it resorted to the same ruthless practices in rate-fixing
as we have seen in the case of the railroads. With the aim of driving
out competitors, it would reduce prices in a particular district; and
having gained a monopoly, it would impose whatever rates it pleased.
The good old principle of the railroad marauders, "Charge what the
traffic will bear!", was evidently appreciated by the heads of Standard Oil. Only by being freehanded with its charges could the Company have achieved dividends such as it piled up during the Nine-
ties. These, according to the report of an Industrial Commission appointed by President McKinley, reached from $11,000,000 to $12,000,-
000 in the years between 1890 and 1894, $16,500,000 in 1895, and
$30,000,000 in 1896; even in depression periods, the net earnings varied
between 11.4 and 15 per cent.

That such returns could be gleaned without overcharges appears impossible. How, after all, expect an unregulated company to refrain from
overcharges, when the orthodox doctrine of *laissez faire* proclaimed that
any returns whatever were legitimate and in the public interest? while
the entire individualistic philosophy of modern business declared that
a man should take what he could, when he could, and how he could—
at least, within the limits of the law.

Doubtless it is in part a question of whether one looks from inside or
outside. To the world, a given act many appear reprehensible; and yet
the doer, within the warped circle of his own perceptions, may see it
as natural and unobjectionable. We have evidence that this was sometimes true in Rockefeller's case. In the matter of the notorious South
Improvement Company, he could take a position of high moral rec-
titude and be sincerely outraged by the attacks upon him. He had dis-

cussed the matter with his religious-minded wife, who joined him in seeing nothing wrong with his course. "We will do right and not be nervous or troubled by what the papers say," he wrote to Mrs. Rockefeller . . . "and leave future events in the business to demonstrate that our intentions and plans were just and warranted." The irony about these remarks, an irony that makes one at once want to laugh and weep, is that they were undoubtedly sincere. The financier simply could not look at his own actions except through the twist of his own personality. To him, as he stood on the inside looking out, those actions were sound and right. He was unable to see that others, as they stood outside looking in, could view his behavior as crooked or dishonorable. And so, though in his own mind he was a moral as well as a religious man, he could proceed blandly with his unfair treatment of competitors.

On his behalf it can be said that he regarded his wealth as a great trust, though he rather naively believed it confided to him by God (the old idea of the divine selection of kings). He appears to have realized that his hundreds of millions were more than any man by his own exertions could earn, more than any man deserved; and in giving out his funds, in establishing foundations for beneficent ends and dispensing the huge sum of $550,000,000, he surpassed all the other great capitalists as a philanthropist, except possibly Carnegie (and even Carnegie did not have so many millions to give away). Nevertheless, the benign use of funds does not justify their illegitimate accrual. One cannot but wonder at the ethics and the code of thought of a businessman who would ruin defenseless rivals and then magnanimously bequeath his ill-gotten gains to public causes. If we could penetrate beneath the quirks of Rockefeller's mind, we might be able to understand the inconsistencies of many another financier.

VI

It was only human that men like Rockefeller, who proclaimed the virtue of monopoly, should think only of situations in which they themselves would have the controlling hand. Naturally, one asks how they would have reacted to combines in which others wielded the whip.

Nevertheless, there are certain undoubted virtues that help to offset the obvious vices of monopolies, and not the least is that they eliminate the competition in which rival businessmen slash and tear at one another like embattled dogs. A long record of remorseless strife proves, if proof were needed, that ordinary business competitors are no more virtuous than monopolists; both, in fact, subscribe to the same business code, and therefore are on the same moral plane. This was shown, for example, by the very men whom Rockefeller drove to the wall. In the story of Standard Oil as told by Ida M. Tarbell, who is inclined to make Rockefeller the villain, we see that his adversaries were no better than he. They sought to keep up the price of crude oil by restricting production; they were willing to side with Standard Oil against the public if that seemed in their own interest; they were on occasion not superior to resorting to sabotage against independent producers. The virtue of Standard Oil was that it could hold together while its competitors could not; but the latter's lack of cohesion is no proof of a higher morality. Over both sides we can see the shadow of the same selfish, the same anti-social desires.

And something similar is true of most other American financial leaders of the nineteenth and twentieth century: Harriman, Armour, Morgan, Du Pont, Mellon, Guggenheim, etc. It is true that some, such as Ford, have been unassailed by scandal; while we can make no such claim for certain others such as Insull, whose activities shook the entire American economy and cost American investors almost $750,-000,000. But whether they were honest or dishonest, whether their methods were those of brigands or of rarely efficient businessmen, those capitalists as a group evoke some disquieting questions.

Why is it that the great names in American industry and finance have been so numerous, whereas during the same period there have been few if any great names in art, music, literature, or philosophy? Is it that the moneyed leaders represent the standards admired by the majority of Americans? Is it that the opportunities in money-making existed because the ways of the money-makers were generally approved and courted? And it is that those who followed the arts and philosophy were not similarly encouraged because they were not running with the currents of the popular mind? May one not suppose that a society, like an individual, will develop the tendencies inherent in it? And if its most conspicuous citizens embrace the religion of acquisitiveness, then it it not because society itself is ruled by the religion of acquisitiveness?

Fundamentally, not public spirit but the spirit of self dominated these men. And was any country, in the deeper sense, ever made greater or more civilized by the spirit of self? It may grow in energy and expand in power; but energy and power are not in themselves civilized forces. Something deeper is needed, something reflecting the heart and soul of man, something such as produced the great flowering of art and literature and thought in ancient Athens, and the artistic burgeoning of Florence, and the literature of Elizabethan England. The American financiers, without having any real artistic appreciation, would play at being patrons or collectors of art; they would regale themselves in rococo palaces, with statues paintings, vases, and rugs expensively imported from Europe or even from Asia; they would go to such fantastic extremes as to set diamonds in their teeth, or to wrap cigarettes in hundred-dollar bills; they would upon occasion pay $65,-000 for a dressing table or $75,000 for a pair of opera glasses, or provide the ladies with gold-embroidered gowns—all in the tradition of the moneyed classes of the decadent days of Rome, or of the France of Louis XIV or Louis XV. But such ostentation is not civilization; it is the caricature of civilization.

Hence, when all is said, the financiers leave one unsatisfied. When all is said, one feels that they failed, because they did little to touch the human spirit, little to develop the relations of man with man, little to improve or expand the mind or to extend culture. There are many who feel what Frederick Lewis Allen has expressed in a trenchant summary of "the lords of creation":

"Through the story of these men's adventures and exploits there runs the thrill of conflict, of immense tasks boldly accomplished and emergencies boldly met, of a continent subdued to the needs of industry; yet the truly heroic note is missing. The note of self-forgetfulness is missing. The dollar is omnipresent, and its smell pervades every episode.

"The men of Wall Street wanted money and got it. All the explanations and extenuations, however genuine, are but accessories after that fact. One wonders what might have been the destiny of America if men of the majestic force of Morgan, the brilliance of Harriman, the utter concentration of Rockefeller, the generosity of Schiff, had been ruled by the disinterestedness of the scientist in his laboratory." [15]

XV

MAMMON, MIDAS, AND TOMORROW

In an intricately branching network, the meshes of modern acquisitiveness reach in every direction and involve almost all things. Within the limits of one volume, accordingly, it would be impossible to consider every aspect of the subject. We might, for example have lingered over political corruption, and the influence of wealth in courts, legislative chambers, high executive departments, and political campaigns. We might have explored the implications of the fact that the higher echelons of the American diplomatic services are necessarily occupied by persons of means. We might have discussed the place, influence, and methods of modern advertising, and its cunning stimulation of acquisitive desires. We might have looked into the subject of the adulteration of foods and drugs, and of inadequately tested and falsely attested patent medicines. We might have glanced at the merchants of human bodies and souls, at commercialized prostitution, and at the various phases of the trade in narcotics (which, to be sure, we have observed in a few of its aspects). We might have noted the spread of alcohol and of alcoholism, and traced the connection between the growth of the traffic and the profit motive. We might have scrutinized the relationship of Mammon to gambling, smuggling, counterfeiting, trading in contraband goods, and organized racketeering and crime. We might have dwelt upon the cornering of markets by self-seeking individuals or groups; and we might have witnessed the encouragement of armaments and of arms races by international cartels.

Then, concentrating upon our domestic economy, we might have remarked the toleration of virtual peonage among migratory laborers, not only Americans but importees from Puerto Rico and Mexico, many of whom have had to live under serf-like conditions while great apple growers and other capitalists profited from their squalor and misery. We might have pursued the labor unions into their day of power, and shown how, having reached a position that labor has never before enjoyed in all historic time, they have succumbed to the philosophy of their one-time exploiters, and in many cases have been ruled by the very acquisitiveness they once berated. We might have dwelt upon the economic cycle of "boom" and depression, and its effects upon millions of the unemployed and underemployed; and we might have considered the plundering influence of deliberately encouraged inflation. Or, turning our gaze abroad, we might have shown how the acquisitiveness of the capitalistic West has been transferred to the Communistic world, concentrating its gaze upon material possessions —even in China, where, until the advent of the present regime, the philosophy of the *Gen* steadily resisted the concentration of wealth. Or we might have pored over the example of Japan, its non-competitive pre-industrial communal life, and the rise of brokers and financiers at the cost of acute popular distress, when a money-economy supplanted the rice currency at the end of the seventeenth century.

Beyond all these, and not less important than any of these, we might have considered the portentous subject of the squandering of natural resources, the devastation of forests, the wastage of watersheds, the pollution of streams and lakes, the destruction of wildlife, the ruination of the topsoil, the exhaustion of irreplaceable minerals, the conversion of grass-lands into dust-bowls and deserts, by which the greed of the few and the principle of private profit are permitted to loot the human heritage and to impoverish mankind for all time.

All these subjects would be interesting to explore; yet none of them would essentially alter the picture. In our glances at acquisitiveness as we have followed it from land to land and from age to age, we have noted its typical phases, and all its characteristic effects. We began with primitive communities, and saw that acquisitions do not mean the same to them as to us: that, indeed, sometimes the purpose of primitive getting is to give away, while sharp property lines are mostly unfamiliar if not unknown. We proceeded to the dawn civilizations, and found that communal ownership existed in varying degrees in many lands, including Egypt and Peru. We traced the rise of the acquisitive attitude of mind, and saw how in part it had its roots in magic and religion, and in part was connected with the spur of adventure, and in part, again, originated in the ferocious desires of the brigand and the pirate, whose get-rich-quick cravings were aroused by the possessions of settled communities.

Throughout the ages, as our whole discussion has shown, the tactics o fthe god Mammon have changed but little. We first see his hand in external warfare, in rapacious thrusts for land, slaves, and booty, as in the conflicts that exhausted the Assyrian empire, and the Syracusan expedition that went so far toward undermining the power of Athens, and the Roman campaigns that devitalized the provinces for the enrichment of the conqueror. Next we find that, within the nations, the cult of the money-god has been insidiously elevated above all other authority. He has captivated the mind until the quest of beauty and enlightenment has been obscured; he has bribed the judge on the bench and the legislator in the assembly; he has dug gulfs between possessors and non-possessors; he has encouraged a luxury and licentiousness that, on the one hand, have sapped morals and constructive endeavor, and, on the other hand, have brought deprivation and misery to multitudes. We have seen all these tendencies in the ancient world, with its omnipresent slave system; in the feudal world, with its vast cleavage between baron and serf; in the medieval Church, with its bishops whose gilded pomp contrasts with the rags of the average parishioner; in the early modern world, with its pre-machine industrialism and the growth of large fortunes side by side with a landless, half-starved proletariat; in the Spanish colonies in America, and in European imperialism in Africa, with the great proprietors who trample the native; in the Spanish and Dutch empires, where self-seeking groups bring ruin to the whole; in pre-revolutionary France and Russia, and most of all in that universe of mechanized industry born in the eighteenth century.

In all these cases, the outstanding fact is that the covetousness of the few dealt disaster to the many—and that, in the long run, the advantage even to the few was illusory. The empire of Cathage failed in large part because her citizens, with their moneyed outlook, refused reasonable concessions to her dependencies; the empire of Athens failed for similar reasons, and her domestic regime broke down when her citizens let the hope of individual gain prevail over their earlier ideals of the State; the empire of Rome was emasculated, among other things, by the merciless exploitation of the provincials, the debasing effects of wealth at home, the venality of administrators, the predatory taxes that ruined agriculture, the unbridled expenditures that bled the energies of cities, the loss of civic pride and virtue amid the orgies of self-indulgence, the decay of the military forces beneath the heel of avarice and corruption, the harnessing of the burdens of the rich upon the bended backs of the poor, and the rise of a hierarchic order of landowners while indigence spread among the masses. Similarly, the medieval Church planted the seeds of her own decline in the wealth that made her authority material rather than spiritual; the feudal lords, by their greedy oppressiveness, frustrated the agricultural development which they sorely needed, sapped their own strength in parasitic warfare, and aroused a spirit of opposition that pointed toward the end of feudalism. In much the same way, again, the financial princes of Genoa and Venice, the Dutch merchant kings, the sheep-

herders of the Spanish *Mesta,* and the nobles and higher clergy of
the old regime of France, all represented privileged classes that,
thanks to a keen regard for profit, enacted the part of blind Samsons
bringing the temple walls of civilization down upon their own unwary
heads.

And recent forces have not been dissimilar. The slave-driver of
Babylon has reappeared in the mines and mills of our early industrialism, where men drudged for their masters' enrichment, not because the
law said they must, but because they had no choice; even in modern
America, where labor in general has a privileged place, we find the
old-time driven wretch among depressed classes such as the migratory
farm laborers.

The proconsul of the Roman provinces, who bled his dependencies
white, has reappeared under other names in more than one colony of
modern Europe; the warrior of Ashur-bani-apal, slaying in the name
of gainful imperialism, has left a trail of blood. And the minor actors
in the theater of Mammon—how many their resurrections! The heritage hunter of the Roman Empire; the patron haughtily dispensing
gratuities to fawning clients; the Grecian advocate secretly accepting
gifts from private sources; the Roman office-holder who grows fat in
ways unrecognized by law; the wealthy landowner exacting tax exemptions while pennies are extracted from the impoverished by means of
the rack and scourge; the viceroy of Heaven, who distributes the favors of the Almighty in return for cash; the monopolist of the medieval
guilds, who drives independent labor to destitution; the baron of the
modern slave trade, the financial wizard who transmutes the blood of
captive Indians into the gold of the mines, the French duke who revels
on royal bounties while the peasant starves, the destroyer of forests
and watersheds who draws profits from the ruin of the future—all
these have made their bow once more, in slightly altered costumes
and under a slightly different light.

There is, however, one significant change: the scope of the drama
has been widened, the dimensions of the stage enlarged, the energy
and powers of the actors vastly augmented. In *kind,* there is little difference between the handiwork of Mammon now and throughout the
ages; in range, degree, and potentiality, we have advanced by mighty
bounds. And this is because industrialism has accelerated all pre-existing forces, and filled the world with unprecedented powers both for
construction and for destruction. Into the hands of man it has put a
tool that has magnified his dominant tendencies, somewhat as the invention of gunpowder (and later of nuclear explosives) has magnified

the potential deadliness of warfare. If those dominant tendencies are creative and humane, humanity must benefit immensely; but if they are repressive and cruel, humanity must suffer crippling blows. And this means that the need for regenerative action is more pressing today than at any previous period.

Beneath the history of Mammon, an ironic and contradictory fact may be noted. Though long revered as the god of wealth, he does not represent actual wealth at all. The true riches of mankind—its art, its poetry, its music, its esthetic appreciations, its extension of knowledge, the insight of its philosophers, the sympathy of its friendships, the joy of creative endeavor—are such as Mammon either overlooks entirely or tends to destroy. For gold in itself has no value except that which the thoughts of men give it; gold, throughout the ages, has been no more than the means to an end, the means to an ampler and fuller life, in which the things of man's mind and spirit may have wider room for expression. But since men throughout the ages have mistaken gold for an end in itself, they have been content merely to acquire it; and from this shortsightedeness a host of evils has arisen, including all those perversions of greed which have caused slave-lashes to raise blisters on cringing black shoulders and shouts to ring out in lockouts and strikes, and which have wiped the green growth from eroded hill-lands and from silted tidal miles.

II

If our discussion has served any clear purpose, it has helped to dispel the widely held view that acquisitiveness is inherent in human nature. A moment's consideration will tell us that if acquisitiveness as we know it were inherent, it would manifest itself in unvarying or almost unvarying patterns, as among animals and birds—as when for example, the squirrel hoards its nuts in the age-old manner of its kind, or when the woodpecker secretes its acorns in the trees, always in the same general way, by the same tapping methods. Such acquisitiveness is of a special type, is species-wide, and is not altered by the whims of individuals or by social traditions.

But quite otherwise is the case among human beings. The Indian of the Pacific Northwest, when he gathers blankets and "coppers" so as to give them away in the exhibitionist orgy of the "potlatch," does not provide a parallel to the American loan agent who charges high interest for the sake of profit. The Zuni who esteems family connections above wealth, but desires property for his religious ceremonials, is not at one with the modern businessman who schemes, connives, bickers, and bribes to get money for its own sake. The islander of the Pacific, engaged in a never-ceasing exchange of necklaces and bracelets that revolve about ideas of magic and of prestige, has nothing in common with the pirate chief or the captain of a slave raid; the Maori, who robs his unprotesting neighbor as a form of punishment and is himself robbed in turn, has few notions as to private property in common with the modern householder. Similarly, the savage warrior who never holds the enemy territory which he overruns, and the tribesman who sees no harm in taking his kindred's property without permission or in having his kindred take his belongings, are responding to concepts of ownership foreign to the modern world. Acquisitiveness among them all does exist; but it is a different force among different peoples; it is shaped by tribal patterns, conventions, and codes of thought, and cannot be considered inherent unless in the most generalized way.

In view of all this, should we not reassess our attitude? Should we not cease to assume that human nature compels the thrust-and-slash of a remorseless competition, in which each man will inevitably take all he can? Should we not recognize that, owing to long-developed social habits along with the special conditions of a great material abundance, we modern Americans have exalted acquisitiveness to a pedestal perhaps never before known? When we look into the past, we find that as soon as men were freed from social restraint and allured by material riches, they would usually help themselves to whatever they could, with the amorality of small children seizing bonbons in a pastry shop. And yet, despite the great number of plunderers and pillagers sulking across the ages, the differences between today and yesterday are glaring. Trade, industry, and finance have had but a low estate in other lands and eras, as we may observe in the ancient Greek scorn of the businessman, and in the medieval churchly decrees against interest-taking, and in the English contempt for the trader, which has continued until comparatively recent times. But in our own age, as I have ramarked—at least, in the United States—the wealthy man has moved into the blank spaces where a titled aristocracy once strutted; a nobility of wealth has been formed, glittering in its palaces like the dukes, marquises, and princes of old. All this has tended to shed glory not only upon the self-made patrician, but upon the riches that paved his way to honor; and the riches have therefore become more of an object in themselves.

But in another, and perhaps even more vital respect, today differs from yesterday. Formerly the gulf between the common man and the person of means was like that between the earth and the moon. The serf, the peasant, the industrial worker, the tradesman, the artisan, the house servant knew that he could no more pass the barriers than he could change the color of his eyes. And this realization, whether or not it was otherwise salutary, did at least bring the sobriety of resignation; did at least restrain popular greed. For while men may at times indulge in gainless dreams, they will not waste much of their life energy in reaching for the rings of Saturn. Petty thievery, petty cunning, petty fraud might indeed continue; but there would be no general concentration on the idea of wealth. Today, however, all is changed. Today, in America, scarcely a boy is not brought up with the notion that he can grow rich. Too many, moreover, are taken with the belief that it is not only possible to become Morgan or Rockefeller the Second, but that this is the most desirable, the most admirable, and in fact the only worthy attainment. In other words, we have something far beyond mere avarice; we have a cultivated creed of acquisitiveness, and this creed has not only possessed the more favored groups, but has percolated down to the majority. In this respect, we differ from all past ages. Largely for this reason, acquisitiveness has become a problem such as the world has not known before.

III

Like all orthodox religions, modern acquisitiveness is built about a series of dogmas, which the worshippers accept as truths above reason and beyond questioning. And the first of these dogmas proclaims that acquisitions are worthy in themselves and for themselves, regardless of any further object, such as the spreading of enlightenment or the relief of poverty. Consequently, any man who accumulates a fortune is likewise worthy. The mere piling up of riches is regarded as a laudable feat, no matter what wasteful, injudicious, or injurious use is made of the wealth (so long, in any case, as the possessor keeps free of the law). The extent of a man's achievement therefore is easily reckoned: it is measured by his assets. He is appraised not for what he is, nor even for what he does, but chiefly for what he *has*.

The second dogma of modern acquisitiveness follows from the first. Since the important thing is *to have*, the question of how a man gets his riches is subordinate to the fact that he does get them. What counts, in other words, is not the means to a fortune so much as the fortune itself This does not imply that crude, raw methods such as

gangsterism and murder are not frowned upon. But we are inclined to
see nothing wrong in phenomena that a less acquiescent age might dis-
approve—such, for example, as nepotism in high office, expensive lob-
bies to influence legislators, privately paid expenses accounts for public
officials, and costly gifts to functionaries able to direct important executive decisions. When a man is immensely rich, few are so churlish as
to refuse him homage because of intrusive questions as to how he may
have gouged his employees, fleeced his creditors, tricked his business
rivals, or bribed, intimidated, or bought his way.

Just as the second dogma of acquisitiveness flows from the first, so
the third proceeds from the second: that, on the highway to wealth,
the public interest is secondary. Here we have an unsavory survival
from Adam Smith: the doctrine that what is for my good as I enrich
myself is for the good of everyone, which makes it unnecessary for me
to consider the general weal. This, of course, is highly reassuring as
I try to scrub the reek of tainted coins from my hands; and since I am
fanatically devoted to my own good, I can look upon myself as a man
of noble principles, who is furthering everybody's interests at the same
time as I take care of myself. True, it may not do to peer at the facts
too minutely, or to ask how *you* have been benefited, let us say, by my
monopoly of land that would normally have been yours, or what it has
gained the community to be stripped of its woods, beaches, or oil
rights. But then, of course, one never peers too closely at a dogma—
not, as least, when it agrees with one's preconceived views.

The acceptance of the three dogmas, along with a whole network of
related beliefs, has had curious results. It has, for example, made possible our orthodox economics, which postulates that if a man has three
oranges and can make less money by selling all three than by destroying one and selling the other two at higher prices, then he should by all
means destroy one. Thus we have the economics of scarcity, which is
unconcerned with the fact that the destroyed orange might benefit
some man, woman, or child, who now may be unable to afford any
fruit at all. And thus, at various times, we have witnessed phenomena
such as the dumping of edible fishes into the sea, the uprooting of
peach trees, and the slaughter of little pigs. Thus, similarly, we have
the strange problem of food surpluses in a world where a major portion
of the consumers are chronically undernourished. Here, certainly, is
something topsy-turvy; on a planet with some ruler other than the
money standard, it would not be impossible for unwanted grain to
reach hungry mouths.

The dogmas of acquisitiveness go far toward explaining all those freaks of wealth which we have observed. They tell us why a man like Carnegie, who at times showed a sense of public responsibility, could wage war against his workers, whom he underpaid and overworked while piling up millions far beyond his capacity to use. They help us to see why Huntington and his railroad partners could connive, cheat, buy legislators, rule by the strong arm, and defraud and dispossess helpless settlers on valley farms. They illuminate the maneuvers of Jay Gould to corner the gold supply of the United States, regardless of the effects on the many whom his strategy shook like a tornado. They underscore the remorselessness of Vanderbilt and of Rockefeller in driving out competitors, the peculations of Insull by which so many were ruined, the ruffianism of the minions of John Jacob Astor, the violence of management in some of the great strikes such as that of the Pullman workers in 1894. The dogmas of acquisitiveness make it easy to understand why political fraud has been common, why "conflicts of interest" in government have been scandalously frequent yet have so often been glossed over or condoned, why adulteration of food and drugs and reckless use of insecticides and weedkillers have not only occurred but have been insufficiently regulated, why unchecked and highly questionable statements as to advertised nostrums are permitted over radio and television, why polluters and destroyers of the earth's natural heritage have been tolerated and in some cases favored, and why lobbyists for wealthy interests have been trying and even now try to obtain for their own selfish purposes whatever they can still monopolize of the surviving natural resources in woodlands, grazing lands, and minerals.

Such results are, of course, all in accordance with the dogmas of acquisitiveness and should cause no surprise.

IV

In the modern world, as already suggested, the greed for possessions does not explain all so-called acquisitiveness; more potent elements have been supplied by civilization. There is, for example, the fact that in many circles money has become the standard of social attainment. Ambitious men, more eager for self-exaltation than for material gain, concentrate upon material gain for the sake of prestige—much in the spirit of the Crow Indian who seeks reputation by a "coup" against the enemy; or in the mood of the Zulu warrior who sets out to kill a foe so as to win the distinction of being truly a man. Whatever society most esteems, whatever it honors most, will be zealously sought; and this

is true whether the means be the severed heads of unoffending neighbors, the display of athletic prowess, or the accumulation of money.
In our own civilization, it merely happens that accumulation is the best
acknowledged means to recognition. The man who seeks a fortune does
not necessarily covet it for itself any more than the scalping Indian
values his bloody trophies for their intrinsic worth.

This is to say that we have come far, very far from the simple
acquisitiveness of the primitive who piles up roots and nuts so that he
may not starve. Acquisitiveness for us has largely lost its economic aspects; it has become a social requirement, a social game in which the
successful player scores dollars somewhat as the baseball "star" scores
hit and runs. And since the score is everything and at the same time
nothing (being but an abstraction in man's mind), we have entered a
realm of make-believe, a fairyland whose heroes fend with shadows for
phantom stakes. Thus the practical becomes the impractical; and the
fortune-seekers wrestle with one another in dominions as far from reality as fabled Camelot or the Castle of Shalott. This is true of all wealth
in its upper brackets—wealth that outdistances the capacity for economic consumption, and so accumulates merely as digits in an account
book and as points in the contest of prestige and power. And such
wealth includes all the great fortunes, all the empyrean of higher finance. The exploration of those stratospheric regions does indeed have
economic effects upon society, and upon the unfortunates brushed
aside in the contest; but such results are merely incidental.

In another way, also our search for profits is at once non-economic
and possessed of a little of the dreamlike, upsidedown qualitiy of *Alice
in Wonderland.* For we moderns, in our money-courting, are by no
means concerned only with the satisfaction of needs, as would be true
were we guided by simple economic law; we are also largely occupied
with the creation of needs. To early man, who in this respect differed
but little from the birds and beasts, life must have been a continuous
battle for the fundamentals of food and shelter. The contest could truly
be called economic, since it aimed to satisfy man's basic needs.
Throughout the ages the poor sheepherder, the farmer, the villager, has
not risen much above the primitive level; his activities have centered
about the satisfaction of needs and therefore have likewise served
economic purposes. But among the wealthy of all ages, this economic
underpinning has been largely forgotten in favor of the creation of
needs—a fact as true of the Roman in his marble-walled villa as of the
eighteenth century Russian in his serf-crowded mansion and of the
lords and ladies of the court of Marie Antoinette. But never has this

been more fantastically the case than since the rise of machine production, which has multiplied the quantity and variety of factory output, and so has created new objects of desire.

We all know what has been happening. To find a market for the new object of desire, business has aimed to increase consumption—to increase it on the basis not of needs, but of desires. It has aimed—to offer but one example—not to supply cotton stockings for the patched daughter of the sharecropper, but to provide nylon for her more fortunate sisters. It has set out to create new wants, regardless of the wants still unsatisfied; and it has schemed to achieve its end by the dazzle of advertisement, coupled with an extension of credit that tempts people to buy what they cannot afford by means of money which they do not possess. Thus civilization has come to be dominated by the psychology of the salesman; this is apparent even in popular speech, in which we talk not of teaching or instilling ideas, but of *selling* and *buying* them. In essence, salesmanship means the breaching of the barriers of desire; you do not have to sell a famished man a crust. But the man who already has bread enough must indeed be sold. Or he will have to be persuaded to throw out his good loaves and buy cake, if only to outshine his neighbors. Thus society, no longer intent on satisfying natural wants, creates artificial wants by salesmanship, though it may incidentally cause good and useful objects to be discarded. And this is to reverse the natural economic order, and to place destruction above production, or else to elevate production as the basic need rather than as a means to the satisfaction of needs.

Not that this is at all illogical under a system of production for profit. But production for profit has caught us in a trap; it is a labyrinth whose entrance all men can see, but whose exit no man can discover. To support its structure, elaborate ramifications have been developed in industry and finance—complicated factories, freight terminals, storage and sales facilities, and transportation and communication systems, involving enormous upkeep and interest charges; and multitudes have been trained in specialized lines, which they cannot abandon without acute strain of readjustment, wrenched lives, and often irreparable loss. Not only that, but a network of smaller industries, upon which other hosts depend, is founded upon each larger enterprise.

No doubt the most obvious case is that of automobile manufacturing, by which the nation's entire economy is affected. Consider what is involved: not only the hundreds of thousands of workers and their families, and the hundreds of thousands or millions of stockholders in the main corporations, but also workers, officials, and stockholders in related industries: the steel industry, the coal industry, the railroad industry, the glass industry, the radio industry, the chromium industry, etc. But we cannot stop even here: there are also the dealers and salesmen in ten thousand cities, the service station attendants, the garagemen and mechanics, the drivers of trucks and other commercial vehicles, the builders and maintainers of highways, along with a horde of tradesmen and others connected in various ways with motor supplies and servicing. Thus, as we can see, a great automobile empire has been established. What if there should be a malfunctioning in that empire? Simultaneously, there would be a malfunctioning in the entire country. It is largely to avoid such a calamity that we have constant sales campaigns, constant paid efforts to whip up desires in the public, yearly new models not for the sake of better products but for the sake of sales appeal, constantly increased power through the result is a litter of bleeding corpses on the highways, and perpetual turnover of serviceable cars in favor of shinier and glossier brand-new substitutes.

What does all this mean? That the automobile industry—and the same may be said of other great industries—has introduced a dangerous specialization into civilization. And this specialization is irreversible or almost so, and hence tends to counteract the protection which nature has given to man as a species by making him generalized. We have, it is important to note, no pronounced physical specialization such as the long neck of the giraffe, the insect-licking tongue of the ant-eater, the armor of the porcupine, the web-spinning mechanism of the spider, or the blood-sucking devices of the flea. Being unspecialized, man has been adaptible; he is rarely caught in the *cul-de-sac* of an environment, but has usually been able to meet conditions by altering with them, instead of perishing with his changing surroundings, as would be the case, let us say, with a potato bug if potatoes ceased to be grown, or with an oak-leaf caterpillar after all the oaks had been felled. To his generalized nature, man can perhaps attribute his survival amid the shifts of lands and circumstances. But now, by the acts of his own hand, man's natural protection has been withdrawn. By his dependence upon processes of production which he himself has set in motion, he has forced himself into a groove, a little like that of the bee which cannot exist without the flowers, or the pilot fish, which depends upon the shark it accompanies and upon whose leavings it feasts. Any form of industrial production, whether for use or for profit, would create something of this concentration upon specific methods, and this consequent specialization. But when the profit motive predominates, the specialization becomes more extreme, for the reasons already mentioned: the emphasis upon the creation of desires rather than the fulfillment of wants, and the resultant enlargement of production in certain directions beyond normal needs, an expansion that must be maintained as the alternative to widespread loss, distress, and even social breakdown. Thus we are enslaved by the child of our own begetting.

Worse still! modern industrial specializations have a grim feature not found to any great extent among specializations in nature. The aphis that relies upon plant nectar, or the silkworm that depends upon the mulberry leaf, can be fairly certain of the essential supplies, which its own activities will not appreciably diminish. But the opposite is true of modern industrialism. Thus, to return to the automobile, the production and use of millions of machines each year depletes our resources in iron and in gasoline, even aside from the cost in the sacrifice of millions of acres to highways, parking lots, and garages. And so we draw nearer to the day when iron and gasoline will not be abundant enough or cheap enough to permit automobile manufacturing on the present scale. Therefore our specialization leads toward a dead-end of disaster. Again, the danger would exist under any form of industrialism; but the process is vastly speeded under the current system, which, by creating an artificial demand, wastes natural resources at a greatly accelerated rate.

At the same time, as if further to hasten disaster, we educate our youth in lavishness, in expenditure, in the creed of paying and getting; and we introduce luxuries until they come to be regarded as necessities. By precedent and example, and through advertisements over television, radio, and the press, we further the idea of material acquisition, of self-indulgence, and of display. Consequently, the young man or woman, growing up in a world of blatantly publicized and costly externals, approaches adulthood with the belief that the only things of worth are those that money can buy; and is subtly encouraged to compete for such valuables. Invariably, of course, the list is large, and is headed by the first of treasures, the automobile. It is for this reason that nowadays on suburban roads, even when conditions for walking are ideal, the only pedestrians one sees are children too young to drive and elderly inheritors of the traditions of a less luxurious age. That our increasing reliance on mechanical acquisitions is right and just, seems never to be questioned. Nor do we ask whether is is salutary to flaunt the money standard more and more before the eyes of youth; or whether it is good to narrow even further the social specializations involved in the creation of wants for the sake of profits.

Ah, yes, one will answer, but how else maintain the industries that give employment to millions? No one, of course, is asking us to abandon those industries. But we might do well to consider whether their further expansion will not deepen the problems of tomorrow and trap us even more hopelessly in the blind alleys of our own specializations. As for jobs for our workers—so long as there are schools, hospitals, and bridges to be built, slums to be cleared, decent housing to be supplied, death-dealing grade crossings to be eliminated, forests to be replanted, erosion to be checked, and irrigation projects to be extended, we need fear no lack of suitable work.

V

There can be, of course, no exact repetition in history. And yet, in general, the present has been recreating the past. Foot by foot, though at a much more rapid pace, we are following the footsteps of Assyria, Greece, Rome, and many another country that was undermined by its own enrichment. The fallacies and allurements of yesterday are the allurements and fallacies of today, accentuated, however, by the modern extension of opportunity to the masses. For whereas of old it was ordinarily the covetousness of the few that brought disaster, today for the first time in history the covetousness of the many has become an important peacetime factor. What remedy, therefore, is there? At one time, I might have argued that since private property was at the root of private greed, our salvation would be to abolish private property. Today, however, I cannot believe the way out to be so simple or easy. First of all, there is the fact that private property, deeply entrenched as it is in our world, could not be uprooted except by some cataclysmic shock, such as the Russian Revolution; and a new regime could be imposed only by a reign of force if not of terror, which would destroy all freedom and make a shambles of all affected regions.

But what of less drastic measures, such as the socialistic enactments of Sweden, England, and other countries that favor the "Welfare State"? Here there is boundless territory for debate, though my personal view is that decisive advantages do lie along these lines. If, for example, we adopt socialized medicine as in England, or if we introduce low-price, publicly sponsored health and hospital insurance, as re- recently in some of the provinces of Canada, we will remove much encouragement to avarice among private practitioners, and much temptation to exploitation. Nevertheless, such innovations, even if beneficent, are at best partial, and scarcely affect the vast realms of private industry, in which production for profit is the law of the day. Only if all industries were state-owned would a remedy be in sight—and such a result, as already suggested, could hardly be acomplished without a calamitous and largely self-defeating revolution. Moreover, even if all industries were state-owned, that would not necessarily put an end to the profit motive, for a change would have to come not only in institutions but in men and in their desires and codes of thought; otherwise, some would still contrive to seize much more of the world's goods than their brothers. And even under a state-owned system, if the emphasis remained on material acquisitions and on production for the sake of production or on job-making for the sake of job-making, the eventual benefits to civilization would at most be questionable.

VI

Acquisitiveness today is so deeply entrenched as a motive in society that, barring a catastrophic shock, it seems likely to remain for a long time; if eventually it is subordinated to gentler and more beneficent forces, the process will be a slow and evolutionary one. This does not mean, however, that we should not immediately consider how to initiate such an evolutionary process. Two possible general courses of action at once occur to one: reduce the incentives to acquisitiveness or else increase the incentives toward other goals. But these two courses are, manifestly, one at root.

Under the first heading, certain steps would be possible were we to revise our social philosophy. Partly as a result of the predatory traditions of centuries, and partly owing to *laissez faire* and related creeds, we assume that any individual has a natural right to dig his fingers into the bag of society and seize whatever he can take. We rarely pause to ask whether there should not be a relationship between taking and giving. We seldom inquire whether it is wholesome that there should be no upper limit to what a man can wall off as his own; and whether it is for the general good that accumulations can be passed on from generation to generation, so creating hereditary financial empires. Certain restraints, such as high income and inheritance taxes, have indeed been imposed; but these, in the United States, have not recognized the principle of a ceiling upon accumulation. We seldom remember that no man achieves a fortune entirely by his own efforts; every man draws upon the facilities civilization has made available to him. The city in which he has his office, the labor that produces his goods and the transportation lines that carry them, the inventions upon which he relies, including telephones, telegraph wires, presses, and business machines, the very financial system and even the units of exchange known as dollars and cents, are furnished by the society he lives in, and owe nothing to his personal efforts or merits. Therefore it is illogical to hold that society has no right to say just how far an individual can use its facilities for his own purposes.

The same is true, even more emphatically, with regard to inherited wealth. When we look into history, we find that bequests were not originally regarded as property rights, but arose in connection with supposed duties to the shade of the deceased: he who took over the possessions of the dead man also assumed the duty of performing the rites for the newly released spirit. And performance of the rites was regarded as primary; possession of the property was a mere outgrowth. Only in the course of time did the idea of a right to inherited property develop; and this so-called right gave birth to many evils, as under the Roman Empire, when, as we have seen, hangers-on would fawn and mince in the train of the rich man.

But is there any natural reason why property, especially in unlimited amounts, should be passed on to a man's sons or daughters or other designated favorites? Actually, the right is an assumed one, honored by custom and by law, but rooted in no basic necessity. If it is found that the laws of inheritance do damage by encouraging the growth of a class of drones or the rise of socially deleterious accumulations, then there is no reason why society in its own interest should not check such harmful developments. If we should decide, for example, that no man should leave a fortune of more than ten millions, or five millions, or half a million, or any other specific sum, then it would be unjust to no one and might benefit us all if the state were to claim every penny above the prescribed amount as an inheritance tax.

Simultaneously, the same type of regulation might be made for incomes over a prescribed amount—incomes far beyond the capacity of any individual or family to use, incomes running into the hundreds of thousands or millions a year. Upon these a tax of one hundred per cent, with no exemption whatever, might be decreed for all intake above the stipulated level. That any person has a right to draw without limit upon the resources of society, selfishly monopolizing more than he can use, is a belief that may have seemed sensible when men did deference to the doctrine of Adam Smith that what is for my benefit is necessarily for your benefit also. But now that this doctrine has been exposed as a hollow shell, unlimited accumulation has become baseless and anachronistic.

Let us assume that we did establish a maximum for incomes, and for fortunes passed on by will. Then would we not have made the first steps toward checking the acquisitive impulse? Ah, but this is just the trouble, some critics will argue. You will have stricken out the incentive to individual initiative—the spur without which men will not push ahead.

This is an easy and common assumption—but how much truth is there in it? First of all, what shall we say of men who (even after fulfilling their own needs) will work for no end but further self-enrichment, or the enrichment of their sons or their sons' sons? Personally, I should suggest that they are men whose activities should be curbed, lest their irrational greed and selfishness should damage the majority. However, I doubt whether such men are as numerous as some suppose. Of the seekers of unlimited accumulation, much the larger number, it seems to me, are merely conforming with socially accepted standards. If there were other socially accepted standards, they would bow to those quite as willingly, and work quite as energetically for their mead of praise and recognition. However, we cannot expect them to turn from an established goal until substitutes have been provided.

What is necessary, therefore, is the social equivalent of acquisitiveness. But just what does this imply? Before attempting to answer, let us pause for a flash-back at other systems and societies.

VII

Throughout the ages, as we know, the money or property motive has been far from the only incentive to action. There has been the magical motive, which has dominated the lives of many uncivilized and half civilized peoples; the religious motive, to be seen behind pilgrimages and movements of peoples, great creative works, persecutions, and wars; the artistic motive, a shaping force in ancient Greece and in Italy of the Renaissance; the adventurous motive, which has had much to do with the distribution of mankind throughout the earth; the motive of intellectual curiosity, the pilot behind our greatest advances in science, philosophy, and scholarship; the motive of power, applause, and glory, a stimulus to the antics of monarchs and the trampling of military captains; and the motive of social commendation and approval, which has ruled with the power of law in certain early communities, as in the Trobriand Islands (according to the anthropologist Bronislaw Malinowki) and in Rome before the days of her expansion and corruption.

And if men in other ages and lands have worked for ends apart from money and from property in any form, men today may also be moved by various incentives, not all of them of a material nature. In a sense, all men must aim for acquisitions of some sort, if life is to contain any object or meaning; but the acquisitions need not be such as one could measure or weigh. Some may seek the impalpable lightness of a song, the rolling rhythms of great prose, the stab and thrill of discovery, the glow of exploration, the illumination of knowledge, or the satisfaction of lifting a helping hand. Some may delight to see shapely edifices rising, some will rejoice in gathering bricks for the foundations of universal brotherhood and peace. But whatever they are seeking, men must have some means of employing their energy, and some satisfaction of the mind and heart in the use of that energy. Here, and here alone, we can find the social equivalent of present-day acquisitiveness.

It does not seem to me that the end is to be accomplished principally by law: formal legislation is effective only when it conforms to preconceived or generally accepted modes of thought and conduct. A community might, for example, decree a thirty-mile-an-hour automobile speed limit; but if defied by motorists, ignored by traffic officers, and unenforced by judges, it would be a dead letter. In the same way, most enactments against acquisitiveness—other than measures such as I have suggested, affecting the great fortunes but applying to comparatively few individuals—would be of little avail unless the public mind had been prepared for them.

Primarily, what is necessary is that our thought and teaching, which have emphasized the desirability of acquisitions, should be turned in fresh directions. What is necessary is that we should set up new goals and objects of competition. And here our schools, churches, and homes have a great responsibility, in helping to dissipate the crass idea that a man's merit lies in what he has, rather than what he is or what he does; and that we should applaud his zeal in furthering his own ends, rather than his readiness to work for the general good. Since approbation and praise are important incentives to conduct, we should provide ambitious youth not only with means to exert its talents but to win acclaim in non-acquisitive pursuits. For example, prizes— not necessarily of a material nature—might be offered for distinctive work in all creative fields; for research, whether scientific or scholarly; and for contributions to the field of human relations. Contests might

be held, in which the normal competitive urge would be allowed full
sway; and the winners might enjoy a repute that would gratify them
far more than the awards of mere money-winning. Great foundations
and public institutions, along with municipalities, counties, and even
the national government, might sponsor some of the contests, which
thus would attract such wide attention that they would tend to draw
the desires of youth away from mere personal accumulation.

But if we are to develop a less acquisitive attitude, we must begin
almost at the cradle, since the instilled traits and tendencies of the
child survive in the adult. One therefore looks a little askance at the
present tendency to emphasize the money motive to the building juvenile. It is not only that millionaires and multi-millionaires are held
up as objects of admiration; it is that the child, very early in life, is
encouraged to believe that nothing should be done except for money.
Does he perform some little job, such as to clean the garage or wash
the car for his father? He is paid in cash. Does he hold down the
fort for an hour with the neighbor's baby? Again he is paid. And
so on and on. Naturally, he comes to believe that nothing at all—no
neighborly service, no act of helpfulness even for his own parents—
should be attempted except for payment. He comes to regard the
compensation as rightly his; he looks forward to it, and subordinates
other considerations. Or if by chance he does help a general cause,
such as a new school gymnasium or a Scout movement, his method is
through the collection of money or the sale of merchandise. What sort
of citizens can we expect to emerge from boys and girls brought up in
this tradition?

One of the ironies of the situation is that, having trained our youth
in an acquisitive atmosphere, we blandly conclude that acquisitiveness
is a part of human nature.

Nevertheless, in a society based upon private possessions, must we
not necessarily turn the mind of youth toward acquisitions? Perhaps
—but with qualifications. Though most children must eventually
enter a paying trade, business, or profession, need the payment be the
only or even the leading consideration? Should we not encourage
young men and women to pick the work that they love, the work they
are best qualified for, the work in which they can do the greatest service? Is there anything crasser than the spectacle of the man or woman
who selects a field of supposed human and humane service, not because he is interested or cares to be of use, but because he hopes to
profit? Too many of us have known physicians who placed the
monthly bill above aid to the sick and disabled, schoolteachers who

viewed their profession merely as an oiled highway to regular checks, lawyers and writers whose only thought was of material returns. I remember the publisher who once told me that he handled books as he might have dealt with hardware. And I recall men drawn by parental suasion or the lure of money into fields for which they were tragically unfitted. I think of one who would have made an excellent college professor; yet he became a lawyer because of the bait held out by a successful uncle, and years later withdrew from his practice amid the wreckage of his life. I think of another who, by nature unworldly, had leanings toward music and the stage, but obeyed the mercantile dictates of a strong-willed father, and dragged out his years as a mediocre and miserable salesman. How many of us have known similar cases, in which the life force has been prostituted to the money impulse! But such cases, of course, would be possible only in a society dominated by preachments of acquisitiveness.

It may be true that, as the modern world is constituted, not all positions can be filled on the basis of aptitude or inclination. But this only means that we should do all the more to provide our workers with a better balanced life, and one less dominated by the profit motive. Among our youth we should encourage the choice of a side activity that can be followed for its own appeal and without thought of profit. One might interest himself in wood carving or woodcuts, another in observations through a private telescope, a third might study the species and habits of birds, still another might devote himself to ceramics, or to sculpture, or to making model railroads or ships, or to experiments with radio, television, tape recording, etc. But these are merely examples; any reader may make his own list. The idea is that the youth would grow up with some activity aside from money-making to engage his mind and time. Even today, many do have such avocations. But the number could be much greater if more encouragement were given in homes and schools and in our educational policy. As a result, we might not only have many more useful and contented citizens, but might reduce crime and diminish the numbers of those who follow socially disadvantageous paths of money-seeking because they must have a way to occupy their time and energies. All this, besides, would tend to isolate and to throw disapprobation upon men for whom profit-making is life's chief objective. And since social disapprobation is one of the strongest deterrents, we would see less of the naked spirit of gain.

VIII

The world provided by nature was rich as well as beautiful, and abounded in forests, rivers, lakes, hills, meadows, birds, beasts, fishes, and minerals. And man, partly out of ignorance and the thrust of circumstances but largely through greed, has slashed down forests, polluted rivers and lakes, eroded hills and meadows, shot, trapped, or poisoned birds, beasts, and fishes, and depleted mineral supplies while extravagance, waste, display, and the covetousness of private exploiters have not only raided the present but robbed the future.

All the while, man has had to live not only with nature but with man, and here too he has sadly misused his opportunities, again sometimes through ignorance, and sometimes through compulsions and phychological urges which he could not understand or control. But often his misbehavior has been spurred by relentless greed. Man has preyed upon man as wolf never preyed upon wolf; pirates have scoured the seas; cities and empires have been plundered; whole civilizations have been overturned; the marauders of politics and of religion and of business have flourished in many lands and ages.

Fortunately, this is not the complete story. There is another chapter, which must not be left out of any appraisal. Though greed has won many a battle, it has also been subdued in many a conflict. Piracy, once respectable and general on all the sea lanes, has been driven from every commercial route. Brigandage, of the type made famous by the Vikings, the Vandals, and scores of other freebooting groups, has become (except in wartime) an unregretted memory. The oppression of class by class, which broke into acute eruption in Rome long before the day of the Gracchi, is no longer seen in the West in its one-time naked savagery. The bleeding of the Roman provinces, which reached extremes of rapacity under the Republic, was largely controlled by the laws of the Empire. Slavery, the disgrace of many a people, was in the process of dying out in Rome before her fall; and although revived with a remorseless cupidity in the modern world, it has been gradually suppressed in land after land. Serfdom, a cousin of slavery, was likewise abolished after centuries, first in Western Europe and much later in the countries of the East. The industrial oppression of the early machine-age, another cousin of slavery, was also in time relieved, though only after much suffering, human wastage, and strife. And raw-toothed predatory individualism, such as built up some of the early American fortunes, has been tempered by public opinion and by law—so much so that it would be difficult today for any financier to act with such self-centered disregard of the general welfare as was displayed by men like Huntington and Jay Gould.

All this, and much more, could be cited to show that acquisitiveness, at least in many of its phases, has been and can be conquered. This great force, to be sure, is still spreading a constant shadow. Shall we keep the unruly giant locked up, while gradually shearing off its power? Or shall we again permit it to dominate—the father of dire inequality, the ravager of natural and human resources, the sower of universal suffering, the formenter of the conflict of men and classes, the progenitor of revolution and war?

We ourselves, by our own actions, shall provide the answer. And our actions shall be conditioned by the strength of our convictions, and the resoluteness of the will to keep the kiss-of-death of Midas from our homes, our schools, our marts, our temples, and our halls of state.

NOTES

I

1. Robert H. Lowie, *Primitive Society*, New York, 1947.
2. Evans-Prichard, Edward Evan, *The Nuer*, A Description of the Modes of Livelihood and Political Institutions of a Nilotic People, Oxford, 1940.
3. *Ibid.*   4. Margaret Mead, *Coming of Age in Samoa*, New York, 1928.
5. W. H. R. Rivers, *Social Organization*, New York, 1924.
6. A. R. Brown, *The Andaman Islanders*, Cambridge, England, 1922.
7. F. E. Maning, *Old New Zealand*, London, 1876.
8. *Ibid.*   9. *Ibid.*
10. R. F. Barton, *The Kalingas, Their Institutions and Custom Law*, Chicago, 1949.
11. Bronislaw Malinowski, *Argonauts of the Western Pacific*, New York, 1922.
12. Ruth Benedict, *Patterns of Culture*, Boston, 1934.

II

1. Sir Henry Sumner Maine, *Ancient Law*, 10th, Edition, London, 1905.
2. Alexandre Moret, *The Nile and Egyptian Civilization*, New York, 1927.
3. Margaret A. Murray, *The Splendour That Was Egypt*, New York, 1949.
4. Philip Ainsworth Means, *Ancient Civilizations of the Andes*, New York, 1931. See also Means' *Fall of the Inca Empire*, New York, 1932.
5. Father Blas Valera, quoted by Means, *Ancient Civilizations of the Andes*, *op. cit.*
6. *Ibid.*   7. Quoted by Means, *op. cit.*

III

1. John Lee Maddox, Ph.D., *The Medicine Man*. A Sociological Study of the Character and Evolution of Shamanism, New York, 1923.
2. *Ibid.*
3. S. Powers, *The Tribes of California*, in "North American Ethnology," Vol. 3, quoted by Maddox, *op. cit.*
4. Quoted by Homer W. Smith, *Man and His Gods*, Boston, 1953.
5. Wilfrid Jackson, *Shells as Evidence of the Migrations of Culture*, cited by G. Eliot Smith, *Human History*, New York, 1929.
6. G. Eliot Smith, *op. cit.*
7. Herodotus, Book IV, tr. by George Rawlinson, New York, 1947.
8. *Ibid.*
9. *The Odyssey*, Book XIV, tr. by J. W. Mackail, Vol. II, London, 1905.
10. Herodotus, Book VI.
11. Diodorus of Agrium, from *Greek Civilization and Character*, tr. by Arnold Toynbee, Boston, 1950.
12. *Ibid.*   13. *Ibid.*   14. *Ibid.*

247

IV

1. Jules Toutain, *Economic Life of the Ancient World*, New York, 1930.
2. *Ibid.*
3. T. Mommsen, *History of Rome*, Vol. II., London, 1901.   4. *Ibid.*
5. Alfred Zimmern, *The Greek Commonwealth*, Oxford, 1924.
6. Plutarch of Chaeronea, *Parallel Lives*, Teubner Text, edited by C. Sintenis, Vol. IV.   7. *Ibid.*
8. *The Republic of Plato*, Jowett translation, Book VIII.
9. J. H. Mahaffey, *Social Life in Greece from Homer to Menander*, London, 1913.
10. *Ibid.*   11. G. Glotz, *The Greek City and Its Institutions*, New York, 1930.
12. Thucydides, V.   13. Mahaffey, *op. cit.*   14. Polybius, VI.
15. Aristotle. *Politics*, II.   16. Polybius, XX.   17. Polybius, XXXVI.

V

1. J. C. Stobart, *The Grandeur That Was Rome*, 3rd edition, London, 1934.
2. W. Warde Fowler, M. A., *Social Life at Rome in the Age of Cicero*, New York, 1924.   3. *Ibid.*
4. Gaston Delayen, *Cicero*, tr. by Farrell Symons, New York, 1931.
5. Fowler, *op. cit.*
6. Joseph Ward Swain, *The Ancient World*, Vol. II. New York, 1950.
7. Fowler, *op cit.*   8. Tacitus, Book IV.
9. Gugliemo Ferrero, *Ancient Rome and Modern America*, New York, 1914.
10. Tacitus, Book IV.
11. Samuel Dill, *Roman Society from Nero to Marcus Aurelius*, London, 1920.
12. *Ibid.*   13. Gibbon, *Decline and Fall*, Ch. IV.
14. Ferdinand Lot, *The End of the Ancient World and the Beginning of the Middle Ages*, New York, 1931.
15. J. W. Thompson, *Economic and Social History of the Middle Ages*, New York, 1928.
16. Samuel Dill, M. A., *Roman Society in the Last Century of the Western Empire*, 2nd edition, revised, London, 1925.

VI

1. Gibbon, Ch. XXXI.   2. Lot, *op. cit.*   3. *Ibid*
4. Samuel Dill, M. A., *Roman Society in Gaul in the Merovingian Age*, London, 1926.
5. G. G. Coulton, *Chaucer and His England*, New York, 1957.
6. P. Boissonade, *Life and Work in Medieval Europe*, New York, 1950.
7. Col. C. F. Young, C. B., *The Medici*, New York, 1933.
8. C. Renard and G. Weulersse, *Life and Work in Modern Europe*, New York, 1926.
9. John Addington Symonds. *Renaissance in Italy*, 7 vols., New York, 1883.

10. Boissonade, *op.cit.*

11. A. Abram, *Social England in the Fifteenth Century.* A Study of the Effects of Economic Conditions. London & New York, 1909.

12. *Ibid.*

13. James Westfall Thompson, *The Middle Ages,* 300-1500, Vol. II, New York, 1931.

14. Johannes Jennsen, *History of the German People at the Close of the Middle Ages,* Vol. IV, London, 1900

15. Quoted by Charles Mackay, Ll. D., *Extraordinary Popular Delusions and the Madness of Crowds,* 8th impression, New York, 1956.

VII

1. Henry Hallam, *History of Europe During the Middle Ages,* Vol. II. Revised edition. New York and London, 1900.

2. Boissonade, *op. cit.*   3. Thompson, *op. cit.,*   4. *Ibid.*   5. Hallam, *op. cit.*

6. G. G. Coulton, *Medieval Panorama, The English Scene from Conquest to Reformation,* Cambridge, England, 1949.

7. Carlo Beuf, *Cesare Borgia, The Machiavellian Prince,* New York, 1942.

8. Thompson, *op. cit.,* Vol. I.

9. Charles Yriarte, *Cesare Borgia,* tr. by William Sterling, London, 1947.

10. Dr. Ludwig Pastor, *The History of the Popes from the Close of the Middle Ages,* Vol. VII, London, 1908.

11. *Ibid.*

12. Geoffrey Chaucer, *Canterbury Tales,* rendered into Modern English by J. U. Nicholson, New York, 1934.

13. F. J. C. Hearnshaw, M. W., Ll.D., "Chivalry and Its Place in History," in *Chivalry, A Series of Studies to Illustrate Its Historical Significance and Civilizing, Influence,* Edgar Prestage, editor, New York, 1928.

14. Henry Charles Lea, *A History of the Inquisition of the Middle Ages,* Vol. I, New. York, 1922.

15. Dana Carleton Munro, *The Middle Ages* (395-1272), New York, 1921.

16. Gibbon, Ch. LX.   17. Bracton, quoted by Coulton, *op. cit.*

18. William, the Austin Canon of Newburgh, quoted by Coulton, *op. cit.*

19. *Ibid.*

20. William H. Prescott, *History of the Reign of Ferdinand and Isabella,* Vol. I, London, 1851.

21. *Ibid.*   22. *Ibid.*

23. Henry Charles Lea, *op. cit.*

24. Henry Charles Lea, *A History of the Inquisition of Spain,* Vol. I, New York, 1906.

25. Lea, *Inquisition of the Middle Ages,* Vol. I.

26. *Ibid.*

VIII

1. Witt Bowden, Ph.D., *The Industrial History of the United States*, New York, 1930.

2. Azurara, quoted by Arthur Helps, *The Spanish Conquest in America*, Vol. I, London, 1855.

3. Quoted by Jean Descola, *The Conquistadors*, tr. Malcolm Barnes, New York, 1957.

4. *Select Documents Illustrating the Four Voyages of Columbus*, ed. by Cecil Jane, 2 vols., London, 1930. Reprinted by Vilhjalmur Stefansson, *Great Adventures and Explorations*, New York, 1947.

5. *Ibid.*

6. Stephen Clissold, *The Life of Don Pedro Sarmiento de Gamboa*, London, 1954.

7. Hakluyt, quoted by Howard Robinson, Ph.,D., *The Development of the British Empire*, Boston, 1922.

8. Walter H. Dorn, *Competition for Empire*, 1740-1763, New York, 1940.

9. Helps, *op. cit.*, Vol. II.   10. Helps, Vol. III.   11. Dorn, *op. cit.*

12. William H. Prescott, *The Conquest of Mexico*, Vol. I, New York, 1922.

13. *Ibid.*, Vol. II.

14. Bernal Diaz del Castillo, *The Discovery and Conquest of Mexico*, tr. by A.P. Maudslay, New York, 1956.

15. Prescott, *op. cit.*

16. Roger Bigelow Merriman, *The Rise of the Spanish Empire*, Vol. III, New York, 1925.

17. Prescott, *History of the Conquest of Peru*, Vol. I, Chicago, 1847.

18. Philip Ainsworth Means, *Fall of the Inca Empire*, *op. cit.*   19. *Ibid.*

IX

1. Morris Bishop, *Champlain, The Life of Fortitude*, New York, 1948.

2. Thomas B. Costain, *The White and the Gold*, The French Regime in Canada, New York, 1954.

3. Sir Alfred Comyn Lyall, *History of India, Vol. VIII*. Edited by A. V. Williams-Jackson, London, 1907.

4. Arthur Percival Newton, *The European Nations in the West Indies*, 1493-1688, London, 1933.

5. *Ibid.*   6. *Ibid.*

7. Sir Alfred Lyall, *The Rise and Expansion of the British Dominion in India*, London, 1911.

8. Francois Cernier, quoted by Lyall, *op. cit.*   9. *Ibid.*

10. Vincent A. Smith, *The Oxford History of India*, Oxford, 1919.   11. *Ibid.*

12. Howard Robinson, Ph.D., *The Development of the British Empire*, Boston, 1922.

13. Henry Dodwell, *Dupleix and Clive, The Beginnings of Empire*, London, 1920.

X

1. Stephen M. Roberts, M. A., *History of French Colonial Policy*, Vol. 1, London, 1929.
2. *Ibid.*　　3. Louis Vignon, quoted by Roberts, *op. cit.*　　4. Roberts, *op. cit.*
5. Nejla Izzeddin, *The Arab World, Past, Present, and Future*, Chicago, 1953.
6. Harry A. Rudin, *Germans in the Cameroons*, A Case Study in Modern Imperialism, New Haven, 1938.
7. *Ibid.*　　　　　　　　8. *Ibid.*
9. Ludwig Bauer, *Leopold the Unloved, King of the Belgians and of Wealth*, Boston, 1935.　　　　　　　　10. *Ibid.*
11. Margaret Goldsmith, *The Trail of Opium. ..The Eleventh Plague*, London, 1939.

XI

1. Renard & Weulersse, *op. cit.*　　　　2. *Ibid.*
3. J. Ellis Barker, *The Rise and Decline of the Netherlands*, London, 1906.
4. *Ibid.*
5. Albert Mathiez, *The French Revolution*, New York, 1929.
6. Henry Troyat, *Pushkin*, tr. Randolph T. Weaver, New York, 1950.
7. George Soloveytchik, *Potemkin, A Picture of Catherine's Russia*, New Edition, London, 1949.　　　　　　　8. *Ibid.*
9. Harry Best, *The Soviet State and Its Inception*, New York, 1950.
10. William English Walling, *Sovietism*, The ABC of Bolshevism—According to the Bolsheviks, New York, 1920.
11. *Ibid.*　　　　　　　12. *Ibid.*

XII

1. Francis Williams, *Magnificent Journey*. The Rise of the Trade Unions, London, 1954.
2. *Ibid.*　　　　　　　3. *Ibid.*
4. Bernard H. Schilling, *Human Dignity and the Great Victorians*, New York, 1946.
5. Dorothy Marshall, *The English Poor in the Eighteenth Century*, London, 1926.
6. J. L. & Barbara Hammond, *The Rise of Modern Industry*, New York, 1926.
7. Schilling, *op. cit.*　　　　8. Hammond *op. cit.*
9. W. Cunningham, *The Growth of English Industry and Commerce in Modern Times*, Part II, *Laissez Faire*, Cambridge, England, 1912.
10. Williams, *op. cit.*
11. Shepard Bancroft Clough & Charles Woolsey Cole, *Economic History of Europe*. Boston, 1946.
12. Allan Nevins, *The Emergence of Modern America*, 1865-1878, New York, 1927.
13. *Ibid.*
14. Bertrand Russell, *The Impact of Science on Society*, New York, 1953.
15. Charles A. Madison, *Critics and Crusaders*, New York, 1947.　　　16. *Ibid.*

17. Edwin Markham, Benjamin B. Lindsey, and George Creel, *Children in Bondage*, New York, 1914.

18. *Ibid.*   19. *Ibid.*

XIII

1. Gustavus Myers, *History of the Great American Fortunes*, New York, 1936.

2. Charles A. & Mary R. Beard, *The Rise of American Civilization*, Vol. II, New York, 1927.

3. Matthew Josephson, *The Robber Barons, The Great American Capitalists*, 1861-1901, New York, 1934.

4. *Ibid.*   5. *Ibid.*

XIV

1. Myers, *op. cit.*   2. *Ibid.*   3. *Ibid.*

4. *Ibid.*   5. Josephson, *op. cit.*

6. Robert Irving Warshow, *Jay Gould, The Story of a Fortune*, New York, 1928.

7. *Ibid.*   8. Josephson, *op. cit.*

9. John K. Winkler, *Incredible Carnegie*, New York, 1931.   10. *Ibid.*

11. H. G. Wells, *The Work, Wealth and Happiness of Mankind*, London, 1932.

12. Stewart H. Holbrook, *The Age of the Moguls*, Garden City, 1956.

13. Allan Nevins, *Study in Power, John D. Rockefeller, Industrialist and Philanthropist*, Vol. I, New York, 1953.   14. *Ibid.*

15. Frederick Lewis Allen, *The Lords of Creation*, New York, 1935.

INDEX

Achaean raiders, 30
Acquisitiveness, nature of, 229ff.
Aeschines, Athenian orator, 45
Africa, colonization of, 133ff.
African natives, 3, 4, 19; and European
  colonizers, 134ff.
Agriculture, English, 177, 178
Agrippa, constructs Pantheon, 58
Akwa people, protest against Germans,
  139, 140
Alaric, sack of Rome by, 68
Alcabala, Spanish tax, 150
Alexander II, Czar, abolishes serfdom,
  162
Alexander II of Egypt, 49
Alexander VI, Pope, 84
Alexis III, Emperor, 90
Algeria, French in, 134ff.
Allen, Frederick Lewis, quoted, 224
Almago, Diego de, compact of, 115
Almanni, the, 68
Altgeld, John Peter, quoted, 185
Amboyna massacre, 123
American Indians, 4, 7, 8, 16, 19, 20,
  229, 230; treatment by Spaniards,
  104ff.; by fur dealers, 204
Americans, in opium traffic, 145
Amon, priests and temple of, 21
Andagoya, Pascual de, report of, 115
Andaman Islanders, 4
Anglo-Belgian Rubber Company, pro-
  fits of, 144
Anne, Russian empress, 163
Antony, 56
Arab tribes, 11
Argos, revolt of poor in, 44
Aristotle, complaints as to venality, 41,
  44
Armour, Philip H., 223
Army, French, under the Bourbons, 158,
  159
Ashley, Lord, statement of, 145
Assyria, ancient, 23, 26, 28, 29; decline
  of, 226
Astor, John Jacob, 203ff, 233

Astor, William B., 205
Atahuallpa, Incan emperor, 23, 110, 112
Athens, and oligarchy, 40; venality in,
  41, 42, 45; opposition to the wealthy,
  44; depopulation, 46; failure of 226,
  227
Attalus III, of Pergamum, 49
Atticus, Roman capitalist, 55
Augustus, 49, 56, 58
Aurelian, 64
Australia, aborigines of, 4
Austria, Jews in, 92
Automobile industry, nature of, 235,
  236
Ayora, Juan de, Spanish captain, 110
Aztecs, the, 11, 112
Azurara, quoted, 101, 108

Babylonia, ancient, 20, 21, 28; property
  in, 33ff.
Ba-Ila, the, 3
Baldwin, in Crusades, 89
Battle of Mussel Slough, 200
Barbarians, ancient, 67ff.
Basle, 75
Bauer, Ludwig, quoted, 142, 143
Beard, Charles and Mary, quoted 195
Behemond of Guiscord, 89
Belgians, in Congo, 141ff.
Belgrave, Lord, remark of, 172
Benedict IX, Pope, 84
Benedict, Ruth, 8
Bengal, revenues from, 128
Bernier, Francois, quoted, 129
Bibikov, Marshal, statement of, 164
Bismarck, and factory laws, 182, 183
"Black Friday," 212
Boccaccio, 97
Boetia, ancient, 45
Boetian Confederation, 40
Boissonade, P., quoted, 75
Boniface IX, Pope, 86
Borgia, Cesare, 84, 85
Boudicca, British queen, 54, 57
Bracton, quoted, 92